Dis-Enclosure

John D. Caputo, *series editor*

PERSPECTIVES IN
CONTINENTAL
PHILOSOPHY

JEAN-LUC NANCY

Dis-Enclosure

The Deconstruction of Christianity

TRANSLATED BY BETTINA BERGO, GABRIEL MALENFANT,
AND MICHAEL B. SMITH

FORDHAM UNIVERSITY PRESS
New York ■ 2008

Dis-Enclosure was originally published in French as Jean-Luc Nancy, *La déclosion (Déconstruction du christianisme, 1)*, © 2005, Éditions Galilée.

This work has been published with the assistance of the National Center for the Book—French Ministry of Culture.

Ouvrage publié avec le concours du Ministère français chargé de la culture—Centre National du Livre.

Library of Congress Cataloging-in-Publication Data is available.

Printed in the United States of America
10 09 08   5 4 3 2 1

Contents

Translators' Foreword   ix

Opening   1

Atheism and Monotheism   14

A Deconstruction of Monotheism   29

The Judeo-Christian (on Faith)   42

A Faith That Is Nothing at All   61

An Experience at Heart   75

Verbum caro factum   81

The Name *God* in Blanchot   85

Blanchot's Resurrection   89

Consolation, Desolation   98

On a Divine *Wink*   104

An Exempting from Sense   121

"Prayer Demythified"   129

The Deconstruction of Christianity   139

Dis-Enclosure   158

Appendix—Far from Substance: Whither and to What Point?
     Gérard Granel   163

Notes   175

Translators' Foreword

The original title of this book was *La déclosion*. That term may be said not to "exist" in the French language, and it is not farfetched to claim that the volume is itself an explication of its meaning. The word recurs frequently in many chapters, particularly the last one. That chapter shares its title with the volume as a whole, explicating the leitmotif of *déclosion* and carrying it to the brink of a further dialectical sublation. Therefore it may be useful at the outset to convey our understanding (without pretending to do any of the hard work Nancy's texts themselves undertake) of *déclosion*.

Nancy uses *déclosion* to designate the reversal of a prior closing (foreclosure), an opening up. This opening is very general: more general than would be suggested by "disclosure," which usage is pretty much limited to divulging classified information. Although Nancy's subject matter is largely Christianity, as the subtitle, "The Deconstruction of Christianity," states, it is not as ecclesiastical as a solution such as "de-cloistering" would have suggested. We have therefore settled on *dis-enclosure*, a term whose existential deficiency (like that of the French title it replaces) may be palliated by the fact that *enclosure* has been used, particularly by British historians, to refer to the movement by which lands previously held privately were made common domain, available for free-range grazing and other communal uses. Now this is, mutatis mutandis, precisely the sense Nancy heralds across a broad range of domains, in which history has closed in upon itself in its indispensable, inevitable, but eventually encumbering assignment of meanings.

This brings us to Nancy's final "title" chapter, in which alongside *déclosion* another term appears (and this one has its ontological papers in order): *éclosion*. The word means "hatching," and for flowers (notably in Ronsard) "opening, blossoming." Why does Nancy need this less complicated companion term for *déclosion*? Because the last, short piece moves the reader to a more cosmïc perspective, one in which the cancellation of sociological strictures is seen in a broader perspective and (perhaps) in collaboration with a manner of spatial burgeoning, a pregnant structuring of the void. Here we have turned to a real but obscure term, *eclosure*. It is used in the field of entomology to designate a butterfly's metamorphosis from pupa to winged fulfillment.

Before leaving the issue of the title, we would be remiss not to mention that French *déclosion* is the usual translation of Heidegger's *Erschließung*, rendered by Macquarrie and Robinson in English as "disclosure."[1] Nancy, whose familiarity with Heidegger may well have suggested the use of the term, appears to extend the notion, from its original phenomenological sense of the way in which things "give themselves" to us to a historical opening up of Christianity in deconstruction. But Nancy's most original addition to the overdetermination of this particular signifier is to see Christianity itself as an opening up of meaning in history. This is what allows him to see his deconstruction of Christianity as a prolongation of Christianity's own historical movement.

Nancy's style presents serious challenges to the translator, not the least of which is his propensity to express crucial points in language that draws heavily on the signifier—the colloquialism, the Gallicism, the essentialist pun. His free and almost lyric interweaving movement, a farandole between signified and signifier, has often led us to resort to leaps in our own register, if not to the confessional footnote. If reading, as Blanchot said, is dancing with an invisible partner, to translate is to do everything he does, as Ginger Rogers is said to have said, backwards and in heels.

At Nancy's request, *sens* has been translated "sense" throughout. As he explained to us, in his usage it signifes precisely not "meaning" but "sense" more or less as in "It makes sense," that is, opening a direction, a possibility of value—a possibility of "meaning" but not a meaning.

The entire text of the translation has profited greatly from mutual criticism and consultation among the translators. The main translator of each essay is indicated in a translator's line at its end. Michael B. Smith would like to express his gratitude to research librarian Xiaojing Zu of Berry College for her technical assistance. Bettina Bergo thanks Philippe Farah, David Bertet, and Héloïse Bailly for their assistance. We both thank Helen Tartar for making this project possible.

—Michael B. Smith

Dis-Enclosure

Opening

Escheat and Piety

It is not a question of reviving religion, not even the one that Kant wanted to hold "within the limits of reason alone." It is, however, a question of opening mere reason up to the limitlessness that constitutes its truth.

It is not a question of overcoming some deficiency in reason, but of liberating reason without reserve: once everything is accounted for, it is up to us to show what remains beyond these accounts.

It is also not a question of repainting the skies, or of reconfiguring them: it is a question of opening up the earth—dark, hard, and lost in space.

> ⌘

It is not our concern to save religion, even less to return to it. The much discussed "return of the religious," which denotes a real phenomenon, deserves no more attention than any other "return." Among the phenomena of repetition, resurgence, revival, or haunting, it is not the identical but the different that invariably counts the most. Because the identical immediately loses its identity in returning, the question should rather be asked, ceaselessly and with new risks, what an identical "secularization" might denote, inevitably, other than a mere transferal. (It has been a long time since [Hans] Blumenberg effectively raised this problem, even if he did not resolve it at the time.)

The return of religion or the return to it can only sharpen—as we readily see—its already critical state and, with that, all the dangers that religion invariably poses to thought, to law, to freedom, and to human dignity.

It is, however, a question of knowing—and here again, with entirely new risks, efforts, and reflective audacities [*courages de pensée*]—what the simple word *human* means. This question denotes nothing less than the sense of humanism. Behind this word, behind what it says, behind what it hides—what it does not want to say, what it cannot or does not know how to say—stand the most imperious demands of thought today.

One may dislike the tone of such a sentence. One may deem it smug, arrogant. One may distrust him or her who claims with sovereignty categorically to point out the essential problems of his or her time. One may and one ought to feel this way. Sometimes, however, comes a time to raise one's voice a bit. And sometimes time is of the essence.

It so happens today that the so-called civilization of humanism is bankrupt or in its death-throes, as we are wont to say, the second term being the preferable one, no doubt. And it is when a form of life has finished aging that thought must rise up. It was no accident that Hegel's old lesson was pronounced at the beginning of the contemporary world, that is, at the beginning of the decomposition or the visible deconstruction of Christianity. The form of life that Hegel observed to be waning and fading into grayness is the form in which religion—the erstwhile providential safeguard of world and existence—loses, along with its legitimacy, the sense of its most specific resources: that which constituted the vitality and vivacity of an act of faith appears only as a dogmatic and institutional control. This also means that that which in faith could previously open the world in itself to its own outside (and not to some world-behind-the-worlds, to some heaven or hell) closes up and shrivels into a self-serving management of the world. This is not new, and this ambivalence is constitutive of what institutes itself as religion, or as the religious character that all institutions conceal (their inner cohesion, the sacred nature of their construction, the superior, even sublime, character of their destiny).

What thinking must then hold together is the void of this opening constituted by an absence of inheritors [*le vide de l'ouverture en déshérence*]. Hegel, Schelling, and Hölderlin were the first to have understood, following Kant's lead, that to make room for a rational faith it was necessary to open rationality to the dimension appropriate to the absolute, or again, to a "higher reason" (our translation of Hölderlin's *höher Besinnen*).[1]

The lesson of the last two centuries is that neither philosophy nor poetry sufficed to assure this, whereas science, for its part, resolutely turned away once and for all from that which seemed apt to sketch out, in it and at a certain point in its development, the same elevation of reason [*exhaussement de la raison*] (at a time when we still believed that science could wholly account for the world [*rendrait raison du monde*]). It was not enough that thinking and speaking sought to take charge of the essential piety, that is, the observance of duty that was incumbent on reason with regard to the unconditioned principle or dimension it requires.

This piety of reason, this service that the *greater reason* (Nietzsche) owes itself in the name of its absolute destiny—this has proved unable to communicate its own fervor. It has found its mystics in mathematics and astrophysics alone, while metaphysics closed in on itself.

The (Sur-)Religious Threat

The civilization of the "death of God," or the emancipation of reason, will have ultimately abandoned reason to hand itself over to understanding. Not that thinking or art have ceased reminding us of the requirement that reason represents. But this reminder—whether expressed in the voice of Nietzsche, Wittgenstein, or Heidegger; whether carried by the tonalities of Cézanne, Proust, Varèse, or Beckett (to name but a few)—has no doubt not hit the precise spot where the void opened. It has not managed to point out the empty heart of the void itself, or it has simply confused this void with nihilism, which is, rather, a congested gaping that fills itself up.

Because we have come to this now, what we can envision as lying before us (in the sense of Gérard Granel's recent remark, "The 1930s lie before us") is not the worsening permanence of nihilism. To put it succinctly, we are at the end, we are in its death-throes (which, for all that, give no clear sign of being brief . . .). What is taking shape, on the contrary, is the possibility of a religious and hyperreligious upheaval or surrection. Where modes of rationality are stuck in understanding (rationalities, or sometimes the ratiocinations of technologies, rights, economies, ethics, and policies), where institutional religions poorly prolong their traditions (in fundamentalist rigidity or humanistic compromise), having been surpassed for four or five centuries, and where, consequently, the void in question was hollowed out—no less than in the very heart of society, or of humanity, or civilization, in the eye of the hurricane of globalization— grows inexorably an expectation, still almost silent, which surreptitiously builds toward the point of igniting.

In other words, what up to now the Enlightenment could not enlighten, what it was unable to illumine in itself, is waiting to go up in flames in a messianic, mystical, prophetic, divinatory, and vaticinatory mode (we distinguish here between these diverse epithets), whose incendiary effects may well prove more impressive than those of fascist, revolutionary, surrealist, avant-gardist, or mystical exaltations of all types. Here again, we will not go into semantics, and this bonfire, if it ignites and spreads, will also go into no semantics in its devastation . . .

Conditions are in place for a delirium that would propagate itself in proportion to the wasteland of sense and truth that we have created or allowed to grow. In effect, the place offered for its unleashing is that which a summons, invariably taken up from "politics," wants obstinately to name. It is in a political refoundation, or again, a refoundation of politics that the demand to do justice to reason in its integrity is intended, repeatedly.

However, it happens that politics has not fallen short of itself by accident [*la politique n'est pas par hasard en défaut d'elle-même*]; it has lost what the expression "civil religion" meant for Rousseau, namely, the element in which is practiced not just the mere rationality of governance but the infinitely higher and broader rationality of a sentiment, even a passion, of being-together in view of or according to one's own existence. Yet, between religious religion and assumption into an apolitical salvation, on the one hand, and the class struggle and assumption into a historical salvation of humanity, on the other (itself not patently "political" in the strict sense), "civil religion" will not have lasted very long. And in our time, it is not the approximate and labile concepts of "subjectivation" or, indeed, "multitudes" that can reheat democratic tepidity.

Perhaps democracy, since Athens, has been nothing other than the renewed aporia of a religion of the *polis*, capable of assuming the succession of or indeed replacing (if either of these words is appropriate . . .) those religions from before the *polis*, those religions that, by themselves, created both social bonds and government. Athens itself, then Rome, and then the sovereign modern state have, each in turn, renewed this aporia.[2]

Both the religion of the priests (as Kant put it) and civil religion have each done their time, the latter born out of the retreat of the former (from Greek times) but never apt to replace it and henceforth clearly extinguished.

Perhaps democracy, as it expands its form to a global scale, reveals that politics will only be capable of redefining or redrawing itself according to one of the branches of the following alternative: either as democracy founded anew qua religion (God willing or not!)—and in that case, not as the "theologico-political," as it were,[3] but as fully theocratic (according to the wont of the fundamentalists)—or as a determinate relationship with a distinct element, or dimension, or some instance belonging to the order of sense, and consequently as a redefinition of the internal-external tension in politics between the governance of society and the projection of its ends or its raisons d'être. In the first case, hyperfascism; in the second, a radical invention to be made—a reinvention, perhaps, of what "secularity" means.[4] At the very least, that should signify the following: that politics assume a dimension that it cannot integrate for all that, a dimension that overflows it, one concerning an ontology or an ethology of "being-with," attached to that absolute excedence [*excédence absolue*] of sense and passion for sense for which the word *sacred* was but the designation.

I would have to reproach myself for appearing to play Cassandra and proffering oracles, if in evoking the threat I qualified it as "surreligious" in order to situate it beyond the wear and tear of established religions. It simply seems to me difficult to avoid recognizing the drying up of humanism [*dessèchement humaniste*] and the correlative temptations of a spiritualizing deluge. Difficult, also, not to take responsibility, as a philosopher, for pointing out a limit: that where philosophy continues to be unable to assume the heritage of the Kantian operation [in regard to religion], its speculative sublation [*relève*], its Kierkegaardian surpassing [*outrepassement kierkegaardien*], or its Nietzschean aggravation. Philosophy (and science with it) has managed somehow to intimidate itself with its proclaimed exclusions of a religion from which it never ceased, underhandedly, to draw nourishment, though without really questioning itself about this "secularization" and—we must return to this—about this consequent "laïcization" or social generalization of secularity.

All this can be said otherwise with another term, that of *world*. When the world becomes simultaneously worldwide [*mondial*] and resolutely worldly [*mondain*] (i.e., without "worlds-behind-the-world," without either "heaven" or "heavenly powers"), how and where is inscribed the necessary assertion that *the sense of the world must be found outside of the world*?[5] To this we should also add: the dissolution or deconstruction of the very notion of sense, and the postulate to which that notion corresponds (the expectation of a signification), do not contradict the preceding assertion, they confirm it.

Dis-Enclosure

Metaphysics Dis-Enclosed

We must work on the limit and intimidation self-prescribed by rational thought, which are becoming intolerable to it. It is not that contemporary thought is of no help here. Since Nietzsche, Heidegger, and Wittgenstein, various forms of an "outside of the world" have been opened up in pure worldly immanence. Since Freud, affectivity is affected by the incommensurable and sense by the unsignifiable. From Derrida and Deleuze, very close to each other on this point at least, comes the invitation to think a secret in which thinking becomes secret unto itself (which amounts to an invitation to think in secret, ultimately, to think a thinking situated in the hollow spaces of its own concealment). We might also say that it is a matter of the other—this time, considering a Levinasian source—but of the other insofar as he or she outstrips any assignation *as* or *in* an other of some kind, whether with a capital or a lowercase *o*. This means not only the *alter*—the other of two—but also the *alienus*, the *allos*, everyone's other, and the senseless.

In all these ways, and a few others as well, the same necessity, the same requirement of reason, emerges insistently: that of casting light on its own obscurity, not by bathing it in light, but by acquiring the art, the discipline, and the strength to let the obscure emit its own clarity.[6]

However, it is really the content of such an expression—of its paradox, its oxymoron, its dialectic, or its *Witz* ["joke"]—that asks for clarification. And, in fact, we are simply pointing out the critical domain of the work to be done.

Here, I will limit myself to one preliminary remark. What must be set in motion can only be effected by way of a mutual *dis-enclosure* of the dual heritages of religion and philosophy. Dis-enclosure denotes the opening of an enclosure, the raising of a barrier. And the closure that should interest us is that which has been designated as "the closure of metaphysics."[7]

This expression has, first, the sense of a tautology: "metaphysics," in the sense by which Nietzsche and Heidegger have marked this term, denotes the representation of being [*être*] as beings [*étant*] and as beings present [*étant présent*]. In so doing, metaphysics sets a founding, warranting presence beyond the world (viz., the Idea, *Summum Ens*, the Subject, the Will). This setup stabilizes beings, enclosing them in their own beingness [*étantité*]. Everything—properly and precisely *everything*—is played out in the mutual referral of these two regimes of beings or presence: the "immanent" and the "transcendent"; the "here-below" and the "beyond"; the "sensuous" and the "intelligible"; "appearance" and "reality." Closure is the completion of this totality that conceives itself to be fulfilled in its self-referentiality.

This fulfillment amounts to an exhaustion: on the one hand, self-reference ultimately immobilizes and paralyzes even *being* itself or the sense of the event that it names, and, on the other hand, the dissociation of the two regimes that the closure affixes to one another ends up proving to be a phantasmatic dissociation between the unimpeachable empirical real and the inaccessible real or intelligible surreal. Thus began what was fulfilled in the "twilight of the idols."

To the degree that Christianity can and must be considered a powerful confirmation of metaphysics—aggravating the beingness of being [*étantité de l'être*] through the production of a supreme, arch-present, and efficient Being—Christianity, and with it all monotheism, merely comforts the closure and makes it more stifling.

But it happens that a careful reading of those who denounce metaphysics most vigorously (Nietzsche, Heidegger, Wittgenstein, Derrida, and Deleuze in his fashion) easily shows that they never shared the somewhat vulgar simplicity of this representation. On the contrary, each of them knew perfectly well that it is from within metaphysics itself that the movement of a destabilization of the system of beings in their totality can take shape; failing that, we would be hard pressed to understand how the shake-up of this supposedly monolithic system could have arisen.

In truth, metaphysics deconstructs itself constitutively, and, in deconstructing itself, it dis-encloses [*déclôt*] in itself the presence and certainty of the world founded on reason. In itself, it delivers forever and anew the *epekeina tēs ousias*, the "beyond beings": it foments in itself the overflowing of its rational ground.

(We might add, by the way, that the illusion of an edifying tale of the liberation of modern reason, rising forth fully armed out of Bacon or Galileo's head and reconquering by its strength alone the whole terrain that was in thrall to metaphysical belief, is doubtless the most tenacious and insidious illusion ever to be concealed in the nooks of our many discourses.)

Each of those whom I have named—and well beyond them, the whole movement of thought during the entire history of metaphysics, that is, since Parmenides and Plato—realized very clearly that the closure, if "closure" there is, does not cut across the course of history (i.e., is neither a revolution nor a revelation) but is instead longitudinal. It is from the beginning and without discontinuities that philosophy and every species of knowledge and rational discourse situate, designate, and contemplate the extreme limits of reason in an excess of and over reason itself (the "of" and the "over" being woven here one into the other). The closure invariably dis-encloses itself: such is the precise sense of the demand for the unconditioned that structures Kantian reason; such is likewise the sense of Heidegger's *Destruktion* of ontology and of Derrida's "deconstruction"—as well as the sense of Deleuze's "lines of flight." As an intransigent rationalist once put it very simply: we will never lose "this tenuous ark that ties us to the inaccessible."[8] To deny this most humble and unimpeachable certainty is just bad faith.

This observation immediately refers to one evoked earlier: the constitution of metaphysics itself proceeded neither by self-constitution nor by the "Greek miracle." Its provenance lies in a transformation of the entire order of "ties with the inaccessible." The West was born not from the liquidation of a dark world of beliefs, dissolved by the light of a new sun—and this no more so in Greece than during the Renaissance or the eighteenth century. It took shape in a metamorphosis of the overall relation to the world, such that the "inaccessible" in effect took shape and functioned, as it were, *precisely as such* in thought, in knowledge, and in behavior. There was no reduction of the unknown, but rather an aggravation of the incommensurable (which was no accident, if the solution to the mathematical problem of "incommensurables"—the *alogon* that is the diagonal of the square—furnished the emblematic figure of the birth of true knowledge and, with it or in it, the modeling or mathematical regulation of philosophy).

As such, the *alogon* can be understood as the extreme, excessive, and necessary dimension of the *logos*: from the moment we speak of serious things (death, the world, being-together, being-oneself, the truth), it has never seriously been a question of anything other than this dimension. It is the *alogon* that reason introduced with itself.

Christianity Dis-Enclosed

The previous observation must be completed by another, which constitutes simultaneously its redoubling and its expansion. If, within metaphysics, Christianity did not occur *merely* as a philosophy (which it also was or which also intervened in its formation; after all, the first Christians were considered to be a species or school of "philosophers"); if Christianity was produced in a conjunction of Greek and Jewish thought; if it was, ultimately, the outcome of two or three centuries during which the Mediterranean world was completely disenchanted or demythified, as much in its religious religions as in its civil religions; if, finally, Christianity represented simultaneously the collaboration and confrontation of "reason" and "faith," all this is not because it constituted a late-contracted sickness in the West, ruinous for what was supposed to be a flourishing state of health. The ever-rehashed condemnation of Christianity by philosophers—and particularly by Enlightenment ones—can only leave us perplexed, once we have understood and recognized without reservation all its excellent motifs. The least we can say is that it is highly unlikely that an entire civilization could be affected by a serious congenital disease. It is not safer for us to wield medical metaphors in light of civilizations than it was for Freud to suppose that the "discontent" ("*malaise*," *Unbehagen*) of our own could be effectively treated.

Not safer, we must admit, than it is still to wield (in a more or less visible, more or less declared way) the discredit attaching to the "obscurantism" or "superstition" of a "Middle Ages," whose very name bears the mark of the unfaltering if not outright arrogant distance that the reason of the Modern age took in regard to it. We must admit that the Reformation and the Enlightenment, with and despite their nobility and their great vigor, also grew accustomed to behave vis-à-vis the European past like yesterday's ethnologists toward "primitives." The recasting of ethnology, more than a little underway today (or the dis-enclosure of its ethnocentrism)[9] cannot fail to hold also for the relationship the West has to itself.

If it need be said, I am not advocating the public or promotional restoration of indulgences. I would wish, rather, that the Church abolish all it has preserved of these. However, it is a question of not resting content with judgments of "primitivism" and "clericalism," which put back into play and question paradigms of "rationality," "freedom," or "autonomy," at least as they have been imparted to us by the epic of humanity's emancipation. Perhaps we should also emancipate ourselves from a certain thinking of emancipation, which saw in it the cure for a *maladie honteuse*.

In this regard, Nietzsche does not simplify our task. But neither does he remain with the pathological simplification that he authored. By way of Nietzsche, we should identify instead the question of a *congenital* disease (Platonism, Judeo-Christianity) in the West, which consequently indicates less a pathogenic accident than the constitution of an essence and therefore another type of "health." A congenital disease is not an infantile one; it is often incurable; nevertheless, it can also give us the conditions for a "health" that does not satisfy norms.

~

It seems to me superfluous to repeat all the grievances that can legitimately be leveled against Christianity, from the divestiture of thinking to the ignoble exploitation of pain and misery. We should even push the accusation farther—indeed, farther *than* mere accusation—to interrogate the conditions of possibility of a so powerful and durable religious domination exerted upon a world that, simultaneously, almost never stopped outmaneuvering and deposing this domination, and that found in it weapons to be used against it (freedom, the individual, reason itself). But that is not our purpose here.[10]

For the moment, one remark must suffice, but it is essential. Christianity designates nothing other, essentially (that is to say simply, infinitely simply: through an inaccessible simplicity), than the demand to open in this world an alterity or an unconditional alienation. However, "unconditional" means not undeconstructible.[11] It must also denote the range, by right infinite, of the very movement of deconstruction and dis-enclosure.[12]

In other words, Christianity assumes, in the most radical and explicit fashion, what is at stake in the *alogon*. All the weight—the enormous weight—of religious representation cannot change the fact that [*ne peut pas faire que*] the "other world" or the "other kingdom" never was a second world, or even a world-behind-the-worlds, but the other of the world (*of every world: of all consistency tied up in beings and in communication*), the other than any world. Christianity can be summed up, as Nietzsche, for one, knew well, in the precept of living in this world as outside of it—in the sense that this "outside" is not, [or] not an entity. It does not exist, but it (or again, since it) defines and mobilizes ex-istence: the opening of the world to inaccessible alterity (and consequently a paradoxical access to it).

Whether we take it from Paul or John, from Thomas or Eckhart, Francis or Luther, Calvin or Fénelon, Hegel or Kierkegaard, Christianity thus dis-encloses in its essential gesture the closure that it had constructed and that it perfects, lending to the metaphysics of presence its strongest imaginary resource.

But only the sharpest sense of the Christian demand for alterity could dismantle the "ontological proof," as well as proclaiming the "death of God" while adding, in a less resounding voice, that "only the moral God was refuted."

Christianity is at the heart of the dis-enclosure just as it is at the center of the enclosure [*clôture*]. The logic or the topology of this complex interweave will have to be dismantled in itself: but it is worthwhile first to recognize the legitimacy of such an interweave. Once again, this legitimacy is found in the demand for the unconditioned, that is, for the *alogon*, without which, or rather without the opening toward which, and without exposure to which, we can give up thinking.

This assertion, or series of assertions, implies the possibility not only of deconstructing Christianity—that is, leading it into the movement by which philosophy deports, complicates, and dismantles its own closure—

but of grasping in it (in it as it gets out of itself), from it, the excedent itself, the movement of a deconstruction: namely, the disjointing and dismantling [*désajointement*] of stones and the gaze directed toward the void (toward the *no-thing* [chose-rien]), their setting apart. We must now concern ourselves with what this might specifically mean.

"Majus quam cogitari possit" [Greater Than What Can Be Thought]

All this being said, the ground of a dis-enclosure is inscribed at the heart of the Christian tradition. It suffices to take as evidence the justly famous *Proslogion* of Saint Anselm, whose fundamental force is not that of an "ontological proof" (which we will have to submit, elsewhere, to the trial of thought concerning the true nature of such a "proof"). The high point of the *Proslogion* is not found in the motif according to which God would be that relative to which nothing higher could be thought (*quo majus cogitari nequit*). It is in the supplementary degree provided by the *majus quam cogitari possit*: greater than what can be thought.[13]

The argument rests entirely on the movement of thought, insofar as it cannot not think the maximum of the being [*l'être*] it is able to think, but thinks also an excess to that maximum, since thought is capable of thinking even that there is something that exceeds its power to think. In other words, thinking (i.e., not the intellect alone, but the heart and the demand itself) can think—indeed, cannot not think—that it thinks something in excess over itself. It penetrates the impenetrable, or rather is penetrated by it.

It is this movement alone that constitutes reason in its unconditionality or in the absoluteness and infinity of the desire through which man is caught up infinitely in it [*s'y passe infiniment*]. In this sense, Anselm is much less a follower of Christianity than the bearer of a necessity that defines the modern world of thought, of the existential ordeal of thought.

"God" is for Anselm the name of this ordeal. This name can assuredly be rejected for many reasons. But the ordeal or trial cannot be avoided. Subsequently, the question may arise of knowing whether this ordeal does or does not require recurrence to a special nomination distinct from any nomination of concepts, and whether "god" or "divine" can or cannot serve as an index or benchmark.

However that may be, the true scope of the "dis-enclosure" can only be measured by this question: Are we capable, yes or no, of grasping anew—beyond all mastery—the demand that carries thought out of itself without confusing this demand, in its absolute irreducibility, with some construction of ideals or with some sloppy assembly of phantasms?

What Follows

A simple warning for those who will not already have thrust aside this book in fury, pity, or discouragement. What follows here does not constitute the sustained and organized development one might expect. It is only an assembly, wholly provisional, of diverse texts that turn around the same object without approaching it frontally. It has not yet seemed to me possible to undertake the more systematic treatment of this object, but I thought it desirable to put to the test texts that have remained little known to the public, even, for the most part, once they were published. In fact, I do not feel particularly secure in this undertaking: everywhere lurk traps. I do not foresee opposition or attacks, or even eager endorsements, so much as I anticipate the extremely narrow margin of maneuver that the operation (if it is one) I am trying to discuss here has available to it. That margin is philosophically narrow, by definition, and socially narrow—caught in its fashion between diverse tensions and complacencies. But so it goes.

I will attempt to advance somewhat farther. For the moment, what we find here is but an *open-air construction site*; that should sum up what we need to know.

〜

It is hardly possible at this stage to propose anything more than this single axiom: it is in no respect a question of simply suggesting that a philosopher could "believe in God" (or in gods)—"philosopher" meaning here not a technician of the concept but first that which is expected, even required, today of common wisdom or conscience [*conscience commune*]. By contrast, it is a question, and perhaps only a question, of wondering whether faith has ever, *in truth*, been confused with belief. In effect, it is enough to observe that belief is in no way proper to religion. There are many profane beliefs; there are even beliefs among scholars and philosophers. But faith? . . . Should it not form the necessary relation to the *nothing*: in such a way that we understand that there are no buffers, no halting points, no markers, no indeconstructible terms, and that dis-enclosure never stops opening what it opens (the West, metaphysics, knowledge, the self, form, sense, religion itself)?

As to the two other "theological virtues" [*"vertus théologales"*], that is, the two other orders and powers of relating to the object of some faith, hope, and charity—to give them their most traditional names—their turn will come later, and we shall thus be gratified or even redeemed moreover [*par surcroît*].

꒘

The order of the texts is only relatively consistent. It is not necessary to follow it, even less so given that they were written under the most diverse circumstances, as we will see. To begin with, "Atheism and Monotheism" should make clear and explicit the perspective sketched above, as does the following essay, "A Deconstruction of Monotheism," which has a more didactic character and an older date. There follow two texts relative to the idea of "faith": "The Judeo-Christian" and "A Faith That Is Nothing at All," relative respectively to Derrida and Granel (a part of whose text, "Far from Substance," follows and is commented on by me). Thereafter, "An Experience at Heart" attempts to restore the "Christian" experience of the "atheist" Nietzsche. *"Verbum caro factum* [The Word Made Flesh]" is a brief and provisional reflection on "incarnation." "The Name *God* in Blanchot" collects a few clues from the author who doubtless has brought the empty relation of belief [*rapport vide de croyance*][14] most closely to that which "God" can (or should it be to that which "God" must?) designate. We then examine the motif of "resurrection," again in Blanchot. This was the point of a discussion with Derrida, of which "Consolation, Desolation" is a trace.[15] "On a Divine *Wink*"[16] examines the gesture to which the "last god" is reduced, for Heidegger, and sets it in relation to "différ*a*nce." "An Exempting from Sense" introduces an atheological reflection on sense, starting from an expression of Roland Barthes. "'Prayer Demythified'" extends the thoughts of Michel Deguy on nonreligious prayer. The text "The Deconstruction of Christianity" is the oldest and remains, to my mind, outside or set apart from the others; yet it points to the first efforts at clearing a narrow and difficult path that seems to me to be necessary. It also points toward the possibility of a deconstructive analysis of the principal elements of Christian dogma, scarcely addressed in the present volume (we will have to return to this later on). Finally, "Dis-Enclosure" provides, in the key of a "spatial conquest"—to put it summarily, in that of the heavens deserted and reopened [*ciel déserté et réouvert*]—a formal variation on the theme of the divine qua opening or spacing, separated by intervals from itself as much as in itself [*de lui-même aussi bien qu'en lui-même espacé*].[17]

Translated by Bettina Bergo

Atheism and Monotheism

> Monotheism is an atheism.
>
> **—Schelling**

1

Not only is atheism an invention specific to the West, but it must also be considered the element in which the West invented itself as such. What we call "Greece" may well be traversed by, or mixed into, a considerable number of religious attitudes; it nonetheless remains true that, before all else, what distinguishes or even constitutes the "Greek" is a space of living and thinking that divine presence (barring that of the gods of the *polis* or those subject to speculation, who are precisely no longer *presences*) neither shapes nor marks out [*balise*]. The Greeks, here, are above all the descendants of Xenophanes, who, well before Plato, scoffed at the anthropomorphism of the gods and thus found himself already caught up in the invention of atheism. (In the meantime, to be sure, the gods of the mysteries pursued their underground fate—another story, which I will leave aside here but which will also come into close relation with monotheism [*s'aboucher avec le monothéisme*].)

This invention of atheism responds to a change in the general paradigm. In the place of a world order given and received in a destinal mode [*sur un mode destinal*] (whether we emphasize the sense of assignation or that of orientation in this term) is substituted a regime in which the world is constructed starting from a questioning concerning its principle or principles.[1] That one starts to speak of "nature" in the sense of a system of elements, of principles and consequences, means that the world can no longer be divided among presences of qualities and diverse statuses (such as mortals, immortals, low, high, impure, or pure qualities). Instead, it must be divided between the totality of the given and the order of the conditions of what can no longer be its mere reception, but must, rather, on the basis of the given, provide its reason in turn. This reason may well be called "divine"; its divinity nevertheless derives solely from the excellence of its axiological position and not from an intrinsic difference [*écart*] in its nature. Contrariwise, this nature shows itself by right as accessible to mortals, even if only after their death (or again, contrariwise and preferably, insofar as their death became the royal road to this access). When Plato writes *ho theos*, as he sometimes does, this designation of the "god," in the singular and lacking a proper name, makes its translation almost impossible for us, since we have to choose between abandoning the substantive and speaking of the "divine," or keeping it and speaking of a "god" as a unique person, of which Plato has no idea—a fitting way to put it, in every sense of the word *idea*.

In Plato's *theos*, we can say that the gods disappear (even if Plato himself can name them in the plural just a few lines after his singular *theos*). This is to say that the paradigm of the given, structured, and animate universe—the same one that will be called a *mythology*, so that a *physiology* and a *cosmology* may be substituted for it—has ceased to function. Its founding representations and stories are no longer recognized as flexible modelings of the world, but only as fictions. Gods are departing into their myths.

Yet if these fictions evince their value only thanks to their various figures, attributes, and scenarios, that is, thanks to the spectacular troop of divine characters enriched with their properties, genealogies, avatars, fury, and desires, then we can also say that the unique *thēos*, deprived of appearance [*figure*] and name, really represents an invention, even the invention, of "god" in general. There is neither "the god" nor "the divine," nor even perhaps "the gods": these do not come first or, again, they do not quite exist so long as there are the people or the species of immortal figures. We find the mortals' immortal partners, but not the ontological distance for which the word *god* will henceforth provide the measure. We must therefore suppose that the invention of "atheism" is contemporaneous and correlative with the invention of "theism." Both terms, in effect, have their unity in the principial paradigm or premise [*paradigme principiel*]. Never did a god—where his or her name was Uranus, Isis, or Baal—hold the position or essence of a principle.

The gods acted, spoke, or watched from death's other shore. They did not convey mortals to that shore, or if they did so, they invariably maintained, at the same time, the river that flowed between the shores. They maintained it gaping and threatening: just as it was when it flowed between Diana and Actæon, for example; just as it would continue to flow between men and their dead shadows.

On the contrary, the premise or premises (but the singular is necessary and required here *in principle*) has no other function than to bridge the gap between the shores. Such is the logical function that is substituted for the mythical fiction: the dual positing of a radical alterity (god and man are no longer together in the world) and of a relation from the same to the other (man is called toward god).

2

It is indispensable that we provide ourselves with these initial givens if we do not want to misunderstand the *vis-à-vis* of "theism" and "atheism," which is always more or less supposed. Assuredly, this *vis-à-vis* exists insofar as one term is the negation of the other. But we should not overlook to what degree this negation retains the essence of what it negates. Atheism states the principle of the negation of the divine principle, that is, of the principle represented in the configuration of an entity [*existant*] that is distinct from the entire world of entities, and for which it would hold the first cause and the final end. It thus poses, in principle, either that the cause and the end belong to another, immanent order, or that these concepts must not be brought into play.

By the first hypothesis, immanence (whether we call it matter or life, history, society, or art), displaces nothing at all in the ideal statuses of cause and end. Further still, the hypothesis changes nothing about their practical statuses, because their principles have not the slightest reason not to become as restrictive, even as coercive, as those of some "divine will" or some "order of salvation." The nineteenth- and twentieth-century West experienced those coercive possibilities to a point not hard to qualify as crucial. Henceforth, we know that atheism is a disaster in that sense. (If there were any need to be more precise, I would point out in passing that not all philosophies of "immanence" [*pensées d'une "immanence"*] place themselves under the atheist paradigm that I just evoked. Some philosophies of "immanence" foil the opposition "immanence"-"transcendence," but this is not the place to discuss that.)

In a way that is paradoxical and worse than contrastive and discordant, we now know both that atheism is the only possible *ethos*, the only dignity of the subject (if I give this word the value of *praxis* rather than that of reflexivity), *and* that this same atheism leaves destitute or threatening the order of the in-common, the order of "culture," of the "together." It is a matter of nothing less here, ultimately (if there is an ultimately), than the unappeased demand that was called "communism." But I will not tarry with that. The in-common finds itself orphaned of all religion, whether religious or civil. And, as a conjunction of atheism and individualism, it is even orphaned, consequently and obviously, in regard to capitalism— which ought to make us reflect.

As regards the second hypothesis—the disqualification of causes and ends—it is no doubt clear enough that a certain state of mind [*état de la pensée*], quite common today, asks no better than to welcome this hypothesis. We sense that "cause" and "end" should not, or no longer, be concepts acceptable outside of determinate technical spheres within which they carry the evidence of axioms. We sense this all the more in considering, not so much the technical systems identified, but the world regime that we could call "technology" (or again, "capital"). And it becomes clear that this regime never ceases dissolving, through its own unfolding, every possibility of finding, imputing, or inventing causes or ends for it. That is, unless we identify this regime more or less with *phusis* itself, insofar as *technē* comes, after all, from *phusis*, before redeploying it for its own purposes. But in doing this we would only end up with a tautological teleology of the world, without ever setting forth, for all that, the new mythology that this tautology should require . . .

We should thus be capable of a strictly anetiological (acausal) and ateleological thinking. It would be easy to show how much this demand has preoccupied philosophy since the beginning of the contemporary world. All things considered, Hegel—who passes for the model thinker of fulfillment processes—also asks to be understood (or again, Schelling, before and with him) as the first to think beyond all teleology. However, being capable of discerning this requirement of interpretation—which bears witness to our own expectations and experiences ever since the suspension of what is called "Hegelian history"—does not make us the more capable of anetiological and ateleological thinking. That is to say, in a word, that we are not now more capable of *atheistic* thinking—the thinking that we know we desire. This is because for us, up to now, such an orientation of thinking—thinking without end, finitude without end, in sum, the infinite—remains privative, subtractive, and, in sum, defective—in much the way that the main tone of every species of atheism also remains obstinately and deafly defective, even if against its own will. (We must, no doubt, hasten to add that this does not authorize any legitimation of the positive assurance of theism: that would only be to set back-to-back the two faces of the Western Janus.) Blanchot understood this perfectly.

3

The day will perhaps come, and perhaps it is not even so far away, when we shall characterize all contemporary thinking as a slow and heavy gravitational movement around the black sun of atheism. With the collapse of that premise—to which all of classical onto-theology bears witness, up to its Kantian dethronement and in its Nietzschean funeral ceremonies—there has followed no new understanding, no unforeseen grasp (revolutionary? creative? emancipatory? salvific?—how would we want to designate this?) of this collapse and of the void that has resulted from it, no new apprehension, namely, one that would be produced through prisms of thought other than those that words like *collapse* or *void* call so banally to mind.

I do not mean that contemporary thought, in all that in it is most alive, has not engaged in disorganizing and delegitimizing those prisms. In fact, it does nothing else. Nevertheless, atheism continues—ultimately, in a very paradoxical way—to close the horizon. Or again, perhaps it is more accurate to say that it continues to form a horizon, precisely where it ought to be a question of something else. For horizons and principles are mutually complicit [*ont partie liée*].

The horizon of a subtraction, of a retreat, an absence, or even the horizon of what I once called "absentheism," to oppose it to atheism, continues to form a horizon. That is to say, it forms a limit, a dead end, and an end of the world. That horizon surrounds our thinking all the more in that the world, in effect, everywhere touches its confines, and this in a physical mode as well as in a metaphysical one. It can no longer be a matter of getting out of the world, but that is not a reason to consider the world a horizon. In other words, finiteness does not limit infinity; on the contrary, finiteness should give it its expansion and its truth. That is what is at stake, and there are no other stakes today. (In a striking sense, physics appears to say something analogous today when it speaks of a finite universe in expansion, but I will not embark upon an analogy that is perhaps merely formal.)

Mutatis mutandis, it is really a matter of nothing other than the nihilism that Nietzsche understood. Atheism *is* nihilism, and if nihilism indicates at the same time that it is through nihilism, on the basis of it, and almost as if in nihilism that any question of "getting out" (if this term is appropriate) can arise, then it has nevertheless not surpassed up to now its own pointing toward something else, except to point toward a repetition of its own *nihil*. Assuredly, this is a repetition that is often powerful, courageous, functional, and inventive—this repetition that is played out around the bounds [*repères*] of the "void," the "absence," the "disaster," the "without-end," the "aporia," or even, in a more ascetic way, around a more or less pronounced renunciation of something other than combinations of "forms of life" and the differentiated truth regimes (with perspectives, at times, more or less akin to Kant's "regulation").

It is always a matter, willy-nilly, of "introducing a new sense, knowing that this introduction is itself without sense," as Nietzsche wrote more or less, expressing a paradox whose structure contains all the force of an injunction and all the difficulty, even the anxiety, of our situation. But how to lift this aporia, when forcing a sense beyond senses (senseless? an absent sense? a hyperbolic or hypertrophied sense?) has given us nothing less than exterminating horror, in so many forms—combined with humanistic impotence, it too in so many forms?

This last word thrusts us anew toward the black core of our vertigo. Humanism was atheism. It was its truth, its breadth, its expression, and its function. Because it turned the essence of god into the essence of man, it merely imprinted on the premise a pivoting or rotation on itself (a revolution?). Thus, on the one hand, it modified nothing in the onto-(a)-theological construction, nor could it situate, on the other hand, its own form as principle in a place worthy of it: "humanism does not think high enough the *humanitas* of man," wrote Heidegger.

What does this so-called "height" mean? Above all, what does it mean if we consider the fact that Heidegger wrote this sentence after passing through his well-known blindness to the "grandeur" of what the word *national-socialism* now stigmatizes? Must we speak in terms of elevation, altitude, or size? That is not certain. But in what terms then? Pascal wrote that "man infinitely passes [*passe*] man." What could this "passing" mean? Surpassing [*dépasser*]? Overcoming [*surmonter*]? Exceeding? Transporting? Transfiguring? Divinizing? Naturalizing? Technicizing? Exposing to the abyss? Annihilating? And still further: Dehumanizing? Inhumanizing? Overhumanizing? As we can see, over some two centuries, we have run through the whole gallery of these figures, rather like the Hegelian Spirit, and we are exhausted, nauseated by this, our Absolute Knowledge from which flows back to us (unlike the knowledge of Spirit) no "infinity" other than that of an infamy, according to which the "surpassing" of man takes the shape of an inexorable domination of humans by a total process that is not even their history anymore, but a mechanism indifferent to their fates and wholly engaged in its own exponential and exponentially tautological development.

This sadness sums up atheism. Even the possibility of the tragic, or the tragic possibility—which may have been that of the Greeks finding themselves deprived, forsaken, or cursed by the gods—is refused us. This sadness retains nothing of the strange, tragic joy to which Nietzsche or the young Benjamin were still witness. This also means, more clearly than ever, that the exit from capitalism—here again, it is a matter of an "exit" (and yet in what valence of this word?)—can only be envisaged as the exit from nihilism. And this, in two ways that share a solidarity. On the one hand, the formal structure of the "exit" is the same (it is an exit from within, as Marx and Nietzsche understood). On the other hand, it turns on the same stake: the one I am designating here, for the time being, as the necessity of an effective modification of the tautology (or, indeed, the consequent necessity of a heterology).

4

If I am undertaking, at present, a meditation on monotheism, it is not to seek in it some way out, some remedy or salvation. "Salvation" represents, on the contrary, the confirmation of the world of nihilism by the necessity of redemption that it asserts. In that sense, monotheism will have represented nothing other than the theological confirmation of atheism: the reduction of the divine to the premise in a logic of dependence on the world. Correlatively, the tautology of the world is simply displaced there into the tautology of God: in effect, the one god is nothing other than the repetition of his immutable being. He does not have any history or form, and it is no accident that, in a decisive moment of his many redefinitions, he was designated and thought as the *logos* present *ēn archē* ["in the beginning"].

In reality, this moment responds to the conjunction of Greek atheism and Jewish monotheism in the elaboration of what, under the name of Christianity, constituted the major configuration of onto-(a)-theology (played out differently in Islam, which would obviously require, in order to be precise, supplementary consideration).

Through the religions of the Book (Judaism, Christianity, Manicheism, Islam), a particularly complex, even tortuous history unfolded. Its driving element or organizing core stands precisely at the point of conjunction of Joyce's *greekjew/jewgreek*—but only insofar as this point forms, at the same time, a point of disjunction and insofar as that intimate disjunction at the heart of atheism itself still demands to be truly experienced and put to the test.

On the one hand, the conjunction conjoins, in effect, two formations of atheism. Jewish monotheism, understood in its unfolding and its spread throughout the Greek world, opens into Christian thought (which we could rightly call Stoic-Christian). It prepares nothing other than the simultaneous evaporation of all divine presences and powers, and the designation of a principle that no longer has as "divine" anything but the name—a name dispossessed of all personality, and even the ability to be uttered [*prononçabilité*].

Considered from this angle, the whole history of "God"—the "God" of the West—unfolds nothing less than the trial or process [*procès*] of atheism itself, in its most rigorous proceedings [*progression*]. To take note of a few indications, this passes through the idea of a "proof" of his existence (which supposes that *one* existence at least could be deduced a priori, on the basis of which all existence will be deduced, and the supposed proof falls back on an ontological tautology), or again through Spinoza's *deus sive natura* (which, notwithstanding, leaves entirely open the question of what the unity of this *deus* consists in, since it exists only in the infinity of its modes). Or, finally, we can see that the process passes through Feuerbach's God, of whom man need only leave aside the imaginary substance in order to reappropriate its predicates. To all this we could add a considerable number of traits, such as Descartes' idea of the perfect being, or the logically necessitated freedom through which Leibniz's God creates the best of all possible worlds. However that may be, we shall end up with this result: *God* denotes the premise or principle of a presupposed totality, founded in unity and in necessity.

In all of this, God names only the tautology of the unitotality thereby presupposed. In Heideggerian terms, God names the consistency of being, understood as principial, founding, and essential. God represents, in the most patent way, being at and as the ground of beings: *ens summum, verum, bonum*. We should therefore not be surprised that Heidegger sees in Christianity (to say nothing of its two fellow religions [*co-religionnaires*]) little more than an epiphenomenon lacking any particular specificity with regard to the destinal and epochal history of being (where "being" itself is understood not as principle but, on the contrary, as a "principle of anarchy," to content ourselves with Reiner Schürmann's paradox, or, again. as a deconstruction of the logic of principles in general). However, as we know, the Christianity of onto-theology is not the Christianity with which Heidegger pursued his "silent elucidation."[2]

It is thus abundantly clear that monotheism will have constituted, all in all, (a)theism's second condition of possibility. The unicity of the god of monotheism must not be set into a numeric relationship with the plurality of gods in what we have called "polytheism." Rather, unicity displaces or converts divinity. From a present power or person, it changes divinity into a principle, a basis, and/or a law, always by definition absent or withdrawn in the depths of being. *Deus absconditum*: we might as well say a "god" that draws into the "one" the entirety of its *numen* inasmuch as it tends to dissolve that *nomen* "god," which, precisely, had never been a divine name!

If this is the situation, then we must nevertheless ask ourselves why the root of atheism should have had—or must have had—a double constitution. The disrepute of Christianity as epiphenomenon of metaphysics, as well as its reduction by Kant or Hegel to the status of a representative transcription of the logic of reason or Spirit, does not account for this phenomenon of lining or doubling [*phénomène de doublure ou de doublage*].

What we ought to say is that reason cannot give sufficient reason for its representations. The idea of a transcription, a travesty, or a religious hijacking of the functions of reason is an idea that definitively commands (with a host of variations on the themes of "representation," "sentiment," "illusion," and "ideology") all that is essential for philosophical denunciation. Now, if in many respects it accounts for the moral, political, and spiritual infamy that religions no doubt share (and especially monotheistic ones, a matter that should be examined elsewhere), it nevertheless cannot account for the peculiar dehiscence of the *logos* and the premise. It cannot account for that separation except by designating an inferior degree of reason, a lack to be raised to the heights of thought, or again by deploring still more directly in religion a veritable perversion or disease (of thought, of culture, of society).

It is strange to think that our civilization in its entirety posits, in principle, the weak, corrupted, or foreign (i.e., non-Greek . . .) essence of what has not ceased to constitute something like its internal lining—and this for more than twenty centuries. It all comes to pass as though atheism refused to consider the possibility that this doubling might be understood in a way other than through infirmity, disease, or even the perversity of priests.

There is no doubt that infirmity, even debility, sickness, and meanness are at work (in alternation or conjunction) from the moment that we attempt to assure ourselves a mastery over and presentation of the premise. The signal weakness of any logic of the premise (should we say, of logic *tout court*?) shows itself at the crucial point where theism and atheism prove to belong to each other [*se coappartiennent*]: insofar as the premise is asserted, or symmetrically denied, it can only collapse in its own positing or in being deposed. The decisive point is this—it ought to be the task of the principle, as we sketched it above, *to exceed qua principle principiation itself*. To put it otherwise and perhaps better, it ought to be the task of the premise to elude itself, to withdraw from itself, to pull away from itself, or again to deconstruct principiation on the basis of itself. A principle or principate [*principat*] (to appeal to this old word here) can only *exempt or make exception of itself in regard to itself* [s'excepter de lui-même]. At least, this is one of the branches of the alternative before which this principate is ineluctably placed: either it confirms itself, infinitely, or it exempts itself by or from itself—and this, no less infinitely. (The politics of sovereignty as the power of the exception reproduces precisely this logic, with the extreme delicacy of its unstable equilibrium, ever balanced between the legitimacy of an illegitimate [prince] and the illegitimacy of a legitimate [prince].) To reuse our earlier terms, either the premise confirms its etiological and teleological tautology, or it is in itself exposed as heterogeneous to any tautology: fleeing into a heterology.

5

Is it not desirable, then, to ask whether the doubling and dehiscence of monotheism and atheism do not communicate with this heterogenesis? In other words, can we be that calmly assured, without further inquiry, that monotheism is but the other, feeble, and clerical side of atheism? After all, the one and the other are forever united in the rigidification of the premise (or of the One), which is also to say in the abandonment or dereliction that is nihilism.

The time has come to understand our own history otherwise than it has heretofore sought to understand itself under the domination of its own principle or premise.

Greek atheism and Jewish monotheism met up at a point at which the unity of the premise and the unicity of the god comforted and opposed each other, reciprocally and at the same time. They did this through a dual and violent movement whose effects have never ceased innervating and irritating our history. On the one hand, the unicity of the god very clearly let itself be subsumed or absorbed by the unity of the premise. In this way Christianity became, by itself, a humanism, an atheism, and a nihilism. The ever more difficult preservation of its properly religious forms (its church, its practices, and its myths) ended up becoming the object of a struggle or of internal schisms. (How and whether this scheme functioned, or was overturned, in Judaism or Islam, as well as in the relation or non-relation between the three monotheisms, will have to be examined elsewhere.)

On the other hand, the unicity of the god refused to come under the sway of the premise. It is no accident if, in the heyday of modern rationality, Pascal, writing his "Memorial," so violently felt the need to separate without reserve the God "of the philosophers and savants" from the "GOD of Abraham, Isaac, and Jacob, the GOD of Jesus-Christ." This separation and its resultant opposition or contradiction are together lodged at the heart of atheism, precisely at the place where the very principle of the premise (as I suggested above) collapses by itself and, in this collapse, signals the possibility, even the requirement of and the call for, a wholly other, anarchic configuration.

It is enough to recall some of the major traits by which monotheism opposes, as much as it comforts, the reign of the premise. (It is my hypothesis or my wager that these traits are at work, silently at least, in Heidegger, and, still more silently, in Wittgenstein; I note this here to point out that what is at stake really has to do with the necessity that has guided thought over the last century.)

In opposition to the relation that forms between a premise and its consequences (or between a condition and what it conditions) stands the relationship between the creator and the creature. Concerning this relationship we must first assert that it radically cuts off any ties with the preceding one, because the latter is a relation of identity, inherence, or consequence (if A, therefore B; if *alpha*, therefore *omega*). By contrast, creation entails a relation of alterity and contingence (if "God," then there is *no reason* why he creates). The idea of *creatio ex nihilo*, inasmuch as it is clearly distinguished from any form of production or fabrication, essentially covers the dual motif of an absence of necessity and the existence of a given without reason, having neither foundation nor principle for its gift (a "gift" for which, doubtless, no concept of gift can prove to be adequate). *Ex nihilo*, which is to say: nothing in or as principle [*rien au principe*], a nothing of principle,[3] nothing but that which is [*rien que cela qui est*], nothing but that which grows [*rien que cela qui croît*] (*creo, cresco*), lacking any growth principle, even (and especially not) the autonomous premise of a "nature" (unless we reevaluate this concept by way of Spinoza).

In the first place, we might say that the *nihil* is posited. Perhaps this is the only way seriously to get out of nihilism. "Nihil*ism*" means, in effect: making a premise of nothing. But *ex nihilo* means: undoing any premise, including that of nothing. That means: to empty *nothing* [*rien*] (cf. *rem*, the thing) of any quality as principle. That is creation.[4]

Without examining further the implications or obligations of such an "undoing," let us simply add two other traits.

First, the relationship of creation is doubled by the relationship between the saint and the sinner. Once again, not identity but alterity is at stake. The saint or the holy is the other of the sinner, in the sense that the sinner is constituted, in his being, by his relation to this alterity. He is a sinner for not being holy, but it is to holiness that he is beholden. Yet holiness is not a principle. Holiness is neither determinable, nor representable, nor prescribable. It opens to man or in man (unless we should say: it opens to the world or in the world, and not for man alone) the dimension and the movement, or gesture, of an "infinitely coming to pass" [*d'un "se passer infiniment"*]. It would not be impossible to interpret, playing on those two expressive possibilities in the French: "*l'homme passe infiniment l'homme*" ["man infinitely passes man"] and "*l'homme se passe infiniment de l'homme*" ["infinitely, man does without man"]. (Does "God," or the saint, do without man, or not? As we know, this question has never ceased circulating in Christianity.)

The last trait that we retain here will be that of faith. If the premise must be known or well known, just as the gods must have been, moreover—and if, additionally, religion is a form of knowledge (the knowledge of observance and scruples)—it is to faith that the saint turns. Faith is not weak, hypothetical, or subjective knowledge. It is neither unverifiable nor received through submission, nor even through reason. It is not a belief in the ordinary sense of the term. On the contrary, it is the act of the reason that relates, itself, to that which, in it, passes *it* infinitely: faith stands precisely at the point of an altogether consequent atheism. This is to say that it stands at the point where atheism is dispossessed of belief in the premise or principle and in principate, in general. This is the point Kant already recognized formally when he spoke, for example, of "the incapacity in which reason finds itself, to satisfy by itself its own needs."[5] Reason does not suffice unto itself: *for itself* it is not a *sufficient reason*. But it is in the acknowledgment of this insufficiency that it fully justifies itself. For in this way it recognizes, not a lack or a flaw for which it should expect reparations from an other, but rather the following: the logic of sufficiency and/or lack is not the logic appropriate to it.

This is why what Kant called a "moral faith" (not a "metaphysical," "speculative," or "doctrinal" one) has its essence not in a failure of reason but, on the contrary, in the firmness with which reason confronts its own dissatisfaction. Not seeing therein an insufficiency, a failing, or a lack that might condemn it to nihilism, moral faith there discovers "non-sufficiency." I use this term in the precise sense in which, henceforth, it is no longer a question of "sufficing" or of "satisfying," for *there is neither sufficiency nor satisfaction possible if there is also no principle to which satisfaction must be granted.* Faith is then the firm fidelity of reason to its own atheology.

What the name "God," or that of the "holy," rigorously attempts to designate in this atheological regime—if we accept using Bataille's term to designate an atheism clearly freed from the schema of an inverted theism—refers not only to a ruining of the premise but, in a way still more contrary to principial logic, refers to "something," to "someone," or to "a nothing" (perhaps to the same *nihil ex quo* . . .) of which faith is itself the birthplace or the creative event. That "God" himself may be the fruit of faith, which at the same time depends only on his grace (that is, exempts itself from necessity and obligation), is a thought profoundly foreign—perhaps it is the most foreign—to the theism/atheism pair. It is the thinking of alterity opened by and exposed outside of sameness, as that which exceeds thinking infinitely without in any way being principial to it. Yet this thinking is not foreign to Christian reflection—no more so than to reflection in Judaism or Islam. Let us cite only Makarios of Magnesia. "The one who does the will of my Father gives birth to me by participating in this act, and he is born with me. He who believes in effect that I am the only Son of God engenders me in some sense through his faith."[6]

I will close here with the following observation: the Platonic precept was to "liken oneself to the divine," whereas the monotheistic precept was to look within for our divine similitude. *Homoiōsis, mimesis,* and *methexis* all together. Now, there are two possible modes by which to liken oneself: either one appropriates the attributes of a subject supposed to be other and principial, or one alters the same into a properly infinite alterity, which proves unappropriable, imprescribable, and an-archic. There remains the question of knowing whether "God" or "the holy" can or do represent names (and on what grounds) for this alterity of reason. While it is established that "atheism" remains a term both equivocal and without a future, no response of this sort has yet been given to the question we have just posed.

Coda

In an abrupt manner, I will introduce in closing the following question: Should we therefore understand today—and if so, in what way—the word that was in a sense Heidegger's last: "Only a god can save us now"?

It is not politically correct to treat this sentence without contempt. Yet it is philosophically necessary. Cut and dried, what does it tell us, then?

First, it states a tautology: if there is some reason "to save" anything, then certainly "only a god" can do so, if "salvation" indeed belongs to a divine order. A tautology then, and empty, inasmuch as reflection on salvation is not developed. Now, "to save" is not something that is thought. But "to save" is not "to heal." It is not a process, and it is not measured against some ultimate "health" (*salvus* and *sanus* are not the same terms). It is a unique and instantaneous act, through which one who is already in the abyss is held back or recovered. "To save" does not annul the abyss; it takes place in it. (Perhaps Buddhist "awakening" takes place in a comparable fashion, if it takes place, right in the middle of the world and not outside of it.)

That same being in or unto the abyss (*Geworfensein*, "poverty," "dereliction,"[7] "sin") is not that *from which* one returns by way of a dialectic, nor that of which we might give ourselves a mimetico-cathartic representation. It is rather that *within* which (more so than *from* which) there is "salvation." At least it is in this direction that we should be able to think.

I will gladly indicate this direction using the words of Rachel Bespaloff (who was, among other things, an astonishing reader of Heidegger): "We must not call God our powerlessness and our despair" (a citation from Nietzsche), nor seek therein a "remedy," but rather expose ourselves "to the peril of salvation."[8]

꒦

But how shall we so much as approach such a thought? Surely not with philosophy understood as the "science of first principles," as "rational knowledge," or as a production of representations of the world. Heidegger indicates this in the context of the same interview with *Der Spiegel* (i.e., "Philosophy is at its end"). And the "god" of which he is speaking designates, before all this, the "nothing other" for which philosophy is neither the site nor the regime. That god, that "last god," as he puts it elsewhere—that "god," insofar as every god is the "last one," which is to say that every god dissipates and dissolves the very essence of the divine—is a god that *beckons* [winkt]. That means, it makes a sign without sense, a signal of approach, of invitation, and of departure.[9] This god has its essence in *winken*. And that sign-making, that blink of the eye comes to pass, starting from and in the direction of the *Ereignis*—the appropriating event through which man, appropriated to or by being, may be disappropriated (*ent-eignet*) of an identity closed in on its humanity. Man may thus "propriate" himself, address himself and dedicate himself (*zu-eignet*) to what is infinitely more than him-"self" [*lui-"même"*].

Perhaps it is simply that this e-levation [*ex-haussement*] of man, of which the all-too-human man cannot so much as dream and to which no philosophical essence of man can be compared (but was there ever a "philosophic essence" of man? Perhaps not; perhaps philosophy always surpasses its own end . . .). Perhaps it is simply that which the word *god* names, or rather signals, "winks at."

Heidegger thus means at least this, that the e-levation takes place without knowledge and outside of sense. Neither firm knowledge (science), nor weak knowledge (belief). Neither belief in God, nor belief in man, nor belief in knowledge, nor even in art. Yet a firmness, yes, and a fidelity, even a *devotion* [*dévouement*] in an extraordinarily strong sense of the word (an act of "vowing or -voting oneself" the way one de-votes oneself to a task or to a devil).[10]

Yet, in this way we would be led back to something that strongly resembles Kant's "practical faith," evoked earlier. This is why it is not without interest to propose here the following, wholly provisional conclusion.

The sentence "Only a god . . ."—or whatever sentence at all that today names "a god" or "the divine"—is nothing other than a reformulation, risky but necessary, imperious even (and neither riskier nor less necessary, when we think about it, than what it reformulates), of a famous sentence:

> I therefore had to abrogate *knowledge* in order to make room for *faith*, and the dogmatism of metaphysics, that is to say the prejudice according to which one might progress, without a critique of pure reason, is the true source of that incredulity that struggles with morality—an incredulity that is, in turn, always very dogmatic, in fact.[11]

What Kant's expression holds open for us is none other than this: a critique of reason, that is to say, a demanding and non-complacent examination of reason by reason, makes unconditionally requisite, within reason itself, an opening and an e-levation of reason. It is not a question of "religion," here, but rather of a "faith" as a sign of the fidelity of reason to that which *in and of itself* exceeds reason's phantasm of justifying itself [*rendre raison de soi*] as much as the world and man.

That the signal "a god"—or again, the "signal of a god"—might be necessary or not here remains once again undecided. That will perhaps remain undecidable—or not. But, for the moment, it is at least beyond all doubt that a signal, whatever it may be, addresses us from the site of our atheist reason.

Translated by Gabriel Malenfant and Bettina Bergo

A Deconstruction of Monotheism

Then there is the persisting legacy of monotheism itself, the Abrahamic religions, as Louis Massignon aptly called them. Beginning with Judaism and Christianity, each is a successor haunted by what came before; for Muslims, Islam fulfills and ends the line of prophecy. There is still no decent history or demystification of the many-sided contest among these three followers—not one of them by any means a monolithic, unified camp—of the most jealous of all gods, even though the bloody modern convergence on Palestine furnishes a rich secular instance of what has been so tragically irreconcilable about them.

Not surprisingly, then, Muslims and Christians speak readily of crusades and jihads, both of them eliding the Judaic presence with often sublime insouciance. Such an agenda, says Eqbal Ahmad, is "very reassuring to the men and women who are stranded in the middle of the ford, between the deep waters of tradition and modernity."

But we are all swimming in those waters, Westerners and Muslims and others alike. And since the waters are part of the ocean of history, trying to plow or divide them with barriers is futile.

—Edward Said, "The Clash of Ignorance"[1]

The West can no longer be called the West on the basis of the movement through which it saw extended to the entire world the form of what might have appeared, up until recently, as its specific profile. This form contains both techno-science and the general determinations of democracy and law, as well as a certain type of discourse and modes of argument, accompanied by a certain type of representation—understood in a broad sense of the term (e.g., that of the cinema and the entirety of post-rock and post-pop music). In this way, the West no longer acknowledges itself as holding a vision for the world, or a sense of the world that might accompany this globalization (*its* globalization), with the privileged role it believed it could attach to what it had called its "humanism." Globalization appears, on the contrary, to be reduced, in its essentials, to what Marx had already discerned as the production of the world market, and the sense of this world appears to consist merely in the accumulation and circulation of capital, accompanied by a clear aggravation in the gap between the dominating wealthy and the dominated poor, as well as by an indefinite technical expansion that no longer provides itself—except very modestly, and with disquiet or anguish—the finalities of "progress" and the improvement of the human condition. Humanism opens onto inhumanity: such may well be the brutal summary of the situation. And the West does not understand how it managed to come to this. Nevertheless, the West has indeed come to this: it is the civilization constructed initially around the Mediterranean by the Greeks, the Romans, the Jews, and the Arabs that has borne this fruit. To that degree, then, it cannot suffice to search elsewhere for other forms or values that one might attempt to graft onto this henceforth global body. There is no elsewhere left, or indeed, and in any case, there can no longer be an elsewhere in the old Western sense of the term (like the elsewhere of an Orient refracted through the prism of orientalism or the elsewhere of worlds represented as living in the "primary" immanence of myths and rites).

Our time is thus one in which it is urgent that the West—or what remains of it—analyze its own becoming, turn back to examine its provenance and its trajectory, and question itself concerning the process of decomposition of sense to which it has given rise.

Now, it is striking to note that, inside the West thus described, although we quite often interrogate, with a view to reevaluating, the philosophy of the Enlightenment (along the model of a continuous progression of human reason) or the will to power of the triumphant industrial nineteenth century—or again, if differently, the diremptions internal [*déhiscences internes*] to the West (the Slavic and Orthodox world as well as the Arabic and Islamic ones) with their complexities and their lost opportunities—we rarely interrogate the body of thought that, as I see it, organized, first in a gestatory or guiding way, if not the West itself, then at least its condition of possibility: monotheism.

We know—how could we ignore this?—that the threefold monotheism of a threefold "religion of the Book" (with which one could associate ancient Manichaeism, as well) defines a Mediterraneo-European particularity and, from there, diverse forms of global expansion by at least the two junior branches, Christianity and Islam. Yet we consider, perhaps too frequently and too simplistically, that the religious dimension (or what we believe, perhaps wrongly, to be simply "religious") behaves like an accident in relation to the facts and structures of civilization. Or, more precisely, this dimension appears as extrinsic, from the moment that it no longer visibly gives, to the globalized West, its face or profile—even though that globalization is also, as I understand it, in more than one respect a globalization of monotheism in one or another of its forms.

Ultimately, if the capitalist and technological economy constitutes the general form of value or sense today, that is by way of the worldwide reign of a monetary law of exchange (or general equivalency) or the indefinite production of surplus value within the order of this equivalency—a value whose evaluation remains impossible except in terms of equivalency and indeterminate growth. Yet this monovalence of value, or this one-way [*sens unique*] circulation of sense hardly behaves otherwise than as the apparently nonreligious transcription of the monoculture whose monotheistic conception it carried: explicitly, the culture of Rome in its European and modern expansion, from Baghdad and Teheran to London and Los Angeles. The mystery of this history is tied to nothing other than the character—simultaneously absolute and invisible, incalculable, indeterminable, and universal—of the value or unidirectionality [*sens unique*] that is placed now in "God," now in "man," and now in the tautology of "value" itself.

Perhaps it is impossible to take a further step in understanding and transforming our history without extending the interrogation into the heart of this structure of monovalence.

⤳

Since the unfolding of modern rationality and its most recent modalities, all of which were at least implicitly atheist in the sense of being indifferent to the question of "God" (whether it was a matter of knowledge or law, aesthetics or ethics), it might seem useless to refer to monotheism otherwise than in a secondary mode, a mode set in second place, either because it referred to the sphere of "private" convictions, or by virtue of a merely historical perspective.

And yet we know—or ought to know, but with a knowledge that is active, mobilizing, and "deconstructive" in a sense that I will attempt to state—to what degree the most salient features of the modern apprehension of the world, and sometimes its most visibly atheist, atheistic, or atheological traits, can and must be analyzed in their strictly and fundamentally monotheist provenance (thus, to put it rapidly, the universal, law, the individual; but also, in a more subtle manner, the motif of an infinite transcendence surpassing man, and within man). Now, "provenance," here as elsewhere, is never simply a past; it informs the present, produces new effects therein without ceasing to have its own effects. It is therefore, no doubt, important to know how monotheism, while reproducing itself elsewhere or surviving itself (and sometimes radicalizing itself) in religious figures, is the provenance of the West qua a globalization over which something entirely different than a divine providence seems to hover, namely, the somber wing of nihilism.

I will call "deconstruction of monotheism" the operation consisting in disassembling the elements that constitute it, in order to attempt to discern, among these elements and as if behind them, behind and set back from the construction, that which made their assembly possible and which, perhaps, still it remains, paradoxically, for us to discover and to think as the beyond of monotheism, in that it has become globalized and atheized.

ॐ

It goes without saying that a program such as this could not be the object of a single talk. So I will immediately narrow the scope of this essay. I will do so in two ways.

First, I will offer a very brief and summary remark on a point that should be developed separately: in speaking of monotheism, I include from the outset the Greco-Roman heritage, understood in its composite character, a heritage both philosophical and state-juridical. Judeo-Christianity would not have been possible if, in the Hellenistic age, a close symbiosis had not come about between Greco-Roman consciousness and the monotheistic disposition. The first of these could be characterized both as consciousness of a logico-techno-juridical universality *and* as the separation between this consciousness and the sphere of some "salvation" (understood as a healing, a delivery from the evil or pain of the world), conceived as a solely internal or private concern. The second—that is, the monotheistic disposition—would be distinguished not by virtue of a single God in the place of many but by the fact that divine unicity is the correlate of a presence that can no longer be given in this world, but rather must be sought beyond it (the presence in this world being that of the "idol," the rejection of which is no doubt the great, generating, and federating motif of the threefold Abrahamic traditions). Between these two providences, the hyphen [between "Judeo" and "Christianity"] represents, in this hypothesis, the very possibility of expressing "god" in the singular, in Plato as much as among the Hebrews, however considerable the differences between those two singulars.

Second, I will limit my analyses here to the form of monotheism that became its most European form—and thus, starting from there, the form that most often accompanied the Westernization of the world, at least up until the middle of the twentieth century—that is, I will limit the analysis to the form that is Christianity. It is also the form of which I am the least incapable of speaking, since it is that of my culture as a Frenchman and a European (which implies, moreover, also a certain distance relative to Orthodox Christianity). But I will do this only on two conditions, which I emphasize as follows:

1. First, we must hold in abeyance, pending the continuation of the work of deconstruction, the other major forms: Judaism and Islam. This is not so much to pass along the same analytic operation from one form to another as to keep in sight the constant interaction in monotheism of its triple determination or of the plural singular that constitutes it. We must therefore also, later on, elsewhere, deconstruct this interaction itself, understand what in the West belongs to the movement by which monotheism has redefined itself at least three times, redefined, taken up, or re-grasped and displaced or transformed itself. This too constitutes our provenance: the association and disassociation, the accord and the disaccord [*la mêlée et le démêlé*] of the Jew, the Christian, and the Muslim.

2. Thereafter, in following the red thread of Christianity, we must take care not to leave in the shadows that which in so many ways ties it together with Judaism and Islam—whether these ways are those of correspondence, of contrast, or of conflict: for that too belongs at once to Christianity itself and to that which, along the Christian vector, shaped the Westernization of monotheism and consequently also its profoundly complex and ambiguous globalization.

☙

I will thus attempt an initial sketch of a "deconstruction of Christianity." First, let me say that what is important is not the Christian marks, so numerous and so visible, that the West bears, and for which the cross is an abbreviation. What is important is, on the contrary, that Christianity is present even where—and perhaps especially where—it is no longer possible to recognize it. The sign of the cross may well decorate sites or practices wholly drained of their Christianity, and that, as we know, has been going on for a long time. Yet a certain conception of "human rights," as well as a certain determination of the relationship between politics and religion, comes straight out of Christianity.

It is thus important to discern in what sense the West is Christian in its depths; in what sense Christianity is Western as if through destiny or by destination, and in what sense, through this Christian occidentality, an essential dimension of monotheism in its integrality is set into play. It is important to think this, insofar as the Westernized world—or again, the globalized West—is experienced as deprived of sense—of sense or value, if we want to highlight the fact that it has replaced all values with the general equivalence that Marx designated as that of "merchandise." In a certain respect, in effect, and at the price of a brutal simplification that nonetheless touches upon an essential issue, the question takes this form: What connects monotheism and the monovalence of the "general equivalency"? What secret, ambivalent resource lies hidden within the organizing scheme of this *mono-*?

In attempting to respond to this question—but of course to do so we shall have to complicate greatly the rough form I have just given it—we may hope to obtain at least three results:

1. First, to be done once and for all with the unilateral schema of a certain rationalism, according to which the modern West was formed by wresting itself away from Christianity and from its own obscurantism (curiously, Heidegger repeated, in his way, something of this schema), for it is a matter of grasping how monotheism in general and Christianity in particular also engendered the West;

2. But we must also cease all our efforts to "cure" the "ills" of the present-day world (in its privation of sense) by some return to Christianity in particular, or to religion in general, for it is a matter of grasping how we are already outside of the religious;

3. And thus, we must ask ourselves anew what it is that, without denying Christianity but without returning to it, could lead us toward a point—toward a resource—hidden beneath Christianity, beneath monotheism, and beneath the West, which we must henceforth bring to light, for this point would open upon a future for the world that would no longer be either Christian or anti-Christian, either monotheist or atheist or even polytheist, but that would advance precisely beyond all these categories (after having made all of them possible).

I will call a "deconstruction of monotheism" that inquiry or search consisting in disassembling and analyzing the constitutive elements of monotheism, and more directly of Christianity, thus of the West, in order to go back to (or to advance toward) a resource that could form at once the buried origin and the imperceptible future of the world that calls itself "modern." After all, "modern" signifies a world always awaiting its truth of, and as, world [*sa vérité de monde*], a world whose proper sense is not given, is not available, is, rather, in project or in promise, and perhaps beyond: a sense that consists in not being given, but only in being promised. Now, is this not a characteristic of Christianity and monotheism in general: the contract or the alliance of the promise, the commitment that commits before all else to be committed to it? In Christianity, the promise is at once already realized and yet to come. (But is this not a theme that runs through all the monotheisms?) Is such a paradoxical space not that in which the presence of sense is at once assured, acquired, *and* always withheld, absented in its very presence?

A world whose sense is given in the mode of not being given—not yet, and, in a certain respect, never—is a world in which "sense" itself defies all received and receivable sense. Could this challenge be the one that monotheism has cast us, and that a deconstruction of monotheism would have to take up?

⟡

In engaging in a "deconstruction of Christianity," in the sense I have specified, we find first this, which must remain at the center of every subsequent analysis and represent the active principle in and for every deconstruction of monotheism: Christianity is by itself and in itself a deconstruction and a self-deconstruction. In this trait, Christianity represents at once the most Westernized form of monotheism—most Westernized and/or most Westernizing, as it were—and a scheme that we shall have to learn to put into play for the entirety of the threefold monotheism. In other words, Christianity indicates, in the most active way—and the most ruinous for itself, the most nihilist in certain regards—how monotheism shelters within itself—better: more intimately within itself than itself, within or without itself—the principle of a world without God.

Today, for this brief talk, I would like only to indicate in summary fashion the principle traces of the self-deconstructive character of Christianity. I will distinguish five traits.

1. The first is a characteristic inscribed in the very principle of monotheism, a characteristic developed most paradoxically within Christianity, yet also exposed in the relations among the three religions of the Book, in their tense and divided proximity. I would state it thus: monotheism is in truth atheism. In effect, its difference from "polytheisms" is not due to the number of gods. In fact, the plurality of gods corresponds to their effective presence (in nature, in an image, in a mind possessed), and their effective presence corresponds to relations of power, of threat, or of assistance, which religion organizes through the entirety of its myths and its

rites. The unicity of god, on the contrary, signifies the withdrawal of this god away from presence and also away from power thus understood. If the God of Israel is an All-Powerful God (a quality he bequeaths to his successors), this is not in the sense of an active power within a differential relation of powers: his "all"-powerfulness signifies that he alone disposes of this power, entirely according to his will, that he can just as well retract it or pull away from it, and that he is, above all, alone in being able to make a covenant with man. Thus, he expects no sacrifices destined to capture the benevolence of his power, but only unconditional faithfulness to his covenant—a faithfulness to none other than the "jealous" election by which he has chosen his people, or his followers, or man as such.

With the figure of Christ comes the renunciation of divine power and presence, such that this renunciation becomes the proper act of God, which makes this act into God's becoming-man. In this sense, the god withdrawn, the god "emptied out," in Paul's words, is not a hidden god at the depths of the withdrawal or the void (a *deus absconditus*): the site to which he has withdrawn has neither depths nor hiding places. He is a god whose absence in itself creates divinity, or a god whose void-of-divinity is the truth, properly speaking. (One might think of Eckhart's phrase: "I pray to God that he make me free of God," or again of Harawi imitating Hallaj: "No one really bears witness to the one God 'that he is one.'"[2]) In its principle, monotheism undoes theism, that is to say, the presence of the power that assembles the world and assures this sense. It thus renders absolutely problematic the name *god*—it renders it nonsignifying—and above all, it withdraws all power of assurance from it. Christian assurance can take place only at the cost of a category completely opposed to that of religious beliefs: the category of "faith," which is faithfulness to an absence and a certainty of this faithfulness in the absence of all assurance. In this sense, the atheist who firmly refuses all consoling or redemptive assurance is paradoxically or strangely closer to faith than the "believer." But that means also that the atheism that henceforth determines the Western structure, which is inherent in its mode of knowing and existing, is itself Christianity realized. (This does not mean that things cannot modulate themselves very differently among the diverse Christianities: for example, that of Latin America is not at all, in this respect, in the same posture as that of North America and that of Europe. But the fundamental stakes are nonetheless the same.)

2. A second self-deconstructive trait flows from the preceding: demythologization. In a trajectory that singularly contrasts those of all the other world religions (we must except Buddhism, here, which is not exactly a

religion and which, for this very reason, has more than one trait in common with monotheism), the threefold monotheism and in it, more specifically, Christianity has a self-interpretative history in which it understands itself in a way that is less and less religious in the sense in which religion implies a mythology (a narrative, a representation of divine actions and persons). It translates itself in terms that are no longer those of a foundational and exemplary narrative (Genesis, Moses, Jesus, his Resurrection, etc.), but in terms of a symbolics deciphered within the human condition (human reason, the human being's freedom, dignity, relation to the other . . .). Christianity tends to erase every distinctive religious sign and all sacrality for the benefit of what Kant called a "religion within the limits of reason alone," or again, of what Feuerbach proclaimed in saying that "belief in God *is man's belief in the infinity and the truth of his own essence*."[3] Henceforth, the democratic ethic of the rights of man and of solidarity—along with the question of the ends to give to that "humanism," or the question of the conquest by man of his own destination or destiny—constitutes, in sum, the durable sediment of Christianity.

3. Christianity presents itself historically and doctrinally as a composition. That is to say, it presents itself not only as a body of narrative and a message (although it does set forth a "good news" proclaimed through an exemplary narrative) but as a complex elaboration, starting with a provenance in and a detachment from Judaism, but also in and from Greek or Greco-Roman philosophy, as much in ontology as in politics. Elsewhere, Christianity also defines itself through a no less complex relationship to Islam, which it rejects while recognizing its co-belonging to and in the Abrahamic faith—and at the same time its role in the history of philosophico-theological thought. In itself, this proclaimed historical complexity—declared, in particular, through various problematics concerning the relationships between "faith" and "knowledge," or between "revelation" and "reason"—already carries the sense of a regime distinct from the regime of a religion *stricto sensu*: as though that regime carried in itself the permanent possibility of dividing or self-interpreting in two distinct registers.

Moreover, the theoretical or dogmatic Christian construction is that of a way of thinking whose center is "the word of God made flesh." Thus, the dogma of incarnation mobilizes the ideas of "nature" or "essence," and of "hypostasis" or "sensuous presentation" in order to establish that the person of Jesus is identically that of a man and that of God in a single manifestation. To be sure, the heart of this dogma is declared "a mystery." But the mystery does not have the characteristics of a myth: it addresses itself to the mind of man; it asks him to consider what (without his being able to understand it) brings light to that mind and about it (that is, once again, concerning an infinite destiny and destination of man). The point of incarnation is obviously the point of an absolute separation from Judaism and Islam. But it is not without value to observe that this point of discord is also that at which, in the first place, the whole question central to monotheism is debated (i.e., What is the covenant or alliance between God and man?), thus the point of the self-ex-plication (i.e., of the unfolding in itself with itself) of monotheism, and the point at which, in the second place, each monotheism can and must find again, in the others, something of itself (e.g., the resurrection, corollary of the incarnation, which belongs also to Islam, whereas the pardon of sins, another corollary, comes from Judaism, and whereas, in addition, the incarnation does not in fact abolish the indivisible absoluteness of the Judeo-Islamic god . . .). This divided unity of self, characteristic of monotheism most properly, and thus also most paradoxically, makes up the unity of the unique god. We could say, including all possible resonances, that this god divides himself—even atheizes himself—*at the intersection of monotheism and/or the monotheisms* . . .

4. Given these conditions, Christianity is less a body of doctrine than a *subject* in relationship to itself in the midst of a search for self, within a disquietude, an awaiting or a desire for its proper identity (we have only to think of the major theme of the annunciation and the expectation, recurrent in the three monotheisms, unfolded paradoxically within Christianity as hope for the event as advent. This is why, just as Christianity thinks a god in three persons whose divinity consists in the relationship to self, so it divides itself historically into three at least (a division of the community which must at the end be reassembled), and so too it presents the logic of the threefold monotheism as a subject divided in itself (i.e., religion of the Father, religion of the Son, religion of the Holy in the Islamic sense).

The relation to self defines the subject. The structure of the subject appears like the caesura between the ancient world and the Christian occidental world. (We should pause here and consider its Greek provenance, its Augustinian, Avicennian, Cartesian, Hegelian elaborations, and consider the fact that this is the history of all the senses and all the figures of what has called itself "spirit.") This subject is the *self* qua instance of identity, certainty, and responsibility. However, the law of its structure entails that it cannot be given to self before being itself related to self: its relation to self—or "the self" in general—can only be infinite. Being infinite, it assumes, on the one hand, a temporal dimension (where it sets about having a history, a past and a future as dimensions of sense and presence—

though presence is not simply in the present), *and* in the last instance it can only escape itself. This escaping of self defines jointly, in this realm of thought, the life of the creator and the death of the creature. But in this way it is the one and the other, and the one in the other or through the other, who are affected by and with the in-finite in the sense of *finitude*.

5. Christianity (and through this prism, monotheism) has been engaged from its beginning in a perpetual process (i.e., a process *and* a litigation) of self-rectification and self-surpassing, most often in the form of self-retrospection in view of a return to a purer origin—a process that reaches up to Nietzsche and continues today, but that had begun already between the gospels and Paul, between Paul and James, in the origins of monastic orders, and, of course, in the various reforms, and so on. Everything takes place as though Christianity had developed like no other, *at once* a theologico-economico-political affirmation of power, domination, and exploitation, for which Rome was the weighty symbol as well as a part of the reality, *and* an inverted affirmation of the destitution and abandonment of self, whose vanishing point is the evaporation of self. The question must thus be that of the nature and the structure of this evaporation of self: dialectical surpassing, nihilistic decomposition, the opening of the ancient to the absolutely new . . . In one way or another, what is in question is: how monotheism engenders itself as humanism, and how humanism confronts the finitude that entered in this way into history.

༈

Today I will remain with this briefest of characterizations. I draw no conclusions from it. It seems to indicate a direction in thinking without which it is impossible to consider seriously, henceforth, the question of the sense of the world such as the West has given it to us as heritage—or as escheat.

If we hold ourselves to a schematized, essential observation, then this direction is at least the following: our task is not to lead toward the fulfillment of a new divine realm, neither in this world nor in another. Nor is it to rediscover the unity proper and immanent to a world of the myth that has decomposed in the Westernization-monotheization of the world. Instead, it is to think a "sense-of-world" or a "world-sense" [*"sens-de-monde"*] in a world divided in its own being-world, in an acosmic and atheological world, which is still a "world" in some respect, still our world and that of the totality of beings, thus still a totality of possible senses—it being understood that this possibility is always also, in and of itself, exposed to the impossible.

Post-Scriptum (February 2002)

The preceding text is that of a talk given in Cairo in February 2001. One year later, that is to say, one "9-11" later, the talk calls for more than one complement (without speaking of the fact that in many respects my work on the subject has been displaced, has opened new paths). If "9-11" made something clear, then it was this: the world is tearing itself apart around an unbearable division of wealth and power. This division is insufferable because it rests upon no acceptable hierarchy, neither of power, nor of wealth. A "hierarchy" signifies, etymologically, a sacred character of the principle or the commandment. Now the world of techno-science, or the world that I have called "ecotechnics"—that is, a natural environment entirely made up of the human replacement of a "nature" henceforth withdrawn—which is also the world of democracy, the universal rights of a human being presumed to be universal, the world of secularism and religious tolerance both aesthetic and moral, not only keeps us from founding in a sacred regime differences of authority and legitimacy, it makes those disparities or inequalities that overtly violate its principles of equality and justice seem intolerable.

What we call the scripting or instrumentation of religions, or indeed the deviation, the perversion, or the betrayal of one or another religion (including the national theism of the United States), in no way constitutes a sufficient explication. What is instrumentalized or betrayed gives, in itself, material for instrumentalization or perversion. This material is given, in a paradoxical but evident way, through the motif of the One: it is Unity, Unicity, and Universality that are evoked throughout in the global confrontation, or rather, in the world structured as a confrontation that is in no wise that of a "war of civilizations" (since Islam is also a part of the West, throughout its entire history, and this even if it is not exclusively such).

To the total mobilization (and it is no accident that I use a concept so recently fascist), proclaimed and telecommanded in the name of a single God whose transcendent unicity effectuates an absolute *hierarchization* (God, the paradise of the believers, the dust of all the rest—all the rest being composed also of a lot of dollars, missiles, and petroleum . . .), claims to respond to the total immobilization of the situation (world capital) in the name of a supposed universality for which the Universal is called "man," but who, in his obvious abstraction, immediately hands himself over to another God (*"in God we trust, bless America"*).

The one and the other God are two figures confronted with the identical Unique when its Unicity is grasped as absolute Presence, consistent in itself and with itself, like the punctual and thus invisible summit of a pyra-mid whose essence it resumes and absorbs. (We could say here, since I am extending remarks made in Cairo: the pyramids of the pharaohs did not draw their value from the null point of their summit, but from the secret of death and life buried deep in their mass. They drew their value from the profound withdrawal into a cryptic obscurity and not from the point of a presence erected as evidence.) And it is certainly permissible to say, without being "anti-American" (a ridiculous category) that this Unifying, Unitary, and Universal model, also Unidimensional, and finally Unilat-eral (which is its internal contradiction) has made possible the symmetri-cal and no less nihilistic mobilization of a monotheistic and no less unilateralist model. We tend to be on guard against this model only be-cause it has become the ideological instrument of the "terrorism" we know too well. But "terrorism" is the conjunction of despair and a Unify-ing will that confronts the other face of the One.

Now, what is thus lost of the very essence of monotheism in all its forms is precisely that the "one" of the "god" is not at all Unicity qua substantial present and united with itself: on the contrary, the unicity and the unity of this "god" (or the divinity of this "one") consists precisely in that the One cannot be posited there, neither presented nor figured as united in itself. Whether it be in exile or in diaspora, whether it be in the becoming-man or in a threefold-being-in-itself, or whether it be in the infinite recoil of the one who has neither equal nor like (thus not even unity in any of its forms), this "god" (and in what sense is it divine? how is it divine? this is what we have to think through) absolutely excludes its own presentation—we would even have to say its own valorization as much as its own presencing

This the great mystics, the great believers, the great "spiritualists" of all three monotheisms knew, and they knew it in repeated exchanges and confrontations with the philosophers, whom they faced, all the while being strangers to them. Their thoughts, which is to say their acts, their *ethos* or their *praxis*, still await us.

Translated by Gabriel Malenfant

The Judeo-Christian (on Faith)

"Judeo-Christian" is a fragile designation. The word appears in the *Littré* dictionary with a historical definition that restricts it to the religion of the first Christian Jews, of those who considered that non-Jewish Christians should first "be associated with, or incorporated into, the nation of Israel." This signification sets aside the partisans of the measures of the order taken in Jerusalem under James's authority and reported in Acts 15. It is no longer the same meaning as in Harnack at the end of the century, which indicates only a preferential place for the Jewish people as the distinctive trait of the Judeo-Christians. Harnack thus distinguishes them from those whom he will call the "pagan-Christians" (who will also be called "Helleno-Christians" or "Hellenic-Christians"). Today, the use of the term *Judeo-Christian* is still less restrictive, as a function of complexities that historians have brought to light. At the same time, certain among them have expressed doubts about the validity of the category, if only because of the diversity of movements or stances that it is able to cover.

In the meantime, usage of the term has authorized a still broader and nonhistorical role when one speaks, for example, of Judeo-Christian culture or tradition to designate a certain interweaving, at the base of European civilization, of the two enemy sisters or, indeed, of the mother and the daughter, the Synagogue and the Church. In truth, this composite term so far has been taken to designate an imbrication or conjuncture essential in our identity or our thought, even "the most impenetrable abyss that Western thought conceals," as Lyotard wrote of the *trait d'u-nion* [hyphen][1] that holds this composition together or de-composes it at its core—which makes of its center a disunion.

The enigma of this noncomposable composition should interest us in more than one respect; in fact, it should interest us in five respects.

1. Insofar as the name *Judeo-Christian* can go so far as to posit a—or even *the*—salient characteristic, that is, the incisive and decisive, if not essential, characteristic of a civilization that will call itself "Western," its stake is then nothing other than the composition and/or the decomposition, in and for itself, of this "civilization."

2. Insofar as its name de-composes what we have agreed to call, in our culture, "religions," it implies, within the determination of Western thought (and in its self-determination) a hyphen drawn between "religion" and "thought," precisely where thought—in the name of "philosophy," itself albeit otherwise self-composed—was determined as non-religious, even anti-religious, thereby drawing its line *over* religion, to destroy it or de-compose it. This name thus implies an irritation or a vexation of the West in itself and for itself.

3. Insofar as it implicates philosophy—if only in the guise of an offense or contradiction—this name communicates in some sense with that other composite: the Greek-Jew and/or Jew-Greek. This composite names nothing other (before becoming a name forged in Joyce's language of de-composition) than the *vis-à-vis* of Judeo-Christianity, understood as pagan-Christianity or Christian Hellenism (and from the latter began properly the missionary expansion of Christianity, which may also be the fact of Jews speaking or thinking in Greek, and designating their new religion, moreover, as one more philosophy). For this motif, there is no Judeo-Christianity, under the circumstances, that is not also Judeo-Greco-Christianity, and philosophy cannot hold itself apart or stand free from this double mark of dis-union.

4. Insofar as this mark multiplies at least once by itself, its reduction [*sa démultiplication*] will not cease thereafter: it draws or traces from itself a general de-composition. This de-composition first dis-unites the three religions called "of the Book," and thus composes with Islam another assemblage and another discontinuity relative to the West; an other disorientation and re-orientation (after all, as we know, the aftermath of historical Judeo-Christianity exerted very specific influences upon the birth of Islam, just as it had, a few centuries earlier, on the formation of Manichaeism). This reduction once again de-composes Judaism*s*, Christianism*s*, and Islamism*s* among themselves, setting in play each time a new form of

contrariety with, or attraction to, philosophy. For its part, philosophy it-self only presumes to be one insofar as (and at the least among other mo-tives) across its extreme synchronic and diachronic disparity; it posits itself as distinct from religion (or again, within religion itself, as essentially dis-tinguished from faith).

5. Insofar as the Judeo-Christian composition thus conceals or stimu-lates what we could call the general dis-position of the West (or indeed, what we should spell, in Greco-Latin, its dys-position), it so happens that this composition espouses formally a schema whose recurrence and ex-tent/amplitude are not insignificant in our entire tradition of thought: this is the schema of *coincidentia oppositorum*, whose declensions include, among others, the oxymoron, *Witz*, the Hegelian dialectic, or mystical ecstasies. From which of these four species the Judeo-Christian composi-tion comes is perhaps not the question to ask, for it may arise from all of them or compose them all. But it is a constant that the most general law of this schema (like the structure of the Kantian schematism, which forms a species of the same genre) is to contain at its center a gap [*un écart*] around which it is organized. The hyphen passes over a void that it does not fill. Upon what could this void open? That is the question that a con-sideration attentive to the Judeo-Christian composition cannot avoid pos-ing. Such a consideration is perhaps virtually a reflection on the composition in general of our tradition and within our tradition; that is, ultimately, on the possibility of the *cum* ["with"] considered in itself. How could the *cum*, how could the *communion*—taken as a generic term (that term of Cicero, taken up later on in Christianity to absorb and sub-late the *koinōnia*, the *societas*, and the *communicatio*)—include constitu-tively the voiding of its center or its heart? How, consequently, can this voiding call to the deconstruction of this composition: that is, the pene-tration in the midst of the possibility, which is a possibility of composition that is both contracted and combated?

(A parenthesis for two axioms. 1. A deconstruction is always a penetra-tion; it is neither a destruction, nor a return to the archaic, nor, again, a suspension of adherence: a deconstruction is an intentionality of the to-come [*l'à-venir*], enclosed in the space through which the con-struction is articulated part by part. 2. Deconstruction thus belongs to a construction as its law or its proper schema: it does not come to it from elsewhere.)

Here, deconstruction is therefore none other than the logic, altogether historical and theoretical, of the construction of what one might readily call in the language of painting "short-stroke composition" ["*la composi-tion au trait d'union*"].[2] To be sure, composition, or the composed or composite characteristic, is not an exclusive trait of Christianity or the West. Nonetheless, Christianity never ceases designating, by itself and as itself, a communication or placing-in-common, a *koinōnia* that appears according to circumstances as its essence or as its *acme*, and it is indeed Christianity that has marked the West, or even as what is Western itself, the intentional drive toward a "pleroma of peoples [*plērōma tōn ethnōn, plenitudo gentium*; cf. Romans 11:25]" whose restored community with Israel must be the touchstone, according to this text of Paul. Likewise, the pre- or para-Christian Judaism of the *Qumran* is a strain that considered the community to be the true Temple. From the religion of the Temple to communitarian or "communal" faith, from the religion of the sons to the religion of the brothers—all the way to republican fraternity and to the comparison Engels developed between the first communists and the first Christians or, more precisely, those Jews he called "still unconscious Christians" (referring, above all, to the John of Revelation)—from this passage, then, which also brings to its end a generalized abandonment of the Temples of antiquity and leads toward the constitution of a "church" which means, above all, an "assembly" (just like a "synagogue"), up to the question of what the *koinōnia* of our globalization or becoming-global and its being-in-common in every sense of the term could mean, there is an insistent continuity of a com-position that would carry in itself, in its *cum* itself, the law of a deconstruction: What is there beneath the hyphen and in the hollow of the assemblage?

Over what and from what is the hyphen drawn? And how is this hyphen drawn from the one to the other—from the one to the other edge and from the one to the other "self"? How is it drawn such that it might withdraw while at the same time remaining intact: not untouchable but intact, remaining intact throughout the entire Greco-Judeo-Christo-Islamo-Euro-planetary history, an intact spacing that has perhaps never yet come to light, having perhaps never to take form or substance, and to remain always residual, the uncomposable and undecomposable non-thought of our history?

I am drawing no conclusions, for the moment, from this enumeration of headings for the uncomposable composition that requires our attention. I propose today to examine only one of the most remarkable tendencies of Judeo-Christianity: that which was incorporated, ultimately, in the Christian canon of the "New Testament," even at the price of remarkable doubts and resistances, which have persisted, in some cases, up to our day. I mean, here, the epistle attributed to James.

That letter is the first of those a very ancient tradition designates "catholic." This name does not designate, at its origin, some particular orientation of these texts toward the Roman Church, but rather, as in the initial expression *katholikē ekklēsia*, their general or, if you will, universal destination. In this sense, rather than being addressed to a community, to a synagogue, or to a determinate church (like the Pauline epistles), they are addressed to a larger whole, which each time arises from the *diaspora*. That catholicity and diaspora might initially have to do with one another is something worth reflecting upon: do the "whole" and the "dispersion" produce a whole out of dispersion, a dispersion of the whole, or, indeed, a whole in dispersion? In a sense, the entire question lies there: I mean that the entire question of the West as totality and/or as dissemination resides therein.

Today, then, for us, the Judeo-Christian will be James. And it will be, in a manner that remains to be discerned, a secret thread or a hyphen that could tie the historic James to that other James [*Jacques*] around whom, or on whose pretext, we have come together here;[3] and who is another Judeo-Christian, or indeed another Judeo-Helleno-Christian. This secret tie has nothing contrived or arbitrary about it; nor am I proposing it as an ad hoc rationalization. At the very least we should venture the risk, here, of its relevance. That relevance would be tied simply to this: if it is possible, at the end of the twentieth century, that a philosopher, and thus in principle a Greek, experience the necessity of re-interrogating a category of faith or of a faith act, or, again, that he or she speak of the real as resurrection—and if it is possible that this philosopher does so in a reference that might be at the same time Jewish (i.e., holiness, borrowed from Levinas) and Christian (i.e., a "miracle of witnessing"), then in what relationship can this take shape within the historical Judeo-Christianity and what could this allow us to discern, and deconstruct, in our own origin or provenance?

(Parenthesis: before reading the Epistle of James, I would like to make it clear that I am going to proceed without furnishing any erudite sources, for that could only be excessive here. Recent studies on the many Judeo-Christianities and on the messianisms of James's time are multiplying. This is no doubt also a sign. But I neither want nor am able to do the work of a historian, no more than I intend a commentary on Derrida: I intend to work precisely between the two.)

The James to whom we attribute the letter in question has been distinguished as "the minor," from James the major, whom all of Europe went to venerate at *Compostello*. The tradition also names him "the brother of Jesus," and we believe we have finally identified him as the head of the

Church of Jerusalem or of the "Holy Church of the Hebrews," who brings down the decision, reported in Acts 15, in favor of the non-Jews by declaring that: "God chose for himself a people in his name . . . so that other men would seek the Lord, all those nations over which his name was invoked." With these words, James confers his authority (and that of a citation from Amos) on the words that Peter had pronounced when he said: "God has borne witness to the nations in giving them the holy spirit just as he did for us." God is a witness, that is, a *martyr*, for all men: the witness of their holiness or of their call to holiness (which is to say, to his proper holiness). Such was the message that the assembly sent Paul and Barnabas, along with a few others, to deliver to Antioch, where tempers had to be calmed in regard to what was due to the Jews, and what to the others. God bears witness for all men insofar as he is the one who "knows human hearts [*ho kardiognostēs*]." Israel is thus the singular site chosen for this witness about hearts: the visible or visibly marked (by circumcision) site starting from which the Holy One attests to the invisible and uncircumcised holiness of all humanity, or of the pleroma of his peoples.

It is from this angle that I will approach the Epistle of James. In it one reads, at 1:18, that God sought "to engender us from a word of truth such that we might be the first-born of his creatures." "We" here is first "the brothers" of the "twelve tribes of the dispersion," to whom the letter is addressed. It is thus the Jews who must be the "first-born of the creatures." The first-born represent the part reserved for the gods of a harvest or a herd. The relation of the Jewish churches to the rest of humanity stands, here, in this single verse. The Jews who have faith in Jesus consecrate to God his own creation. Now, the letter reminds us further on that "men are made in the image of God" (3:9). (No doubt, the "we" of this verse can just as well tend to designate all men as the first-born of creation in its entirety: we shall come back to that.)

The resemblance of men to God, and with this a thematic and problematic of the image that are infinitely complex, belongs to the essential core of biblical monotheism. This resemblance occupies an important place in the thought of Paul, for whom Jesus is "the image of the invisible God" (Colossians 1:15). But the Epistle of James stops at this mention of the well-known verse of Genesis and ventures nothing in particular about the relationship between man-as-image and Jesus. The mediation of this relation remains at a certain distance. As we shall see, it is not the economy of a Christo-centric salvation that organizes James's thought: it is, as it were, directly, a certain relation of man to holiness that becomes an image in him.

Before proceeding we must make a remark about methodology. An absence of Christology, and even of theology in general, characterizes this text—which we could call more parenetic or spiritual than doctrinal—to the point that this has aroused suspicion about its authenticity, or about whether to consider it simply a Jewish text. In passing, it is remarkable that Harnack does not even mention James in his *History of Dogma*: in fact, one can grant him that this epistle doesn't provide us much, by contrast to those of Paul, for the development of a discourse about the contents of faith (I would readily put it as the contents of a knowledge of faith, but that would be to anticipate too much). The epistle is wholly given over—as we shall show—to the act of faith.

I am not claiming to reconstitute (others have done so much better than I could) the backgrounds or the implicit thematic (Essene, in particular) of this text. I am taking it in the form in which it is given. Now it is given at once as a text rather thin in theological speculation (as Luther said, "an epistle of straw") and as a text whose intention is not to oppose Paul but to correct a tendentious interpretation of Paul that tended to cut faith off from all action. James's theological reserve seems therefore intentional. But that means we must look here not for theological thinness but for a retreat of theology, or for a theology in retreat, that is, a withdrawal of any representation of contents in favor of an active information by faith—which is also to say that we must look for that alone which activates the contents. It is not another theological position, even less an opposed thesis: it is the position that stands precisely between two theological elaborations, and thus perhaps also between two religions, the Jewish and the Christian, like their hyphen and their separation [*trait d'union et d'écartment*], but also of their com-possibility, whatever the status of this "com-" might be: like their construction and their deconstruction taken together. That is to say that this position is like one of those points, one of those situations, in which the construction in question, like any construction, according to the general law of constructions, exposes itself, constitutively and in itself, to its deconstruction.

Let us return, then, to the internal logic of this letter. If humans were engendered according to the image (*gegonotes kath'omoiōsin theou*), then what is this *homoiōsis*? To what or to whom are humans similar or *homogeneous*? The God of the letter is described rather briefly. He is unique, to be sure, but therein does not lie what is essential to the faith, which concerns more the works of man than the nature of God (James 2:19: "you believe that there is but one God, and you do well. The demons also believe this and they tremble," which is to say, this is not enough to qualify your faith). This God is not the God of Israel in his jealous exclusivity, but neither is it properly speaking the God either of the Trinity or of love (nonetheless, the love of others plays a primordial role in the letter).

God is "Lord and Father" (James 3:9), and this is uttered in the same verse that mentions *homoiōsis*, just as in 1:17–18, where it is said that he "engendered us as the first-born of his creatures." The father is father of and in his resemblance (we could even say that paternity and resemblance share a reciprocity here), just as in Genesis, in the second story of creation, the resemblance of Adam to God passes into the resemblance between Adam and his son Seth: in this way opens the genealogy that will lead through Noah to Shem, Ham, and Japheth. This resemblance distinguishes man in creation; it makes of him the first-born of creation, which is to say that it is (and that through it man also is) the mark or the homogeneous trace that dedicates the world to its creator. This resemblance therefore does not depend on generation (as we are accustomed to thinking); it is rather generation that consists in the transmission of the trace. The created world is less a produced world than a marked world, a world traced, simultaneously imprinted and traversed by a vestige (as Augustine will say later on), that is to say, traced by that which remains withdrawn and by the withdrawal of an origin.

From what, then, is this *homoiōsis* made, this trace of the creator as such? The letter names him "Father of lights" (1:17)—he who opens the world in the division of light from what it illuminates (according to a very ancient cosmogonic schema). Immediately thereafter, it is said that from him comes "every beautiful gift, every perfect donation [*pasa dosis agathē kai pan dōrēma teleion*]": that is, every action of giving and all things given, the first being literally called "good," and the second "fulfilled," "completed." God is first the giver. And it is as such that he is the "Father of lights, with whom there is nor change nor a shadow of variation." He gives as light and what he gives is first, essentially, his light (the Latin allows us to specify: *lux*, illuminating light, not *lumen*, the glimmer of the illumined thing). He gives not so much some thing as the possibility of the clarity in which alone there can be things. If the logic of the gift is indeed, as the other James [*Jacques*] enjoys thinking, that the giver abandons him- or herself in his or her gift, then that is what is taking place here. In giving, in fulfilling the gift, God gives himself just as much as he remains in himself without shadows, since it is this dissipation of the shadow, this clearing of light that he gives, and since he "gives to all, simply" (James 1:5). To give and to withhold, to give oneself and to withhold oneself, these are not contradictories here and, correlatively, to be and to appear would be identical here: a phenomenology that is theological, but not theophanic.

The logic of the gift and the logic of the *homoiōsis* are superimposed: the *homoios* is of the same *genos* as that which engendered it (this theme, which displaces the pre-Greek and pre-Jewish relation of man to the divine, runs from Pythagoras via Plato up to Cleanthes, from whom Paul will borrow in addressing himself to the Athenians), and that which engenders or which engenders itself, gives itself, gives precisely its *genos*.

Further on, the letter names the thing given. In James 4:6 we read: "He gives a grace better than covetousness," and again, "he gives this grace to the humble" (a citation from Proverbs 3:34). Grace is favor, that is, at once the election that favors and the pleasure or the joy that is thereby given. Grace is a gratuity (Émile Benveniste shows that *gratia*, which translates *kharis*, gave us both *gratis* and *gratuitas*).[4] It is the gratuity of a pleasure given for itself. In verse 4:6, the *kharis* is opposed to the desire that is *pros phthonon*, the desire of envy or jealousy. The latter is associated with voluptuous pleasures (*hēdonai*). But the logic of the text cannot be reduced to the condemnation of the *philia tou kosmou* ("the love of this world"). Or again, perhaps this condemnation should be understood according to the ampler and more complex logic in which it is inserted. James says, in effect, that the desire of envy proceeds from lack: "you covet and you have not, so you kill" (4:2). *Phthonos* is the envious desire for the good or for the happiness of the other (as we know, the *phthonos* of the Greek gods takes aim at the man whose success or happiness irritates them). Now, James continues: "but you have not because you ask not." And then: "you ask and you receive not, because you ask wrongly, in order to spend for your sensuous pleasures." There is thus a logic of lack and of jealous appropriation here, as well as a logic of asking in order to receive that which cannot be received other than by the gift or as the gift, that is, the favor of grace. This *kharis* is the opposite neither of desire nor of pleasure: it is desire and pleasure qua receptivity of and to this gift. This receptivity must equal the donation in gratuity.

This gift gives nothing that might be of the order of an appropriable good. (We must also remember, so as to come back to it again shortly, that this epistle is the most vehemently opposed to the rich in the entirety of the New Testament.) This gift gives itself, it gives its own gift's favor, which is to say, a withdrawal into the grace of the giver and of the present itself. The *homoiōsis* is a *homodōsis*. To be in the image of God is therefore to be asking for grace, to give oneself in turn to the gift. Far from coming out of an askesis, one may justifiably say that this logic of grace arises out of enjoyment, and this enjoyment itself comes out of an abandon. That supposes, no doubt, according to the letter of the text, "unhappiness" and "bereavement," "weeping" and "humiliation," but these are not a sacrifice: they are the disposition of abandon, in which joy is possible. To be sure, something is abandoned, and it is lack, along with the desire for appropriation. But that is not sacrificed: it is not offered and consecrated to God. James is not preaching renunciation here: he is laying bare a logic separated as much from envy as from renunciation. And this logic is that of what he calls faith.

As we know, the letter of James—while it may not be as opposed as one might think to the thought of Paul—is clearly distinguished from the latter, at least by its great insistence on the works of faith. (That was, moreover, the first reason for Luther's severity toward this text.) But it is important to understand clearly that the works of faith in question here are not opposed to faith: they are, on the contrary, faith itself.

The relationship of faith to its works is set forth in chapter 2, whose most famous verse is the eighteenth: "show me your faith without works, and I will show you my faith by my works." The injunction or the challenge does not concern the necessity of proving one's faith. Besides, the preceding verse has just stated: "without works faith by itself is dead [*kath'heauten*, by itself, in itself, as to itself]." These works do not stand in the order of external manifestation, or in that of a demonstration through the phenomenon. And faith does not subsist in itself. This is why what is in question here is to show faith *ek tōn ergōn*, on the basis of works, and coming out of them. Instead of works proceeding from faith, and instead of works expressing it, faith here exists only in the works: in works that are its own and whose existence makes up the whole essence of faith, if we may put it that way. Verse 20 states that faith without works is *argē*, that is, vain, inefficient, and ineffective (curiously, the Vulgate translates this term by *mortua*, like the *nekra* of verse 17). *Argos* is a contraction of *aergos*, which is to say without *ergon*. James is thus stating a quasi-tautology. But it means: the *ergon* is here existence. That also means, then, that the *ergon* is understood in a general sense, as effectivity much more than as production; it is understood as being-in-act much more than as the *operari* of an *opus*.

This logic is so precise and so restrictive that it obliges us to set aside a certain comprehension of the *ergon* to which we are more habituated, and even our Platonic and Aristotelian understanding of *poiēsis*—a word that appears in 1:25, tied to *ergon*, and which everything makes us think, following several translators, in the sense of "practice" (thus, of "*praxis*"), that is, if *praxis* is indeed action in the sense of *by* or *of* an agent and not the *praxis* exerted *upon* an object.

One might say: *pistis* is the *praxis* that takes place in and as the *poiēsis* of the *erga*. If I wanted to write this in a Blanchotian idiom, I would say that faith is the inactivity or inoperativity [*désœuvrement*] that takes place in and as the work [*dans et comme l'œuvre*]. And if I wanted to pass from one James to the other [to Jacques Derrida], I would say that faith, as the *praxis* of *poiēsis*, opens in *poiēsis* the inadequation to self that alone can constitute "doing" ["*faire*"] and/or "acting" [l' "*agir*"] (both concepts implying the difference within or unto self of every concept or the irreducible difference between a *lexis* and the *praxis* that would seek to effectuate it). Extrapolating from there, I would say that *praxis* is that which could not be the production of a work adequate to its concept (and thus, production of an object), but that *praxis* is in every work and it is *ek tou ergou*, that which exceeds the concept of it. This is not, as we commonly think, that which is lacking in the concept, but rather that which, in exceeding it, thrusts the concept out of itself and gives it more to conceive, or more to grasp and to think, more to touch and to indicate, than that which it itself conceives. Faith would thus be here the *praxical* excess of and in action or in operation, and this excess, insofar as it aligns itself with nothing other than itself, that is to say, also with the possibility for a "subject" (for an agent or for an actor) to be more, to be infinitely more and excessively more than what it is in itself and for itself.

In that sense, this faith can no more be a property of the subject than it can be the subject's "work": this faith must be asked for and received— which does not prevent it from being asked for with faith, quite the contrary. (In James 1:6, one must "ask with faith without turns or sidestepping": there is at the heart of faith a decision of faith that precedes itself and exceeds itself.) In this sense, faith cannot be an adherence to some contents of belief. If belief must be understood as a weak form or an analogy of knowledge, then faith is not of the order of belief. It comes neither from a knowledge nor from a wisdom, not even by analogy. And it is also not in this sense that we should understand Paul's opposition of Christian "madness" to the "wisdom" of the world: this "madness" is neither a super-wisdom nor something symmetrical to wisdom or to knowledge. What James, for his part, would have us understand is that faith is its own work. It *is* in works, it *makes* them, and the works *make* it. Taking a step further, even a short step, we could extrapolate from James a declaration like the following: "It is false to the point of absurdity to see in a 'belief,' for example, in the belief in redemption by the Christ, that which characterizes the Christian; only Christian *practice* is Christian, a life like that *lived* by him who died on the cross"—a declaration that we could read in Nietzsche.

Spinoza, for his part, asserts that "God demands, by the Prophets, of men no other knowledge of himself than that of his divine Justice and his Charity, that is to say those attributes which are such that men might imitate them by following a certain rule of life," by which he is referring implicitly to the citation from James's epistle, which he mentioned earlier in the same text.

That faith might consist in its practice is the certainty that commands James's interpretation of Abraham's act or of that of Rahab (Genesis 2:21–25). Contrary to Paul (Romans 4), James maintains that Abraham is justified by his work, designated as the offering of Isaac. For his part, Paul does not mention this episode, but rather that of Sarah's sterility (in Hebrews 11:1 ff., the sacrifice is evoked, but the fundamental argument remains the same). According to Paul, what is important is that Abraham *believed* that God could give him a son, against all natural evidence. His act thus depended on a knowledge postulate (or it consisted in one; in the text of the letter to the Hebrews, we find the word *logisamenos*: Abraham judged that God could). For James, on the contrary, Abraham did. He offered up Isaac. It is not said there that he judged, considered, or believed. (Likewise, Rahab the prostitute saved the emissaries, and James says nothing, by contrast with Paul, about her belief in the promise the emissaries had made her, whereas the Letter to the Hebrews reminds us that Rahab expected that her life would be saved.)

In a certain sense, James's Abraham believes nothing, does not even hope (Paul says that he "hoped without hope": even this dialectic is absent in James). James's Abraham is not in the economy of assurances or substitutes for assurance. Abraham is neither persuaded nor convinced: his assent is not in the *logismos*. It is only in the *ergon*. If the notion of "faith" must be situated in the "logical" or "logistical" order (as the origin of *pistis* in *peithō* would invite us to think: "to persuade," "to convince"), then this faith resides in the inadequation of one's own "*logos*" to itself. The reasons that this faith has "to believe" are not reasons. Thus it has nothing, in sum, with which to convince itself. This faith is but the "conviction" that gives itself over in act—not even to something "incomprehensible" (according to a logic of the "I cannot understand but I must or I may still believe," and still less according to a logic of the *credo quia absurdum*), but to that which is another act: a commandment. Faith is not argumentative; it is the performative of the commandment—or it is homogeneous with it. Faith resides in inadequation to itself as a content of meaning. And it is in this precisely that it is truth qua truth of faith or faith as truth and verification. This is not sacri-fication but veri-fication. That is, also, the contrary of a truth *believed*. This faith, above all, does not *believe.* It is neither credulous nor even believing in the current sense of the term. It is a faith not believed. *It is a non-belief whose faith guarantees it as non-believable.*

The concept of "trusting oneself to" [*"se fier à"*] or "confiding in" [*"se confier à"*] opens on two sides: on the one hand, it is a matter of a kind of assurance, of a postulated certainty, something wagered, by a confidence poised upon some anticipation risked toward an end (analogous to the Kantian postulates, which are precisely those of a rational or reasonable belief into which Christian faith metamorphosed or by which it was eclipsed). But faith, according to James, is effected entirely in the inadequation of its enactment to any concept of that act even if it be a concept formed by analogy, by symbols, or by as an "as if." The work of Abraham is the acting or the doing of this inadequation: a *praxis* whose *poiēsis* is the incommensurability of an action (to offer Isaac up) and of its representation or its meaning (to immolate his son).

Faith as work could very well be knowledge—or nescience—of the incommensurability of acting with itself, that is, of the incommensurability of the agent, of the actor, or of the acting entity insofar as it exceeds itself and *makes* itself in the act, or *makes itself* exceed itself, or be exceeded by itself therein: thus, radically, absolutely, and necessarily, it proves to be the being-unto-the-other of its being-unto-self. In this, faith would be the very act of a *homoiōsis* with the gift itself, understood in the sense of its act. *Homoiōsis* as *heteroiōsis*, the identity of the concept (of "knowledge" or of "thought") qua the incommensurability of the conceiving in act. This incommensurability would be tied to the following: this faith ("persuasion," "wager of confidence," or "assurance of faithfulness") must come from the other, this faith must come from outside, it is the outside opening in itself a passage toward the inside.

This faith would be—or, again, the Judeo-Christian and Islamic faith would be—the act of a non-knowledge as non-knowledge of the necessity of the other in every act and in every knowledge of the act that could stand at the level of what James here calls (5:21, 24–25) "justification": that which makes just, that which creates a just one (which could never be, could above all not be in the adequation of the knowledge of its own justice). This act would be tied first to faith in the other—which the other James, or Jacques [Derrida] calls "the relation to the other as the secret of testimonial experience," if by "testimony" we mean, as he does, the attestation of truth that all words postulate in the other or from the other, and in me qua other to myself (just as, Platonically, I "dialogue with myself"). The just one or the justified one would be he who lets himself be attested, borne witness to, in the other.

This truth and this justice open most precisely where it is no longer a sacred presence that assures and guarantees, but the fact itself—the act and the work—of not being assured by any presence that might not be of the other, and other than itself, other than the presence of sacred gods: in a sense, or if one wishes, the sacred itself or the holy (to fuse them for an instant), but as not given, not posited, not presented in an order of divine presence—on the contrary, "God" "himself" as unlike any god, as gift and as the gift of the faith that is given to the other and that believes in nothing. With this, then, the Judeo-Christianism of James as deconstruction of religion and, consequently, also as self-deconstruction: leaving nothing subsisting, if this is indeed subsistence at all, but the hyphen and its spacing.

This is why the work of faith, the *poiēsis-praxis* of *pistis*, presents itself in the letter under three aspects: the love of the neighbor, the discrediting of wealth, and the truthful and decided word. In these three forms, in question each time is an exposition to what cannot be appropriated, to what has outside itself, and infinitely outside itself, the justice and truth of itself.

In question is what the letter calls "the perfect law of freedom" (James 1:25 and 2:12). Unlike Paul, James does not sublate the law (supposedly ancient) into freedom and/or into a law (reputedly new). The "law of freedom"—of which no precept is really foreign to Judaism—is the arrangement or framework that would have it that acting should expose itself to the other and be nothing other than this very exposition: it is the *acting* of relationship or proximity rather than the *doing* of desire or appropriation; the *acting* of the word and the truth, rather than the "logistical" *doing* of representation and meaning. This formula—"law of freedom" (*nomos tēs eleuthērias*), which is perhaps a *hapax* in the Scriptures—could be understood with a Stoic resonance, and we would have, in that case, one of the marks of the implication of philosophy in this Christianity *in statu nascendi*. If something like this could be attested, then that should refer us to the deepest level of Stoicism's understanding: not the submissive acceptance of an order that escapes me, but the sharing (*nomos*) of the event as the opportunity of a becoming-self. In this we can hear Jacques Derrida's text on Abraham resonate with Deleuze's lines on Stoicism: "to become worthy of what befalls us, thus to want it and to set it forth in its event, to become the son of one's own events . . . and not of one's works. For the work is itself only produced by the son of the event." The *nomos* is thus the following: that we are only liberated by the truth that does not belong to us, that does not devolve to us, and that makes us act according to the inadequation and the inappropriation of its coming.

It would be outside the scope of this conference to analyze the triple determination of the "law of freedom" according to love, the word, and poverty. I will therefore not attempt to do so today and I will conclude simply with that which can no longer be deferred: namely, Jesus Christ.

In a certain sense, the only indubitable attestation of the Judeo-*Christian* composition of James's letter is his mention of Jesus. This mention is made from the first verse, in the formula, also used by Paul, "James, servant of God and of the lord Jesus Christ." Then, in the first verse of chapter 2: "my brothers, you who have faith in our Lord Jesus the Christ of glory." On the one hand, as I have already noted, this mention of the Christ stands withdrawn from any Christology. On the other hand, and at the same time, this mention alone determines faith, no longer according to its (praxical or operative) nature, but according to its reference, its scaffolding, its support or its guarantee. Mere faith in the uniqueness of God, as we have seen, is not, by itself alone, truly faith. Faith, in order to be, that is, in order to act, draws its consistency from somewhere else: from a proper name. Being the carrier of no specific theology, the proper name does not turn into a concept. This proper name is no introduction to a logic of the mysteries of incarnation and redemption. At the most, we may suppose, beneath the name *Jesus*, an implicit reference to the teaching transmitted by the gospels, especially that of the "Sermon on the Mount." For everything else, this name only serves to identify Christ, that is, the messiah. If the messiah is named, it is because he is come, because he is present in one way or another. He has presented himself. The name states this presence come to pass. A reader unaware of this would have no reason to think that this Jesus is no longer of this world. This presence is not that of a witness who would give reasons to believe, or some example of faith. The presence named here refers only to the messianic quality.

The expression "messiah of glory" could be, itself, a *hapax*. The messiah is the anointed one. Anointing is, in Israel—which inherited it from other cultures—the gesture that confers and signs the royal, sacerdotal, or prophetic function (a later Christology will attribute these three functions to Jesus). To be sure, whoever says "messiah," in Israel, understands this triple function, and foremost, the first one, that of the reign—which verse 2:5 names here, speaking of the "reign that God promised to those who love him" (four verses after the "Christ of glory"). A reflection on messianism cannot forego consideration of this royalty or kingship. (Without wanting to go into details here, I would say that the somewhat biased reduction of the meaning of *messiah* to the idea of a "savior" overlooks the functions implied by anointment and the fact that this "salvation" requires these functions—which also implies, eventually, a dehiscence or a disparity between these functions, like that between priesthood and prophecy.) A messiah "of glory," whether he be anointed with glory or glory be the splendor of his unction, is an absolutely royal messiah: resplendent with the magnificence that the Scripture never ceases to attribute to God, and which the oil, luminous and perfumed, reflects as it flows over the hair and onto the beard of the anointed one. Royalty according to glory is not first of the order of power. Or again, it is not of that order without being identically in and of the order of light and dispensation, the order of the "beautiful gift and perfect donation."

(Glory, *éclat*, or splendor is a very ancient attribute, divine and/or royal, in Assyrian and Babylonian representations, in whose context one also finds it allied with seduction and pleasure, especially on the part of feminine deities: this is the splendor associated with favor. In this regard, a great Hellenist once wrote: "It is with the Greek notion of *charis* that the *rapprochement* is unavoidable between charm, external grace, power of seduction, but also the luminous sparkling of jewels and materials, bodily beauty, physical wholeness, sensual delight, the gift that woman makes of herself to man.")

Ultimately, there would no longer be messianism here, but charisma, an inappropriable gift.

Glory purely and simply gives itself, and precisely as that which is not appropriable—not even by the one from whom it emanates—it is only admirable, and perhaps admirable to the point of not being able to be contemplated. Faith in glory or faith of glory (*pistis tou Kuriou Iēsou Christou tēs doxas*) is faith in the inappropriable: and once again, as the inadequation of the work or the inadequation at work. This faith receives itself from inappropriable glory, it is in glory in the sense that it comes from glory, where that glory provides faith its assurance, which is not a belief. The *doxa* of Jesus is his appearing: the fact that he is come, that the glory of his reign has appeared, already given as faith. *Jesus* is thus the name of this appearing—and he is this *doxa* qua name: the proper name of the inappropriable (that is, as we know, the very property of the name or, if you prefer, its divinity). And it is thus a name for any name, for all names, for the name of every other. The whole verse says: "take no account of persons in your faith in the Lord Jesus the Christ of glory," in order to introduce considerations about the poor. In a certain sense, we can only attempt to understand, likewise, that it is a matter of not taking account of the person of Jesus (either his face, his *prosōpon*, or his *persona*).

Thus a deconstruction comes to pass even before construction, or during construction and at its very heart. The deconstruction does not annul the construction, and I have no intention to reject, in James's name, the subsequent study of Christian construction—I don't want to take out the gesture of "returning to the sources" and of "puri-fication" of the origin, so obsessive in Christianity, monotheism, and the West. But this deconstruction—which will not be a retrocessive gesture, aimed at some sort of morning light—henceforth belongs to the principle and plan of construction. Deconstruction lies in its cement: it is in the hyphen, indeed it is *of* that hyphen.

For the present, here, of the hyphen in "Jesus-Christ" there remains but the dash that ties a name to glory. There remains this dash or hyphen, like a schema, in the sense of the conjunction of a concept and an intuition, but above all, in the more precise sense according to which, in this conjunction, each of the edges, exceeding the other, remains incommensurable with it. And so there remains the schema like a name, which is always the name of an other, the way the name *James* is the name of more than one James (as the other would say), always the name of an other, even if it were my own—and the *doxa* of what shows itself, the fame of the name so far as it puts faith to work, and a faith that creates a work, as at first blush, the deconstruction of religion as of the onto-theology that awaits it in its history—that awaits it to deconstruct itself therein.

But now, glory is only what it is insofar as it does not shine like gold or silver (unlike the jewels and the clothes of the rich man in verse 2:2). Glory is monstration, the exhibition of faith in the act (the *deixon* of the "show me your faith" carries the same semantic root as *doxa*), and yet for all that, glory is the exhibition of inadequation or incommensurability. It is in that way that glory is the anointing of the messiah: that is, the messiah exhibits the withdrawal of that with which he is anointed. This withdrawal is not a sacred separation: it is, quite precisely, the withdrawal of the sacred and the exhibition of the world to the world. To be sure, anointment is a consecration. But it is the non-sacrificial consecration that is not attached to offering the transgression of sacred separation, but which pours upon the world, in the world and as the world—as the work of creation—the very withdrawal of the divine.

James's letter says, toward the end (5:8), that "the coming of the Lord is near [literally: has approached, has become near]." The *parousia* is nigh: this is to say that *parousia* is and is not in proximity. Proximity is what never ceases closing and opening itself, opening itself in closing (it is not promiscuity, which would be a mixture). *Parousia* is—to be set apart from the very thing that approaches, to be a gap with and in itself [*l'écart de soi*]. *Parousia*—or presence close to—differs and is deferred: in this way it is there, imminent, like death in life.

What is changing, in the instituting configuration of the West, is that man is no longer the mortal who stands before the immortal. He is becoming the dying one in a dying that doubles or lines the whole time of his life. The divine withdraws from its dwelling sites—whether these be the peaks of Mount Olympus or of Sinai—and from every type of temple. It becomes, in so withdrawing, the perpetual imminence of dying. Death, as the natural end of a mode of existence, is itself finite: dying becomes the theme of existence according to the always suspended imminence of *parousia*.

The conclusion of James's letter recommends anointing the sick with the "prayer of faith" and the mutual confession of sins. The Catholic Church will found what it calls the sacrament of extreme unction on precisely this text, albeit much later. We must understand that the unction supposed to "heal," as the text says, heals the soul and not the body ("the prayer of faith will save the ailing one, the Lord will pick him up, and the sins he committed will be forgiven him" 5:15). This is to say that unction signs not what will later be called a life eternal beyond death but the entry into death as into a finite *parousia* that is infinitely differed or deferred. This is the entry into incommensurable inadequation. In this sense, every dying one is a messiah, and every messiah a dying one. The dying one is no longer a mortal as distinct from the immortals. The dying one is the living one in the act of a presence that is incommensurable. All unction is thus extreme, and the extreme is always what is nigh: one never ceases drawing close to it, almost touching it. Death is tied to sin: that is, tied to the deficiency of a life that does not *practice* faith—that cannot practice it without failing or fainting—at the incommensurable height of dying. Yet despite this, faith gives; it gives dying precisely in its incommensurability ("to give death," "the gift of death," he says):[5] a gift that it is not a matter of receiving in order to keep, any more than is love, or poverty, or even veridicity (which are, ultimately, the same thing as dying).

Not sacrifice, or tragedy, or resurrection—or, to be more precise, no one of these three schemas, insofar as it would give to death (one way or another) a proper density or consistency, whereas death is absolute inconsistency, if it *is* at all. (Hegel writes: "Death, if we would give a name to this non-effectivity.") Each of these schemas gives consistency to death: sacrifice seals in blood the reconciliation of a sacred order; tragedy soaks in death the bloodied iron of destiny (the utter rending of the irreconcilable); resurrection heals and glorifies death within death itself. Whether in one mode or another, each of these schemas gives a figure to the defunct and substance to death itself.

No doubt, each of these schemas can be understood differently. Each one, or all three together, in some composition that remains to be set forth and that could well be, precisely, Christianity in its most elaborate form.

But we can draw from these still another thread or splinter; that is, an inconsistency of death that would be such that the mortal does not "sink" into it, and still less escapes into it or from it,[6] but rather, remains safe from it at the precise point where he disappears qua mortal (and thus disappears "in death," if you will: but in death there is nothing, no inside, no domain). At this point where he dies, the mortal touches, making the only possible contact, upon the sole immortality possible, which is precisely that of death: it is inconsistent, inappropriable. It is the proximity of presence. The only consistency is that of the finite so far as it finishes and finishes itself.[7] For this reason, death can do nothing to the existent—except that, in its irreconcilable, inadequate way, it makes that existent exist, after a birth expelled it into death. Death thus puts the existent in the presence of existing itself.

In the Epistle of James, everything unfolds as though faith, far from being a belief in another life, that is, some belief in an infinite adequation between life and itself, were the setting in act [*la mise en œuvre*] of the inadequation in which and as which existence exists. How did faith, one day, with the West, start composing a decomposition of religion? That is what places that curious day still before us, ever before us, ahead of us, like a day that would be neither Jewish, nor Christian, nor Muslim—but rather like a trace or hyphen drawn to set space between every union, to untie every religion from itself.

Translated by Bettina Bergo

A Faith That Is Nothing at All

1

Among his singular characteristics, Gérard Granel presents a singularity more singular than others: that of being one of the very rare contemporary philosophers, if not the only one, to have affirmed, for a time, his belonging to the Catholic confession and Church—this while practicing a philosophy clearly tied, on the one hand, to Heidegger and, on the other, to Marx. Broadly speaking, we could say that he is one of the few, if not the only one, to have held together without confusion a religious faith and his engagement in philosophy (no "Christian philosophy," here, to the contrary!). He did this without maintaining, between the two orders, the exteriority and heterogeneity always invoked (if not well established) by other philosophers (Levinas or Ricoeur, for example). Everything comes to pass as though a singular point of contact, never stated explicitly, had held together over some twenty years a coupling without identity. This point existed de facto. How was it traced de jure (for Granel is not a man to leave things in empirical complacency)? This is what I am wondering about. I will pursue it starting from another question: Is a trace of this point visible thereafter, and at the conclusion of the work? And can this trace, if it exists, give us the import of the initial mark?

Before going to the "conclusion of the work" that I have announced here, I would like summarily to situate its beginnings. Up to the 1970s, Granel presents the singular form of a Heideggerian who is Marxist and

Christian (and who, into the bargain, if I may say so, recognizes early on in Derrida one of those "works that inscribe their age in its essential outlines").[1] I will not implicate myself in analyzing the hybrid [*composé*] thereby synthesized or syncretized—a kind of monster, to use a word that pleased him. There was indeed an organizing principle in this monstrosity, no doubt less teratological than *monstrant*. According to this principle, the destruction or the deconstruction (Granel uses both words) of metaphysics—understood as onto-theology, that is, as an assignation of the beingness of being [*de l'étantité de l'être*] (and thereby of its substantiality and its foundation in a supreme reality and *causa sui*)—was essentially the same as, on the one hand, the radical critique (that is, starting from "man" as "root") of political economy and, on the other hand, the no less radical reform (albeit in no way Protestant) of the Church, within which he called for a "struggle" against it without concession.

In the limited space of this volume, I will not attempt to retrace the path that this thought took and its attitude toward the Church (including dogma, morality, and pastoral practice). I will note only that, for Granel, it amounted to the task of conjoining—which is a singular stance for a Heideggerian—the deconstruction of onto-theology with an affirmation of faith. He wrote in 1971: "The possibility of faith remains ever open, even its reality often alive, if only beneath its ashes. It suffices, for it to appear or set itself back into movement, either that a Christian life lets us glimpse something of the truth of God (resembling however slightly these two signs of the early times: 'Look how they love one another' and 'They are afraid of nothing'), or even that the path of the truth of God's *work* becomes viable anew, simply in itself (as "ontological" truth), and without any reference or order to God being considered in this."[2] Faith, then, as love and courage, and/or as the thinking of being in its totality qua "works" [*"œuvre"*] detached from any craftsman . . . (created then? is "creation" not a work [*ouvrage*]? I would ask the reader to keep this on reserve until the last of these pages).

By one or the other of these traits, indeed. by the three taken together, the faith in question—the *"quid proprium* of faith"[3]—can only be a relation to God, not only the God "hidden" but the one who "wanted himself hidden," as Pascal says.[4] A relation to the will to hide itself and to remain hidden is a relation to something other than to an essence transcendent and beyond access. It is here not a matter of a *Deus absconditus* (i.e., of a subject predicated as *abscons*), but rather of the divinity of the *absconditus*. The relation of faith is thus an access to this "to will itself hidden" as such: an access, consequently, to that which cuts off or withdraws access. We have already understood this: it is the trace of this "faith," or the glowing beneath the ashes, that I want to question further in Granel's thought, which completely breaks with the Church and the confession of faith.

Later on, in fact, scarcely later, Granel apparently left Catholicism, theology, and even any will to "destruction." He abandoned Christianity to its metaphysical destiny and to the suspicion that it was renewing, by way of "globalization," the domination of a "Christendom" carefully disguised as modernity.[5] For all that, he did not seem thereupon to have explicitly determined the destiny of his "faith." In a manuscript text discovered later (was it ever published? we don't know—it was dated by hand Spring 1970), Granel spoke a propos God of the "old blasphemy of the *ipsum esse subsistens*."[6] Such a formula readily leads back to an opposition of faith to the onto-theology of the God who is Supreme Being. In a text published in 1973,[7] he again writes: "As we do not see what a 'general unity of practice' might mean (as a concrete, political, collective historical practice)—at least as we no longer see what it might mean (and no longer want to) under the form in which the Christian Faith, degenerating into 'Christendom,' had long usurped—and fulfilled—this function. . . ." As we can see here, this discourse, which wants to arrive at the idea of a non-metaphysical politics as a politics of "the Difference," remains in a state of indecision about this faith that might not have "degenerated." As "degenerate," this faith had filled and usurped the role of a concrete collective subject (which is already not nothing). However, as non-degenerate, what has it done, if it ever was active?

But I will not seek further sense from those rare texts in which we discern the twinkling vacillation of a tiny ember. I will retain only the idea that "faith" as such is not formally destroyed or crossed out of thought. And without tarrying, I will turn straightaway to the last text published by Granel: "Loin de la substance: jusqu'où?" ("Far from Substance: Whither and to What Point?").[8]

2

This text has as its subtitle "Essay on the Ontological Kenosis of Thought since Kant." It thus sets itself explicitly under the sign and the concept of a word consecrated (the term is apposite here) by Paul in his theological usage (God emptying himself of his divinity in Jesus Christ). By declaring his intent to assign this term to "an ontological index that is no longer theological" (535), Granel undertakes, in this respect, to pursue as far as possible a thinking of the ontological void, all the way to the extremities that the title pushes toward the irresolution of a question, *Where to?*—a question in which the "far" will not cease moving away and, in sum, exhausting itself. But whither? Perhaps nowhere, in no assignable site, in an excess of thought over any grasping by thought? But let us follow Granel's thread.

This thought is one that he several times calls, elsewhere, "the emptying out of being" ["*l'évidement de l'être*"], and which he here calls, with regard to Kant, a "transcendental emptying out" (535). Using these expressions, he transcribes Heidegger's "sense of being" insofar as this sense is understood as that of a being [*d'un être*] that is not substantive but verbal, and, moreover, verbal in a transitive mode. If being is thought as that which a being *is* [*comme ce qui* est *l'étant*] (as though the being "did" this or "gathered" this or "exposed" it without itself being confused with any of these actions), or indeed, if being "is" nothing other than the event itself (*Ereignis*) of a being, then being *as and in being a being* [*alors l'être en étant*] empties itself of all substantiality. Granel asserts that this emptying out gives us the red thread of modern thought, from Kant to Heidegger and passing through Husserl. At the end of the text, we learn that the emptying out is understood as the finitization of being [*la finitisation de l'être*]: it is "the pure and simple finitude of Being itself" (544), which will ultimately name the most distant or removed thinking that we will have been able to approach.

The progression of this approach can be analyzed insofar as it operates in three registers, tied to each other but relatively distinct, which function now simultaneously, then in alternation, relaying each other in some manner within the construction of the argument. There is a strictly philosophical register and, by contrast, a register constituted by a series of transpositions, metaphors, or borrowings of an unspecified nature, on the basis of a theological register, itself alternately Christian and "pagan."[9] The third register is of a wholly different nature: in it, Granel presents himself as himself and in the first person, as he who cultivates the ambition and risks "to venture" (535) going farther than others, "even Heidegger" (535), in thinking the *kenosis* in question. Farther, therefore, than any philosophy up to now, Granel advances "alone" (535): Whither and to what point? Up to what thinking experience of the—and in a—"void of being" [*vide de l'être*] (535)? It is he who asks us this question, as though he defied us to guess, or as though he invited us to follow him into this distance, where he is, nonetheless, alone in venturing.

These three registers have quite different statuses in the text: the first constitutes its true fabric, the second hardly occupies more than a dozen lines in these nine pages, and the third registers still fewer. I would like, however, to weave the three together in a tight braid that makes up the true functioning of the text.

It seems to me, in effect, that we are not concerned here with the body of a philosophical analysis that is elsewhere embellished by a few images (theological ones, incidentally) or with the contingent expression of an ambition (whose pride, no doubt, is foreign to no thinker, but very rarely exposes itself in such a defiance of the conventions of false modesty). What is more, it would be disregardful of Granel to judge that we are dealing with an amalgamation of heterogeneous registers. On the contrary, we must understand how the prideful or courageous? (can we distinguish these?) requirement and the theological or atheological? (can we distinguish these?) figure are here incorporated (I do not use this word without intent, as we will see) into the philosophical and, more precisely, the ontological investigation. We must understand how the demand [*revendication*] (the *Anspruch auf*, to speak Kantian) for an extremity that is proper to thought *and* the apparently allegorical resource of the theological have, between them, and in the midst of the philosophical *propos*, an alliance as unassuming, or secret, as necessary. And how this alliance is required in order to carry the arguments *to their farthest reach*, up to their "final stage" (543), however "strange" this might be.

3

The analysis of the "transcendental emptying" comes down to objecting successively against Kant and Husserl that they produce a substantial or substantializing waste [*scorie substantielle ou substantialisante*].[10] In this respect, the text presents some developments whose relative extent must be recognized as not being absolutely necessary, the less so in that they proceed from results that Granel obtained a long time earlier. Moreover, he himself indicates that he is "taking up various examples of what he [had] once called 'the ontological equivocation of Kantian thought'" (535), and he notes farther on that he has "shown clearly enough elsewhere" (542) how Husserl falls back, with each argument, "into a substantializing regime of discourse presumed to be descriptive" (542).[11] The text we are reading is thus a text of self-surpassing: Granel wants to go farther than he had up to that point, and that means going farther than "the entire Tradition" (540). *Traditionis traditio*: he draws himself with the tradition outside of it, farther than it, a carrying along and away [*entraînement*], a stretching, an extraction, a promise of some decisive excess. ("But one should not promise too much . . ." [535], he says with reserve, and as though he does realize that all promises contain a structural excess.)

This passing outside of and beyond a tradition, and of self, corresponds to a "purpose . . . alas!—more ambitious than all the critiques" (542), already addressed to the various substantialisms of the object or, above all, of the subject. (Why write "alas!"? No doubt because this ambition is exposed to an immoderation [démesure] that Granel deplores—sincerely? that is another question—and desires at the same time. The whole secret of the text is there, indicated and hidden.) Beyond the critiques, we must "seek the very root of this 'stubbornness' of Substance" (542) within the entire tradition. "And the response I will venture consists in saying that what escapes could be called *the Ungraspability of Being* [l'Insaisissabilité de l'Être]" (542). In a sense, the risk taken on, this response, consists in not responding: taking being away from any grasp, Granel empties or voids it [*le vide ou l'évide*] of all sub-stance, or of all "stance" in general. He empties being of all being, and thus empties the entire tradition of all its pretension to grasp being, whatever that might be. There results a void of being and of ontology or of philosophy—but to the benefit of what?

It is here that the surpassing of Heidegger is played out, if more subtly. This surpassing is sketched, suggested, rather than shown with the imperious certitude that pronounced the givenness of the "critique." The sketch of this surpassing takes shape when Granel declares that "there exists for 'things' a primitive mode of being that is different from the one described by the existential analytic, that is, the perceptual mode in which they are, as we say, 'given'" (539). I cannot stop here to examine the considerations called for by a reference limited only to the Heidegger of *Being and Time*. What is important is to grasp how Granel opposes to what I will call, in an attempt to restore his intention, the existential norm of "care" (a "pragmatics" of the world) another transcendentality or existentiality: perception, understood not as a pragmatics but as a poietics of the world.

4

(Here, a remark must be made to which I cannot give the requisite space. The "poetry of the World" appears early in the text [536]. The signal capacity of the poet, to name "the reserve [*pudeur*] of the World" [536] was designated as a sovereign challenge to any philosophical effort. This challenge is tied to "writing" [536], and the same page touches on examples of this writing ("the cry of a harrier streaking the gray sky," etc.), which quietly constitute writing in its ultimate truth as a phenomenological "description," which, precisely, would no longer be, in truth, phenomenological. This poetry or *poïesie* is nothing less—as his examples show, being all sketches, colors, and subtle touches [cold, red, outline of branches . . .]—than the regime of art in general. Art as perception, this is what is to go farther than Heidegger. But did Heidegger not also come back, later on, to what, for him, implicated art in the division [*partage*] of sky and earth, of "the open and the closed" [540]? What I am emphasizing here under the name of Granel's "poietics" is a comparable division between sky and earth: an upsurge of the world. But as we will see, the text also evokes another division of sky and earth, doubling or prolonging that of art, unless it is in fact the same one, differently intended.)

If, in this unattached [*déliée*], delicate way, we are advancing farther than Heidegger, then that is in order to touch—if we can say this—the "ungraspability of being" and to touch it in the mode of a "poietic perception," which is also to say a "creative perception" [*"perception créatrice"*], to put this word on hold once again. This ungraspability has nothing of any "sublime mystery, analogous to the Unknowability of God" (542). It is, writes Granel, "the withdrawal of the 'how' that occurs in every phenomenal field—at once its finesse, its total novelty, and its unproducibility" (542). "How it is that there is a world"—and not "how is the world"—or the fact that it is, always new and non-produced, not founded on a substrate or in a subject of "consciousness" (544), but rather ingathered, in "a sort of hollow" (542), or in "the Open" (542), which, each time, opens and gathers the world in this way: this is what sets in play the emptiness or void of being.

Now, it is here that Granel's solitary step forward takes place: it is here that he will "venture" (535), and it is here that it is a matter of establishing a condition of experience, an "ideality" or a "formality" of the world, which no philosophy has managed to state (540). This "formality" will have to respond to the question of knowing how a world appears to me without there being "on my part a movement of appropriation of the real" but also "no movement of reference to me, on the part of the real." Granel then declares: "Courage, we must state the strange, or simply remain blocked here" (542).

The "hollow always gathers up the seen" (542) and likewise forms the Open where "I am" at the very site of the appearing of things, without being "in the midst" of them, or before them like a subject. Granel identifies this site—a site that is not localized but localizes all taking-place—as Heidegger's *da* (543). But the ultimate step is taken when this *da* sees itself interpreted by a term that is no longer Heideggerian, that of the "body."

Granel does not explicitly thematize this last gesture, by which he distinguishes himself from the tradition in its final representative. But it is certainly there that he completes it. The "body" in question is not the symmetrical material counterpart of a soul or the "body proper" of Merleau-Ponty (543). This body is the primary "formality" of the world qua "site of diversification of the a priori of the visible (544). It is "a sort of black rectangle in the midst of a painting, which functions like a dispatcher of regions" (543). The term *painting* is not there by accident: painting is hinted at from afar as the true site of the formality-body and of the exposition of the world.

With painting, and in it once again, the poïesie of an outer-phenomenological "description" (outer in the sense of beyond or on the in-side of aiming, in an opening of the unintentional view), it is art that forms the object of the remarks. The "black rectangle," "principle and blind spot" of spatial regionalization ever reborn in the perceptual (544)—this is not an eye, it is an art: the art in which or as which a painting / a world is opened (the painting of a world as the world of a painting). That there might be no convocation of time indicates, here again and in an excess over Heidegger, that the spatial diversification—creating gaps, spacing, "regionalization"—governs the expansion as the opening of the open. I imagine, attempting to account for what Granel does not say, that the diversity of regions imposes itself as the form absolutely prior to any possible succession and movement (which does not mean one cannot sense therein, as well, the extension of time).

5

This body is therefore nothing other than the diverse aspects of the open, and therein lies the pluralizing trait that Granel insists on inscribing as surcharge (rather than as a crossing out) of the *da* of the *Dasein*. There results "this utterly surprising result . . . that the very thing that constitutes the purest field of thought is, as it were, *laid* [*posé*] upon our body" (544). This "poised on" challenges at once the autonomy of a pure subject of consciousness and the idea of an "incarnate spirit" (543). The body is not something in which and with which the spirit would have to do. It is, "rather, totally out of the picture" (543). It is ultimately, itself, the ontological void, vacuity as a diversifying opening of appearing. The principle of the world is set or *poised* on this void: nothing else organizes it.

Granel then concludes: "wanting to know more about this would be like wanting to enter into the creative act of God" (544). We can know nothing about or *on* [sur] the position of the appearing of the world, *on* the "black rectangle." We can posit or poise nothing above the being-on of the opening poised upon the void. We can know nothing, for this reason, of that art of the void or of that artist-void of the world and its "creative" *poiein*.

A double displacement takes place gently and secretly here. On the one hand, Granel introduces the theological register without clearly stating what is involved in this introduction: "It would be like wanting to enter . . ." This comparison leaves unclear whether the thing compared (the theological) has the status of a distinct reality or whether it is a purely figurative analogy (but figurative of what? what does "creation" figure other than getting out of the void?). On the other hand, by writing "wanting to know . . . ," Granel is referring less to an impossibility than to a prohibition. We must not seek to penetrate the aesthetic void [*vide artiste*]. The tone recalls a sacred taboo. Do we not find, then, yet another "surprising result," before which we must say, for our part: "Courage, we must state the strange . . ."?

In his final sentence, Granel appears immediately to defuse and disavow everything that seemed to bring us to such a reading. With a kind of jolt, he declares: "What then!—might we say, on the contrary, that the invention of a divine creation is only a flight, on our part, from all that is terrible in the pure and simple finitude of Being itself?" (544).

How can we avoid making two remarks? The first is rhetorical: Why introduce the "creative act of God," whatever the argumentative register of this introduction might have been, if only to expel it immediately from the space of thinking? Why, if not for the reason—at least for the reason—that this "creative act" offers the least bad analogical recourse, in our culture, for pointing out the stake of the void-artist-body [*corps-vide-artiste*]? But then should he not have said a bit more about the "creative act," whether we take it as an image or as a truth of faith (since its contents remain the same)?

The second remark obliges us to renew this question and extend its reach. This time the remark concerns concepts. "Creation" in the last sentence evokes, manifestly, according to a current use of the word *creation*, an operation that produces the world, giving it the foundation and the guarantee [*l'assise et la garantie*] of its producer or founder. Yet the "creative act" of the penultimate sentence is not less manifestly tied, through its comparative function, to the theme of the ontological void. From one creation to the other, Granel has changed concepts. From an *ex nihilo* understood strictly in the sense of a *nihil* opening as world [*un nihil ouvert en monde*], he passes to the fable of a producer supposed to produce without material (but certainly subject and substrate of his work). The most exigent theology, and in any case mysticism, in the three monotheisms will not have failed to underscore the opposition between these two thoughts. I will not develop this here,[12] but the difference must not be overlooked. Either God empties himself of himself in the opening of the world, or God sustains himself as being, by himself, subject and substance of the world. It is not at all the same "God" here. By dismissing the second possibility—the God of religious representation—did Granel fail to see that he was not dismissing the first? Or would he have, on the contrary, recognized in this, in an infinitely unassuming, secret, complex, and delicate way—the stake of his audacity vis-à-vis the tradition?

Or again, and more precisely: in dismissing the second "creator," Granel dismisses God, without a doubt. He does not dismiss a god emptying himself of God, or a "divine" that would be the exhaustion of all divine substance (that is to say, of all substance in general, if divine self-sufficiency defines substantiality itself, and absolutely). But this divine of exhaustion is precisely that of *kenosis*, whose mark or emblem this text carries. By the same token, the change in sign for *kenosis*—bearing an ontological, and no longer theological, sign—proves to be an operation less simple than it might appear. We cannot avoid asking why he has recourse to the Pauline term, if this term must simply transcribe in Greek what one has no difficulty calling "emptying out" [*"évidement"*] in French, and if, in addition, the transcription risks burdening (as we see that it does) the entire text (to which it gives its title) with the difficulty of untangling the precise reach or thrust of the dismissal given to theology within a regime nevertheless still "theological," insofar as it at least speaks of God (or again: insofar as it makes "God" a feature of its writing . . .).[13]

6

We must concede without hesitation that this regime might not be ontotheological, in the precise sense of the term that Heidegger intended. We must concede that, in this sense, it would be more accurate to say that it might be *neither* theological *nor* ontological. Granel does not say this, but he could have. He could have attempted to say, for example, that a "kenology" displaces all onto-theology here. If he does not do so (and if the term *kenosis* only appears in the subtitle of the text), then I would risk the hypothesis that this has the following motive: a kenology would have placed him under a summons—it would place us all under summons—to state what happens to the *logos* therein. It is likely that there is not a *logos* for the *kenos* the way there is one for "being" or for "god," inasmuch as we take being or god to be objects of discourse (of a founding discourse in reason), something the *kenos*, perhaps, tolerates with difficulty.

What happens, then, to the *logos*? Perhaps a double displacement befalls it.

On the one hand, and as we have discerned over the entirety of the text, it must be identified in some way with the "description" of the appearing of the world according to the "hollow" and according to the "unreal 'how' of all that is real" (538). This description is only a scription: "poetry" and "writing" (536). In sketching out the aspects [*allures*] of this "co-participating in the space of emergence or eclosure" (542) in all things of this world, like the "harrier" or the ray of light that does not separate from the sparkling of the sea (538), Granel wanted himself to be, sought himself, or hoped himself (promising? fearing to promise himself too much?) on the side of the poet (and not on that of the literary hack: he separates from the latter with an "I hope not," which proves his presentiment of a possible mistake, a possible decorative heaviness, and the extreme fragility of an approach to the poetic by the philosophical, even though this approach, extending all the way to contact, might appear precisely inevitable here, and more pressing than ever. In fact, this approach does press Granel, it troubles him. But it goes toward this point of contact, fugitive and pulsating, wherein "A Measure of Gathering" ("Mesure du Recueil") is exactly the sense of the Greek *logos* (542).

But, on the other hand and at the same time, the discourse and its poetic escapades have borrowed the resources of a metaphorics of the divine, and this still calls to be deciphered. True, the "mysteries" of Christian theology have twice been set aside: that of the incarnation (535, in regard to *kenosis*) and that of the "sublime mystery of the Unknowability of God" (542). If it is necessary to set them aside, then this is because confusion would be possible. In both of these cases, confusion would come down to identifying that which, in Christianity, proceeds from an outside the world (God coming into the world, God remaining inaccessible to the world), along with what must be understood of the world as the "formality" of its "opening": the latter is not outside the world, although it is not inside it either; it is not an other world, nor is it a beyond-the-world, since it opens this world to itself.

If confusion threatens, then this is because there is resemblance here, and if there is resemblance, then this is perhaps not without witness to some filiation leading from Christianity to the thought of the ontological void, or even from a paradoxical fulfillment of Christianity in its own exhaustion. But I do not want to follow that path here, as nothing in Granel authorizes it. I will stay with the clear distinction: that which is of the world has nothing to do with an outside of the world, nothing to do with a "pure spirit" or with a "supernature" (and *nothing to do* is here the right expression, in this text where everything is concentrated around seeing or its possibility).[14]

But that which is of the world and which constitutes its opening—like the edge, the dis-cerning limit—nonetheless contains the "divine." Never is the divine lacking in Granel,[15] so much so that he can speak, in another text, of the "god-world," which he opposes to the "god of the philosophers" (but the latter, assuredly a god of onto-theology, is not, for all that, the god of faith: I am speaking, in a sense, of nothing else, in Granel, than that shadow of a Pascalian trait). This divine is always a way of naming, in regard to the world, the constitutive alterity of its opening. Divine is the division that creates a world.[16] Here, this denomination *divine* is posited as nomination itself, favoring an appropriation of the metaphor at work in the word *god*: *dies*, "the light of the day, the Cerne or ring, compass, border [*le Cerne*], of which we spoke as the condition of perceptual discernment and which, for that reason, is in itself nothing that one might discern" (540). *Dies*, which is also, for Latinity, a goddess "mother of Sky and Earth," that is, of "all of this division that is truly original, and thus divine," this division according to which it is possible to have the order of things and (distinguishing itself from them in order to distinguish them) of the "non-thing of the Sky" (540): that is, ultimately, the opening of seeing, itself qua formal body or qua the *form-body* of which we spoke.

7

That the divine might not thus descend to "incarnate" itself does not make it any less divine, according to a dissimilar logic that is not totally heterogeneous (and that permits us to modify the sign of the *kenosis*)—a divine itself, the form-body of the luminous (or illuminating) opening: the "birth of the divine" (540) as the dawn of the world. Not incarnate, "the purest field of thought," that is to say, the perceptual aperture [*l'apérité perceptive*], which "is, as it were, *laid* upon our body" (544). "As it were": What does this mean? What does "laid" mean? The text has already utilized this participle, at the beginning, when it evoked or wrote/described [*(d)écrivant*] "an evening, on an earth of vanishing fields, an exalted color, as though it had just been laid down" (536). "Laid" is the *laid down* of the touch of a brush: it is precisely the touch of a seeing that opens a color—a "detail," a "suspension," an "emergence" or eclosure [*"éclosion"*]. Such a touch is consubstantial—if this word is possible here!—with the opening itself. "Pure thought" *upon* or *at the level of* the spatializing body is the simultaneity of the open and the ringed, the bordered, the cerned or dis-cerned, and the simultaneity of the void and of the divided out—of the divided out by way of the withdrawal of the "how"—"at once its finesse, its total novelty, and its unproducibility" (542). Unproducible is what is created in the sense of that which comes out of nothing. Laid down is the ungraspable touch of an *ex nihilo*, the clarity of a *dies divus formalis* [day divine formal], giving place to the world.

God there empties himself of substance and the divine there becomes the measure of the dividing of light and shadow, of the seeing and the visible. This site, this body, is thus the site, the hollow of God emptied out and of the divine void. Or again: what remains of the divine—what remains divine of the divine—would be this name *dies/divus*, which would gather in itself a *kenosis* wherein atheology would come to show itself as destitution and the truth of the "mystery." I in no way want to insinuate the suspicion of some remainder of piety in Granel. Quite the contrary. I would simply like to pose this question, to which it seems he has induced me: How do we recognize "the ungraspability of being"? How do we accede to this hollow body of which we must not "want to know" anything more? How do we touch, or let ourselves be touched by, the opening of the world / to the world? How, if not by a gesture that lays down, poses (or deposes) more and less than knowledge, by a gesture that passes outside of knowledge without unreason, by a precise reason [*raison juste*] attuned to the "*manifestly*" divine aspect of the manifestation itself and its division (540)? This gesture or act, which measures neither knowledge nor certainty, an act neither objectifying nor subjectifying, the necessary accomplice of a writing (of a song, of a tone, of a touch), could we not, must we not call it "faith"? A faith that would stand up unflinchingly to the atheism without reserve in which it would be nothing other than the "courage" invoked to say the "strange." The strange: a divine body discerning.

This is how I believe I can understand the part played in this text by the ostensible pride of Granel, who alone has ventured farther than all the philosophers—farther, but to what point? To this faith that is nothing at all: a fidelity thinking beyond the concept of the "nothing of that primitive All" (535), a thinking given over to that which comes to it from elsewhere because from nowhere, from *nulla partes*, from the null part of the nothing [*de la part nulle du rien*],[17] and thus a faith that, in sum, is nothing—nothing but this tiny extreme touch of thought laid upon that nothing [*posée sur ce rien*].

And above all, no religion! No belief, or some correlate of a represented substance, but a certainty with neither subject nor substance that receives itself and gathers itself out of "the pure and simple finiteness." Alone to the end, an open *black rectangle*.

Translated by Bettina Bergo

An Experience at Heart

Let us not discuss Nietzsche here, nor even a theme from his thought; instead, let us answer the question "What does Nietzsche tell us today?"

To respond to this, I would like to take the attitude that Bataille wanted to have toward Nietzsche and that I, in turn, want to adopt toward both Nietzsche and Bataille himself (from whom I will not separate Blanchot: perhaps you will be able to discern why). Nothing other than the attitude of thought toward each thinker: neither citing him, nor studying him, but rather learning him by heart, that is to say, by the organ that, in order to comprehend, must take and must be passionately taken. This is a platitude, but it is this that asks to be revived: such is also, and firstly, the sense that lies in naming "Nietzsche" today, without naming, for all that, a rubric from the history of philosophy. (Yet, to put it precisely: this is not simply philosophy.)

Nietzsche tells me nothing without also communicating an experience to me. This contagion between the discourse and the ordeal thoroughly marks an oeuvre that, for this reason, does not cease to exasperate, to be exalted, and to vacillate, uncertain, between outrageousness and suffering.

The experience is always that of the death of God. The death of God is always the fact of this immense destitution of the representation of the premise, and with that destitution, of representation in general: for, once the premise has crumbled, there can no longer be a question of representing anything. From then on, everything throws presence directly into question, directly into play. And everything makes a game of presence and plays it out. The evil genius.

1

Nietzsche knew, first, the agitation that takes hold when presence comes to tremble as the premise withdraws. (In a sense, it is too much to say "Nietzsche . . . first": he was the second after Plato, or the fourth after Plato, Augustine, and Kant. But our entire history has had no stronger jolts than these, and we are still trembling.) Presence no longer breaks free from its ground; it does not disappear into it either: presence stands, vacillating, at the edge of appearing in a world where there is no longer a rupture or opening between being and appearing. It has itself become presence, this rupture. (There is no longer a rupture between being and appearing, or again: there is no longer anything but rupture between them.)

Presence torn, wrenching presence. Presence is to the world in not being in that world. It stands before and in withdrawal from itself. What thus occurs to presence is what occurs to the order of the world itself. Without a principle, the world no longer provides justification to the order that organized its significations (what is above, what is below, the known, the unknown). Authority, virtue, value are given over to anarchy. They no longer have their -archy but are in play beneath and inside the archy. The anarchy in question is not some muddled grandiloquence directed against any type of constraint, it is the power that ought to begin all things, to signify all things, without any given sense.

2

We should understand Nietzsche's *Umwerten* in this sense. It is necessary to *um-werten* ["re-value"] the *Werte* ["values"]: "*um*" always has a valence of "making a turn around or through" and, as a prefix, it frequently indicates the reversal, revival, or recapitulation that returns. We must transvaluate, reevaluate, counterevaluate the values. It is not at all necessary to overthrow them (i.e., devalorize them), rather, it is necessary to *reevaluate value* itself. It is necessary to reform value (in the two senses of the word) or revolutionize it (likewise in all of its senses). That means: we must rethink value's price, considering it as an absolute price and one no longer dependent on a principle that sets it fast, fixes it.

Value must have value without measure. Bataille expressed this in calling value "heterogeneous": The "homogeneous" is the exchange of values, a general equivalence. In order to have value properly, it is necessary that value be heterogeneous to that equivalence. (In so speaking, we pass from Nietzsche to Marx via Bataille, but we also do justice to the contemporaneousness of Marx and Nietzsche, which is, not accidentally, a contemporaneousness of philosophies of value, even if they were unaware of one another.) The heterogeneous is not a matter of usage or of exchange: it is a matter of experience.

3

Who, then, has had the experience of absolute value (that is to say, value detached from a measure) and absolutely foreign to the fettered order of the world (of use and exchange)? Who, then, introduces *into* the world this *withdrawal* that is the heterogeneous—in the place of the principle that founded and provided measure?

It is he who saves the world in its absence of value, of that generalized equivalence into which the world appears to have sunk. Nietzsche calls him the redeemer.[1] Nietzsche gives him the title of Christ, and it is thus that he makes the Antechrist[2] the very sign of salvation: for Nietzsche, antechrist is he who overturns Christianity to make what he calls "the redeemer type" arise out of this overturning.

This type is that of the "sole Christian that ever was," he who "died on the cross." Nietzsche is alone in knowing him; the only one who knows how to recognize, behind the interested deformations of the first disciples themselves and of the evangelists. Assuredly, this is a "*decadence type*": but it is also from decadence that he will save. The redeemer presents a form of departure from nihilism: not the most active form, but a departure, and perhaps this departure—as I would suggest—is the weak, bloodless departure that nevertheless comes into contact with an affirmative and vigorous departure. (The entire question of getting out of nihilism is suspended between a weakness and vigor, both of which are necessary, and both perilous.)

This redeemer is he who founds no religion, who does not proclaim a god, who demands no belief in a doctrine or in any type of belief. He is the one whose faith is a behavior, not the adherence to a message. He is in the act and not in the significance, or again, his significance, his sense is wholly in his act. He effectuates pardon; he is pardon given and received, redemption effected here as coming from elsewhere, for redemption, or pardon, consists precisely in inscribing elsewhere in here. He erases sin, which is to say that he no longer makes of existence a fault or a lapse. On the contrary, existence consists in having, in the world, the experience of what is not of this world, without being another world for all that.

The opening of the world in the world is the result of a destitution or a deconstruction of Christianity, which goes back or which advances in it all the way to the extremity at which nihilism breaks up the presence and the value of God, breaks up the sense of salvation as an escape from the world, erases all value inscribed upon a heaven, erases heaven itself, and leaves the world intact *and* touched by a strange gaping that is grace and wound at the same time.

4

In the dissipation of nether- and hinterworlds, with their misty shroudings, lies the secret of salvation. Salvation saves us from other worlds: it restores to the world, it restores us to the world, and it sets (us) into the world anew, as new. It sets (us) into the world,[3] according to the novelty of an experience that is not of this world because it is that of value: the values of this world are measured, that is, evaluated, by the necessities and the interests of this world. But he who does not let himself be measured by that evaluation, he who has for himself the experience of value—he withdraws from the world in the very midst of that world. Not at all that he might become the subjective source of a value that would be his own: it is rather that he becomes the site of an experience that, in itself, is or creates value, absolutely.

This experience is "inner" experience, which is not at all the fact of some interiority qua subjectivity. The "inner" or the "interior" is not here some hidden depth that it would be necessary to find afresh or to express, some sense buried and to be interpreted: no, it is without interpretation, the literal and simple text of the retreat of the homogeneity of equivalent, measurable, and exchangeable values.[4] The same goes for "the one in love, who does not merely displace the sentiment of values, but who has more value and who is stronger." Love ("even the love of God" [*Liebe zu Gott*], Nietzsche specifies in the same fragment) is but the increase of value in itself, without available measure.

Inner experience is the experience of what places me outside of the outside of the equivalence of values, even of the valence of values in general, and thus outside of all subjectivity as of all property, whether this be the property of mercantile goods or of spiritual goods (competences or virtues).

This outside of the outside envelopes an "interior" where expectations are disarmed, knowledge disconcerted, as also certitudes and doubts. In place of representations and significations is substituted the affirmation of existence itself. Not speculation over its value, but value in itself as the affirmation and exposition of existing—which is to say, existing qua existing, nothing more, but above all nothing less.

This affirmation that existence is experience: that it does nothing else, cut loose from the goal or the project of the will—does nothing else but expose itself to the unforeseeable, the unheard of of its own event. Experience simply—we should say—"events" [*"s'évenir"*], "comes forth of itself."[5] This *évenir* opens *within* the world an *outside* that is not a beyond-the-world, but the *truth* of the world.

5

Truth is value reevaluated: a devaluation of every measurable value, a devaluation of every given by which one evaluates. Value is existence, which, in eventing evaluates itself: it becomes value without equivalence. That is the absolute price of existence without price. The same price that the existent gives itself, when it lets itself be evaluated by nothing. It gives itself a price without price, one that it can neither measure nor pay. It has nothing to pay: neither fault nor debt. It has neither sinned nor borrowed: it is redeemed from and for its being in the world through its withdrawal from the world. However, this withdrawal comes to pass in the midst of the world: it is contemporaneous with existing, it events with existing, as existing.

The redeemer is thus an inimitable "type": he is not a type; he is the experience of existing—with nothing other than this exposure to being nothing that might take on a price, or weight, or sense through something other than its step within/without the world [*son pas dedans/dehors le monde*]. This brief beating or pulsing has worth: it is itself evaluation without measure.

The redeemer is thus he who saves man from God, from that death mummified in the mausoleum of sense. The divine, henceforth, is the empty tomb: it is the void of the tomb qua affirmation of an eternal return of that which has no price. Value returns eternally, precisely because it has no price. The absence of price is what is inscribed and excribed with each existence as its eternal presence, immediately in the world out of the world, instantaneously eternal.

This is why the world of the homogeneous presents evaluation now as an equivalence of mercantile value, now as one entailing the sacrifice of existence to a supreme omnipotence. It is always a traffic. It is always one fundamentalism of value against another: one value being valued as a fundamental, a principial measure, God or money, spiritual or stock-market value. Yet heterogeneous value is worth nothing, or it is worth what the "valent" [*"valoir"*] in itself is worth: an ex-posure to some measure when that measure is but the other of all measure, or its infinity in act.

6

Nothing other, in this sense, than the Good *epekeina tēs ousias* ["beyond being"]: beyond all being-ness [*étance*], thus being not, being neither a being nor a nonbeing, but existing nevertheless. Neither God nor humanity, but yet the world as that *in* which an *outside* can open itself, and become experience. This experience is an "experience at a heart"—*eine Erfahrung an einem Herzen*:[6] an experience that forms itself right at a heart [*à même un coeur*], which is that heart itself beating with the beating of the inside/outside through which it ex-ists and, in ex-isting, senses and feels itself within/without the world, senses and feels itself as the interval between the within and the without, like the nonsite of what is its ownmost taking place, and like the unevaluatable value of this absolute property, without goods of its own.

According to this redeemer, "the kingdom of God" is nothing one might await; it has neither yesterday nor tomorrow, it will not come "in a thousand years"—this is the experience at a heart: it is everywhere, it is nowhere . . .[7]

Translated by Bettina Bergo

Verbum caro factum

For the time of a brief note, for the moment, let us analyze this central proposition of Christianity: *verbum caro factum est* (in Greek and in the Gospel of John: *logos sarx egeneto*). That is the formula of the "incarnation" by which God makes himself man, and that humanity of God is indeed the decisive trait of Christianity, and through it a determinative trait for the whole of Western culture—including the heart of its "humanism," which it marks indelibly, or may even be its basis (in return for a "divinization" of man—to stick to a short summary treatment).

The term *incarnation* is usually understood in the sense of the entry into a body of some incorporeal entity (spirit, god, idea); more rarely in the sense of the penetration of one part of the body by another part, or by a substance, usually foreign, as one speaks of an "ingrown nail." It is a change of place, the occupation of a body by a space initially not connatural to the given reality, and this sense can easily be extended to that of "representation" (the actor "incarnates" the character). According to that current acceptance (and it is assuredly not the major theological one), incarnation is a mode of transposition and representation. We are within the space of a way of thinking in which the body is necessarily in a position of exteriority and sensible manifestation, as distinct from a soul or spirit given in interiority, and not directly representable.

It suffices to read the Christian formula of the *credo* literally to see that it does not in the least, of itself, point toward that interpretation. If the verb *was made* flesh, or if (in Greek) it *became* flesh, or if it *was engendered* or *engendered itself* as flesh, it is surely the case that it had no need to penetrate the inside of that flesh that was initially given outside it: it became flesh itself. (Theology has made superhuman efforts—one might quite appropriately say—to think this *becoming* that produces, in one sole person, two heterogeneous natures.)

ↄↄ

Let us add here—in reserve for future analyses elsewhere—two supplementary givens that it is not vain to recall. With nuances, even important differences between "Catholic," "Orthodox," and "Reformed" Christianities, the human maternity of the *logos* (with or without virginity of the mother) and the "transubstantiation" (whether real or symbolic, it matters little here) of the body of Christ into the bread and wine of a "communion" represent two developments or two intensifications of the incarnation: on the one hand, in giving the man-god a provenance, already, in the human body, and in the body of a woman (in a sense, the incarnation takes the sexes into account), and, on the other hand, in giving his divine body the capacity to change again into inorganic matter (thus causing a lowly parcel of space-time, as well as a reality—bread and wine—issued from a transformation of nature by human skills, to be invested by "god").

ↄↄ

In this sense, the Christian body is completely different from a body serving as an envelope (or prison, or tomb) to the soul. It is none other than the *logos* itself that makes itself body as *logos* and according to its ownmost *logic*. This body is none other than the "spirit" having exited itself or its pure identity to identify itself not even *with* man but *as* man (and woman, and matter). But that exiting of the spirit from itself is not an accident that befalls it. (I will allow myself a vast ellipsis here, around the question of sin and salvation, which I will provisionally leave aside.) In itself, the Christian divine spirit is already outside itself (that is its Trinitarian nature), and we would probably have to go back to the monotheistic god common to the three religions "of the Book" to consider that he is already, himself, essentially a god who puts himself outside himself by and in a "creation" (which is not at all a production, but precisely a putting-outside-oneself).

In this sense, the Christian (or even the monotheistic) god is the god who *alienates himself.* He is the god who *atheizes himself* and who *atheologizes himself,* if I may for the moment forge these terms. (It is Bataille who, for his own purposes, created the term *atheological*.) Atheology as a conceptualization of the body is the thought that "god" made himself "body" in emptying himself of himself (another Christian motif, that of the Pauline *kenosis*: the emptying-out of God, or his "emptying-himself-out-of-himself"). The "body" becomes the name of the *a-theos* in the sense of "not-of-god." But "not-of-god" means not the immediate self-sufficiency of man or the world, but this: no founding presence. (In a more general sense, "monotheism" is not reduction to "one" of the number of gods in "polytheism": its essence is the disappearance of presence, of that presence that the gods of the mythologies *are*.) The "body" of the "incarnation" is therefore the place, or rather the taking place, the event, of that disappearance.

꒛

Neither the prison of the soul (sensible and or fallen body), then, nor the expression of an interiority (body "proper" or "signifying" body, which I will go so far even as to call the "sublated" body of a certain "modernity"), but neither pure presence (body-statue, sculpted body, redivinized body in the polytheistic mode in which the statue is itself the entire divine presence): but extension, spacing, putting aside of disappearance itself. Body as the truth of a "soul" that takes off (disrobes, drops its robe: the stripping bare of an infinite breakaway).

But the syncope that the body *is*—and that it *is* in one uninterrupted block, sustained from the cry of birth to the last breath, a block that is modulated in a singular phrasing, the discourse of "a life"—is not simply a loss: it is, as in music, a beat; it adjoins (syn-) in cutting (-cope). It adjoins the body to itself and bodies among one other. A syncope of appearance and disappearance, a syncope of utterance and of sense, it is also a syncope of desire.

Desire is not a melancholic tension toward a lacking object. It is tension toward what is not an object: namely, the syncope itself, in that it takes place in the other, and that it is "one's own" only in being in the other and of the other. But the other is only the other body to the extent that the latter, in its distance [*écart*] from mine, makes it possible to touch distance itself, the body open to the syncopated truth.

Here a (Socratic) erotics passes through the (Christic) incarnation as if by means of a fold internal to the *logos*: it is that erotics that would have it that the love of bodies leads to "conceiving beauty in itself," which is no other thing, in Plato, than to seize—or be seized by—the only one of the Ideas that is visible per se.[1]

A circle thus leads endlessly back from the visibility of the Idea—or from the manifestation of sense—to the syncope of the soul—or to the breaking away of the true. One in the other and one through the other, to the full-contact combat in which the body trembles and suffers and feels pleasure.

Translated by Michael B. Smith

The Name *God* in Blanchot

This title is not a provocation, no more than it is a cover for an insidious kidnapping attempt. It is not a question of trying to smuggle Blanchot over to the side of the new *political correctness* (and thus indecency) that takes the form of a "return to religion," as unsound and insipid as are all "returns."

It is merely a question of this. Blanchot's thought is demanding, vigilant, uneasy, and alert enough not to have thought itself obliged to adhere to the atheistic *correctness* or requisite expression of antireligious feeling that was de rigueur in his day. Not that his thought was in any way caught up in a countervailing declaration of faith. It is true that Blanchot affirms a form of atheism, but he does so only to dismiss atheists and theists alike.

(That takes place in a major text in *The Infinite Conversation*, "Atheism and Writing: Humanism and the Cry," in which atheism is associated with writing.[1] I shall return to this point, without, however, quoting or analyzing this text, no more than I will any other. In the context of and space allotted for this note, no analysis can be carried out. I will limit myself to allusions to a few Blanchotian topoi in order to suggest a direction for subsequent work.)

To reject in the same gesture both atheism and theism means to consider first and foremost the point that the atheism of the West (or the double atheism of monotheism: the one it causes and the one it secretly bears within itself) has thus far never pitted against or set in the place of God anything other than a different figure, instance, or Idea of the

Supreme punctuation of a sense: an end, a good, a parousia—that is, an accomplished presence, especially that of man. It is for that very reason that what is at stake in the association of atheism with writing—a provisional one, preliminary to the joint deposition of the claims of theism and atheism—is the displacement of atheism in the direction of an absenting of sense, of which, it is true, so far no notable atheistic figure has been capable (unless it may be in the figure, so close to Blanchot, of the *atheology* of Bataille—of which I will say no more here).

The "absent sense," that expression Blanchot sometimes risks, does not designate a sense whose essence or truth is to be found in its absence. That would be transformed ipso facto into a modality of presence no less substantial than the presence most assured, most *being*. But an "absent sense" makes sense in and by its very absenting, in such a way that, in sum, it never stops not "making sense." Thus it is that "writing" designates for Blanchot—as well as in the community of thinking that connects him with Bataille and Adorno, Barthes and Derrida—the movement of exposure to the flight of sense that withdraws signification from "sense" in order to give it the very sense of that flight—an élan, an opening, an indefatigable exposure that consequently does not even "flee," that flees flight as well as presence. Neither nihilism nor the idolatry of a signified (and/or a signifier). This is what is at stake in an "atheism" that owes it to itself to deny itself the position of the negation it proffers, and the assurance of every sort of presence that could substitute for that of God—that is, the presence of the signifier of absolute signification or signifiability.

Now it so happens that Blanchot's text is devoid of any interest in religion (beyond the fact that a Christian—a specifically Catholic—culture shows through here and there in a remarkable way, which will have to be examined elsewhere), yet the name *God* is not simply absent from it. Precisely, one might affirm that it occupies, with the text, the very particular place of a name that flees and yet returns, finding itself alternately (not very frequently, but often enough to be noticeable) firmly distanced, then evoked in its very distance as the site or as the index of a form of intrigue of the absenting of sense.

(Again, although it is totally out of the question to go into the texts here, I simply suggest a rapid re-reading of *Thomas the Obscure* [first and second versions], *The Infinite Conversation*, and *The Writing of Disaster* or *The Last to Speak*,[2] to verify at least from a formal point of view the presence of the word *God*—even if at times only latently—and the manifestly diverse, complex, or even enigmatic modalities of its role or tenor.)

If the name *God* comes in the place of an absenting of sense, or in the line of flight, so to speak, and in the perspective at once infinite and without depth of field of that same line of flight, that is primarily because this name does not involve an existence but precisely the nomination (and this is neither designation nor signification) of that absenting. There is, then, in this respect, no "question of God" that is to be asked as the ritualistic question of the existence or nonexistence of a supreme being. Such a question cancels itself out automatically (as we have known since Kant, and in fact from much earlier), since a supreme being would have to be indebted for its being or for being altogether to some authority or some power (terms obviously very inappropriate) impossible to classify within the order of beings.

This is why the most precious gift of philosophy is, for Blanchot, not even in the operation of the negation of the existence of God, but in a simple shrinking away, a dissipation of that existence. Thought does not think unless it be from this point of departure.

Blanchot, therefore, neither asks nor authorizes any "question of God," but he additionally posits and says that that question "*is not to be asked.*" This means that it is not a question, that it does not correspond to the schema of the demand for the assignment of a place within being ("What is . . . ?" or "Is there . . . ?"). God is not within the jurisdiction of a question. That does not mean that he falls within an affirmation that would answer the question in advance. Nor does he fall within a negation. It is not that there is or is not a God. It is, quite differently, that there is the name *God*, or rather that the name *God* is spoken. This name corresponds to a *statement* of the question, whether it is a question of the being (the "What?"), of the origin (the "Through what?"), or of sense (the "For what?"). If all questions intend a "what," a something, the name *God* corresponds to the order, the register, or the modality of what is not, or has not, any thing.

Moreover, this name sometimes appears in Blanchot alongside words such as *being* (as taken from Heidegger), or *neutral*. For them as well, the question is not to be asked, for it is already deposited within them. But they are words (concepts), whereas *God* is a name (without concept). The name *God* must, then, represent something other than a concept here, more precisely, it must bear and bring to a head a trait common to names as such: to be at the extremity and the extenuation of sense.

The same may be said, no doubt, of this name and of the name *Thomas*, who might be called the eponymous hero of Blanchot's writing. In the story titled *Thomas the Obscure*, a narration in the course of which God appears and intervenes on several occasions, the name *Thomas* is sometimes referred to as "the word *Thomas*." The word *thauma*, in Greek, means marvel, prodigy, miracle. As a concept, "Thomas" presents the miracle or mystery of the name qua name.

The name *God* is said by Blanchot, on occasion, to be "too imposing." That qualification, mixed with fear or reverence, is open to two interpretations. Either this name is too imposing because it claims to impose, and impose itself, as the keystone of an entire system of sense, or else it is majestic and awesome to the degree that it reveals the nonsignification of names. In the second case, this name names a sovereign power of the name that beckons—which is very different from signifying—toward that absenting of sense such that no absence can come to supply a supposedly lost or rejected presence. "God," then, would name neither the God subject to sense nor the negation of this in favor of another subject of sense or non-sense. *God* would be the name of that which—or of he or of she who—in the name escapes nomination to the degree that nomination can always border on sense. In this hypothesis, this name would de-name names in general, while persisting in naming, that is, in *calling*. That which is called, and that toward which it is called, is in no regard of another order than what Blanchot designates, on occasion, "the emptiness of the sky." But the appeal to this emptiness, and in it, inserts in this name a sort of ultimate punctuation—though without a *last word . . .* to the abandonment *of* sense that also forms the truth of an abandonment *to* sense insofar as the latter exceeds itself. The name *God* would indicate or proffer that call.

To the coupling of atheism with writing, Blanchot adds, in the same text and under the same title, the association of humanism and the cry. The humanism of the cry would be a humanism that abandons all idolatry of man and all anthropo-theology. If it is not exactly in the register of writing, it is not in that of discourse either—but it cries out. Precisely, it "cries out in the desert," Blanchot writes. It is no accident that he takes up a watchword phrase of biblical prophecy. The prophet is the one who speaks for God and of God, who announces to others the call of and recall to God. There is no motif here of any return to religion, rather, an attempt to extract for himself, out of the monotheistic heritage, its essential, and essentially nonreligious, trait—the trait of an atheism or of what one might call an *absentheism*, beyond all positing of an object of belief or disbelief. Almost in spite of himself, and as if at the extreme limit of his text, Blanchot did not yield on the name *God*—on the unacceptable name *God*—because he knew that it was still necessary to name the call unnamable, the interminable call to in-nomination.

Translated by Michael B. Smith

Blanchot's Resurrection

The theme of resurrection does not seem, on the face of it, to play a major role in Blanchot. At least it is only rarely encountered in the so-called "theoretical" texts. It may be more frequent in the narratives, but in them it is harder to isolate themes per se. Yet resurrection is indissociable in that work from death and dying, with which we are more used to associating the name *Blanchot*. And if the phenomenon of dying is, in turn, not only indissociable from literature or writing but consubstantial with them, that is only to the degree that it is engaged in resurrection and does nothing but espouse its movement. What is that movement? That is what I will attempt to approach, while setting aside the project of reconstituting an entire economy throughout Blanchot's work, for that would be the object of an entire book.

Let us first be attentive to the major chord. The resurrection in question does not escape death, nor recover from it, nor dialecticize it. On the contrary, it constitutes the extremity and the truth of the phenomenon of dying. It goes into death not to pass through it but, sinking irremissibly into it, to resuscitate death itself. To resuscitate death is entirely different from resuscitating the dead. To resuscitate the dead is to bring them back to life, to bring life back where death had destroyed it. It is a prodigious, miraculous operation, which replaces the laws of nature with a supernatural power. Resuscitating death is a completely different operation, if it is an operation. At any rate it is—not far from that concept—surely an *oeuvre*, or of the order of the *oeuvre*, the *oeuvre* in its essential *désoeuvrement*.

But in point of fact *désoeuvrement* itself cannot be understood otherwise than by starting out with the resurrection of death, if, by means of the *oeuvre*, "the word gives voice to death's intimacy."[1]

Now the "resurrection of death" is a rare but decisive expression in Blanchot. He may have used it only once, but in such a decisive and striking way that that sole occurrence seemed sufficient to him—being at the same time too daring not to become dangerous were he to use it repeatedly. For it is dangerous, of course, and may open up all sorts of ambiguity. Blanchot knows this and is determined to avoid the risk, though not without assuming a portion of it carefully, one might even say in a delicately calculated manner. That part retains at least partially the monotheistic and, more precisely, the Christian root of the thought of resurrection.

We must begin by dwelling for a moment, without forfeiting the right to return later in more detail, on this Christian source. Blanchot could have silenced it, or even suppressed it entirely and replaced *resurrection* with some other term. We may imagine he might, for example, have used *désoeuvrement* ("*oeuvre* without fulfillment"), or "madness," or "insomnia," "reversal," or "overturning,"[2] or yet again "recognition," whose movement and "extravagance" Christophe Bident has taken pains to discern.[3] Up to a certain point that substitution was thinkable, and relieved him of the burden of religious connotation. But what would have been lost thereby is obvious: the immediate and manifest connection with death—the deliverance and exit from which the term *resurrection* expressly designates. Everything therefore seems to have happened as if it were not possible to dispense with the use of a term destined to function as a logical operator in a relationship with death posited as essential to writing—no less than in a relationship with writing (with the spoken word, the cry, the poem) posited as essential to dying or human mortality. But that is not entirely sufficient: one must take into account that which, by its very presence, cannot help but function also as the taking up of a theological motif.

At this point we must extend the examination to the entirety of the theological or, if I may hazard the expression, theo-morphological given in Blanchot's text. That will be for another work. I note only, on the subject of resurrection, that that given becomes clear in a very singular manner in texts not far from this motif. It becomes clear through an expressly evangelical reference to a figure that may be said to be eponymous with resurrection: Lazarus in the Gospel of John. Indeed, Lazarus first appears at the same time as the first and perhaps sole occurrence of the expression "death resurrected." This happens early on in Blanchot's work, since it appears in 1941, in the first edition of *Thomas the Obscure*.[4] The text is retained in the second edition, yet the two sentences that precede and follow the statement that names Lazarus are modified. This shows the attention given by the author to the following sentence, whose subject is Thomas: "He walked, the only true Lazarus, whose very death was resurrected."[5]

Let us point out immediately that six lines earlier the text has these words: "he appeared at the narrow gate of his sepulcher, not resurrected, but dead and having the certainty of being torn away at once from death and from life." This last sentence transforms somewhat, by lightening it, the turn of phrase of the first edition, in which the order of words is the reverse: "from life and from death." As for the lightening, it resides in the modification of this inserted modalizing clause: "having suddenly, through the most pitiless of sudden blows, the feeling that he was torn away." These micrological specifications are instructive. Whereas the gate to the sepulcher continues to recall the evangelical episode as well as the name *Lazarus*, the state of mind of Thomas has moved from "feeling" to "certainty," and the latter is stripped of any "devastating" ["*foudroyante*"] and spectacular qualifiers. From a sort of commotion we have moved toward the affirmation of a certainty—which is never, in a general sense, very far removed from the order of a Cartesian *ego sum*. From an over-whelming impression, Thomas has moved to a kind of dead *cogito*, in or of death. He knows that he has been "torn away" as much from death as from life (hence the importance of the change in the order of the terms). Though "dead," he is not plunged into the thing: "death." He becomes the subject dead from having been torn away from death itself. That is also why he is not resurrected, that is, does not regain his life after having traversed death. But, while remaining dead, he advances in death ("he walked") and it is death itself that is resurrected in this "only true Lazarus."

Death is the subject: the subject is not, or is no longer, its own subject. Such are the stakes of resurrection: neither subjectivation nor objectiva-tion. Neither "the resurrected" nor the dead body—but "death resur-rected," as if stretched out over the dead body and thus setting it upright without lifting it up. Nothing but that. *Wo ich war, soll es auferstehen*.[6]

The other Lazarus, the one in the Gospels, is not, then, the true one. He is the character from a miraculous story, of a transgression of death by the most improbable of returns to life. Truth does not reside in such a return: it resides in the simultaneity of death and a life within it that does not come back to life, but that makes death live qua death. Or yet again:

the true Lazarus lives his dying as he dies his living. So it is that he "walks." The text goes on, ending the chapter (and also transforming, lightening the first version, in which, moreover, the chapter was far from ending): "He advanced, passing over the last shadows of night, losing none of his glory, covered in grass and earth, going, beneath the falling of the stars, with measured steps, with the same gait that, for men not enveloped in a shroud, marks the ascension toward the most precious point of life." That subterranean, glorious advance amid the *disaster* proceeds with the same gait as the one with which we go toward death. Thomas is wrapped in a shroud, just like Lazarus, while the men's walk is that of an "ascension," another Christian term designating, this time, the manner of advancing peculiar to the Resurrected par excellence. Thus, the distancing from the Gospel is only validated by a renewed appeal to its reference. The true Lazarus is not an entirely distinct figure from the Lazarus resuscitated by Christ (by the one who says, in this same episode in John, "I am the resurrection"): there remains within him something of the man who was miraculously cured.

But it is not exactly the miracle: it is rather the sense that the story of Thomas gives to the miraculous narrative. This sense, or this truth, is not a crossing through death, but death itself as a crossing, as transport and transformation, from itself into itself withdrawn from its thingness, from its objective positivity of death, in order to reveal itself—"the most precious point of life"—as the extremity at which there is a turning inside-out and a laying bare of life's access to that which is neither its opposite nor its beyond, nor its sublimation, but only—and at the same time infinitely—its obverse and illumination by its darkest face, that of Thomas, the face that receives a light of shadows and is therefore able to renounce the exclusive light of possible senses.

Must it be further specified? *Thomas the Obscure* presents us with nothing other than the story of a resurrection, and better yet, the story of the resurrection. For Thomas himself *is* the resurrection, following the example of Christ, another of whose utterances is recalled apropos of the death of Anne,[7] whereas Anne is the resurrected one, the dead woman whose "body without consolation"[8] is at the same time the presence that "bestowed on death all the reality and all the existence which constituted the proof of her own nothingness."[9] Thus, as the monologue of Thomas, who keeps watch over her, goes on to say: "Neither impalpable nor dissolved in the shadows, she imposed herself ever more strongly on the senses."[10] Now that last sentence, which impresses on the reader the affirmation of the strong physical presence of the body, must also be read in accordance with the narrator's express indication to the effect that Thomas speaks "as if his thoughts had a chance of being heard,"[11] and consequently, according to that orality, the plural "on the senses"—an expression, moreover, slightly unusual in this context—becomes inaudible and is elided into a singular that is calculated to be understood, without, however, formally imposing its concept.[12]

In any case, Blanchot will confirm it for us: the resurrection designates access to that which is beyond sense, the advance into that beyond by means of a step that goes nowhere but to the repetition of its equality. We know that writing is the trace or mark of this step—but only in that it opens onto a "space in which, properly speaking, nothing has any sense yet, but toward which all that has sense returns as to its source."[13] Let us ignore, for the moment, the fact that this text from 1950 speaks a language that is somewhat distinct from the one Blanchot would speak later on. The divergence is certainly not a matter of indifference, and Blanchot remarked on it,[14] without that preventing (quite to the contrary) the impressive reiteration [*ressassement*], the remarkable obstinacy of a thought across necessary variations. Thus it remains the case that the space of the resurrection, that space that defines it and makes it possible, is the space outside of sense that precedes sense and follows it—if we accept that here anteriority and posteriority have no chronological value but designate an outside-of-time that is as endless as it is instantaneous, eternity in its essential subtractive value. (But the remark thus made about the displacement of terms in Blanchot after the period of *The Space of Literature* should open onto another inquiry: to some degree, Blanchot proceeded in this way to a putting in abeyance or an interruption of the mythical register. And yet, beyond the interruption, what is it, perhaps—or even surely—that insists and can only insist? This insistence is allied, in Blanchot, with that of the name *God*, to which I turn elsewhere.[15])

Life withdrawn from sense, the dying of life that constitutes its writing—not that of the writer only, but that of the reader and, further yet, the writing of those who neither read nor write, whether they be illiterate or have renounced all learned commerce, writing, in short, defined by the "dying of a book in all books,"[16] to which the following definition also applies: "To write, 'to form' in the informal an absent sense"—that life is life withdrawn from sense, which does not resurrect as life but resurrects death. It removes death from its advent and its event, it takes away, from the death of mortality, the dying of immortality by which, incessantly, I know this radical retreat of sense, and thus truth itself. I know it, I share it, that is, I withdraw my death, my due date, from all property, from all presence proper. It is thus from myself that I am disengaged and that I "transform the fact of death."[17] Doubly so: death no longer befalls me as the cutting off inflicted on "me" but becomes the common and anonymous fate that it cannot help but be, and, in a corollary way, death resurrected, absenting me from myself and from sense, exposing me not only to the truth but exposing me at last as myself the truth—myself the dark glory of the true in act.

In a subtle way, Blanchot's life—whose intimately withdrawn nature made possible the affirmation and exposition of an entirely other life, a life whose declared absence involved the most insistent public presence of a life extracted from the death of objectified existence and identified in the person and the work, the life of Blanchot, which was thus not hidden but, on the contrary, the most published of all—was a life resurrected during his life by the very publication of his death, always at work. There is, no doubt, some ambivalence in that attitude, but its coherence and performance offer food for thought. What is certain, at any rate, is that Blanchot never took his lead from any reanimation or miracle but was able to grasp (if we can use "grasp" here in the sense of "comprehend"; at least we can use it in the sense of "take") his life as dead from the outset, and thus turned around in resurrection.

That there is here neither reanimation nor miracle is made clear in the text "*Lazare, veni foras*" in *The Space of Literature*. Blanchot sets himself the task of describing reading as the act of accessing the work, which is "hidden, radically absent perhaps, covered up in any case, obfuscated by the visibility of the book."[18] He identifies the "liberating decision" of reading with the "*Lazare, veni foras*" of the Gospel.[19] This identification opens in fact on a considerable shift, by which it is no longer a question of bringing a dead man back from the grave but of seeing the tombstone itself as "the presence," whose "opacity" is not to be dispelled but recognized and affirmed as a truth of the awaited transparency, or as "obscurity" (that of Thomas, once more) qua true "clarity." Now, if the operation of reading, in its revelatory capacity, can be considered a "miracle" (a word Blanchot puts in quotation marks, indicating at once an ordinary way of saying "miracle of reading" and the operation carried out by Christ on Lazarus), it is only in understanding its revelation by following the lead of the stony darkness that we are also "perhaps enlightened about the sense of all thaumaturgy." Blanchot makes or slips in this remark in an incidental manner. Yet it is nothing less than a clarification of the sense of miracle. "Thaumaturgy": this term distances itself from the evangelical miracle, pushing it in the direction of a scene of the magical or marvelous. (This last term comes a few lines further on, it too with a slightly deprecative connotation.) Let us note here, however—as a general point of information—that Blanchot uses the name *Thomas*, which, treated at times as a word rather than a name in the eponymous book, does not leave off, perhaps, beckoning toward a "marvel" that is more marvelous, because less dazzling, than all the marvels of the Gospel, or . . . of the literature of the marvelous. In any case, the upshot is that "the sense of every" miracle is given in that of reading, namely, by no operation that defies nature as given, but by the "dance with an invisible partner" that characterizes, in sum,[20] the "light" reading that is not learned, which also means—it is specified—a reading not "permeated with devotion and quasi-religious,"[21] the only reading that does not freeze the book into an object of "worship" ["*culte*"], which can even be "uncultivated" ["*inculte*"], and thus is open to the withdrawal of the work. The sense of the miracle is to give rise not to a sense that exceeds or subverts common sense, but only to the suspension of sense in a dance step.

That image itself may bother us. It has about it something too immediately seductive not to be too facile. Yet it does suggest as best it can the relationship between lightness and gravity around which Blanchot delineates it. Indeed, he concludes: "where lightness is given to us, there is no want of gravity."[22] That gravity, which is not wanting but remains unassuming, stands in opposition to the heavy gravity that fixates thought on the thing, on being, on substance. It also stands in opposition, then, to the thought that is fixated on the substance of death and intends to lighten it and console itself about it by the thaumaturgy of a ponderous return to life. Dancing gravity does not click its heels in the air before the grave; it experiences the stone as light, it puts or feels, in the heavy stone, the infinite lightening of sense. Such is the opposition between death resurrected and the resurrection of the dead.

Hence, as another text expresses it, everything happens "as if, in us alone, death could be purified, internalized, and apply to its own reality that power of metamorphosis, that force of invisibility whose original profundity it is."[23] *In us alone*: the context makes it possible to specify that what is referred to here is not only us as human beings, but us as dead. "Us alone" is also us in our solitude and in our desolation of the dead, and of mortals, "we of all beings the most perishable,"[24] as it is said further on. In this text, devoted to Rilke, it is to the poem and its song that the light gravity of the resurrection of death has been consigned. "There the spoken word," he writes, "gives voice to the intimacy of death."[25] That takes place "at the moment of the break," at the moment the spoken word dies. The swan song seems always to have been the *basso continuo* of Blanchot's texts. This means two things, which in combination make up the difficult, strange, and obstinately fleeting thought of resurrection.

On the one hand, this song only sings, or this step only dances, at the moment of its breaking off, in the breaking of its breaking off, and it cannot do otherwise than entrust to its own dying the task of sustaining its note, of dancing its step. It must therefore be that way throughout the length of the writing: at each point it must be the case that what is ex-scribed from it [*s'en excrit*] is inscribed, and that there is nothing else to say, no ineffable, nor any return of yet another word of truth, but the cessation of speaking. But there is no reprieve from this ex-scription, and poetry—*sive philosophia*—is a vain word only up to the point at which it thus dies. At this point, dance or song follow no arabesque, and in a sense no longer appear. Their only contour is that of the address, an address stretched toward and entrusted to that which—it, he, or she—there is no possibility of reaching. As Philippe Lacoue-Labarthe writes apropos of another of Blanchot's texts: "a sort of confidence, or—which is the same thing—confession. This text is quite simply *entrusted*, it appeals to a faith and a faithfulness."[26] Elsewhere, we will have to return to the "faith" that apparently is presumed by everything involving "resurrection" or whatever its name may be, "poetry" or the leveling of all names. For the moment, let us say simply that indeed dying *entrusts* what death in fact steals and buries beyond appeal. Dying is the appeal.

On the other hand, resurrection is not simply borrowed as a convenient or provocative image from the vocabulary of the miracle. It also presents itself as a rewriting of Holy Writ: a sanctity taken from the marvelous of religion, but also taking from that marvelous a nongullible and nonpious access to what it is no longer appropriate to call "death" (the reality of an unreal) but "consent," the reality of a correspondence with the very real of dying. This word comes up several times in Blanchot's texts, both the ones I have cited here and others.[27] Consent, dubbed later, I believe, "patience of passivity,"[28] by which it is given "to answer to the impossible and for the impossible,"[29] neither submits nor resigns: it grants a sense or a feeling. It agrees precisely with the sense and the feeling of the insensitive and of sense *in absentia*. It is nothing other than the infinitely simple—and by that very fact indefinitely renewed, indefinitely reinscribable in us—experience of being without essence and thus of dying. Resurrection—or let us say it in Greek, *anastasis*, erects dying, like the thick and heavy gravestone, like the stele on which the name of an inviolable and uninscribable identity, always ex-scripted, is inscribed . . . to be ultimately obliterated. That stele raised before the void and devoid of any beyond, without consolation, comforting, with all of its mass, a grief already borne very far from itself and from lamentation. An infinitesimal, unassuming, and insistent lightness, which constitutes the consenting of this consent to the insensate. Whoever does it or writes it, if writing is the name (as inconsistent as any other, but inevitable . . . as much so as "poetry" or "sanctity") of the refusal of all belief in a consistency foreign to the world. The consent to resurrection consents primarily to the refusal of belief, just as faith denies and rules out that same belief. But in reality belief is never believable, and always within us some obscure something or someone knew it for us. Always this presentiment of the absolutely unbelievable, defying beyond appeal all credulity and entrusting itself, absolutely, has carefully prepared for us the cul-de-sac of consent.

If consent, or resurrection—the raising that erects death within death like a living death—obtains within writing, or literature, that means that literature can stand the cessation or the dissipation of sense. "Literature," here, does not mean the "literary genre," but any sort of saying, shouting, praying, laughing, or sobbing that holds—as one holds a note or a chord—that infinite suspension of sense. It is understandable that this holding or sustaining has more to do with ethics than aesthetics—but in the end it eludes and undoes these categories as well. It may be said yet otherwise: To the extent that these categories belong to philosophy, they also make us aware that philosophical onto-theology practices embalming, or metempsychosis, or the escape of the soul—but never resurrection. Thus metaphysical practices always designate a "forward, march," the future of a renaissance, a kind of possible and of power, whereas literature only writes the present of what has always already happened to us, that is, the impossible into which our being consists in disappearing.

Translated by Michael B. Smith

Consolation, Desolation

In the Preface he wrote for the volume entitled *Chaque fois unique, la fin du monde* (*Each Time Unique, the End of the World*),[1] a collection of memorial addresses, Jacques Derrida emphasizes how much the "adieu" should salute nothing other than "the necessity of a possible non-return, the end of the world as the end of any resurrection." In other words, the "adieu" should in no way signify a rendezvous with God but, on the contrary, a definitive leave-taking, an irremissible abandonment—as much an abandonment of the deceased other to his effacement as an abandonment of the survivor to the rigorous privation of all hope in some kind of afterlife, whether that of the other or indeed, ultimately, of the survivor himself: I, who salute the other, whom another will salute, some other day.

This necessity is tied to that according to which we must recognize, in each death, the end of the world, and not simply the end of a world: not a momentary interruption in the chain of possible worlds, but rather the annihilation with neither reserve nor compensation "of the sole and unique world," "which makes each living being a single and unique one." We must say "adieu" without return, in the implacable certainty that the other will not turn back, will never return.

A salutation [*salut*] "worthy of the name" rejects all salvation. It salutes the absolute absence of salvation [*il salue l'absence absolu de salut*], or, again, it "foregoes salvation [*salut*] in advance," as Derrida wrote already in *Le toucher—Jean-Luc Nancy*.[2] Just as he then addressed that salute to me, that salute dismissing salvation, he again directs to me the monition of this "book of adieu." He specifies, in effect, that "resurrection" must be refused, not only "in the usual sense, which imagines bodies that have come back to life get up and walk about; but even in the sense of *anastasis* of which Jean-Luc Nancy speaks."[3] In effect, the latter "continues to console, were this with the rigor of a certain cruelty. It postulates both the existence of some God and that the end of *one* world may not be the end of *the* world."

1

I would like, in turn, to salute this salute and not reject the rejection it carries, but rather attempt to clarify it differently, so far as it is possible to bring whatever light there might be to this material, and so far as it is not necessary—to the contrary—to abide with it with eyes closed, definitively and obstinately closed, to everything that is not related to a night and a sleep without tomorrows and awakenings. Eyes open, consequently, to the night, in the night, and as themselves nocturnal: eyes that see the end of the world, not represented before them, but unleashing in them the collapse of the vision and touch of the night itself. Night against eyes like other eyes, which would arrest and drown in them all possibility of vision, of intentionality, of direction, orientation, and recourse outside the adieu without return.

If my salutation is to be worthy of its name, it must salute without salvation, but it must salute. The noun *salut* denotes address, invitation, or injunction with a view to being safe. Safe (*salvus*) is that which remains whole, unscathed, intact. What is safe is thus not the saved, separated from the injury or the pollution that had touched it, rather it is that (or that one, he; that one, she) which remains intact, out of reach—that which has never been touched. In this way the dead carry off with them, as we say, the unique and sole world each of them was. They carry off, this way, the entire world, for never is the world a world if not unique, alone, and wholly intact. *Solus, salvus*: there is salvation only of the sole, the single, yet the sole or single is the *desolate* par excellence: devastated, deserted, given over to a total isolation (*desolari*).

No more than the word *consolation* has anything but assonance with the word *desolation* (*solor*, "comforting," is foreign to *solus*), no more can there be a consolation for desolation, if consoling signifies soothing the pain, restoring a possible, retrieving the presence and the life of those who are dead. Everything must, on the contrary, "console" in the sense of fortifying the desolation, of making its harshness inflexible and untouchable. Touching the intact: this is what death offers us, and that means that the deceased disappears in the absolute isolation of his or her untouchable death, while the living one who salutes him or her stays on this side, which no other side confronts, for there is no shore on which to land, and no possible contact (neither sensible, nor intelligible, nor imaginary) with the intact. It is precisely this that the salutation salutes: the salutation touches the untouchable in the form of an address that confirms, to itself, its disappearance, which gives back to itself in some way its foreclosed absence, and the world in it that is over. To say "adieu"—Derrida said it in his *Adieu* to Levinas[4]—is "to call him by his name, to call his name." The salutation salutes the other in the untouchable intactness of his or her unsignifying propriety or ownness, his or her name plunged henceforth into the nonsignificance which is that of the proper name and, through it or in it, each time that of the world as a whole. Saluting the name [*nom*] and the no- [*non*] placed upon that name, the salutation desolates it as it desolates itself: I am alone, each time absolutely alone before this isolating, this isolation of the other "facing," which, properly speaking, I can no more stand than I can touch it without flinching or failing, deprived of this very sense and, in it, of all sense.

It remains nonetheless true that the salutation salutes and that in so doing—in doing nothing, moreover, in producing nothing, only desolating—it addresses and invokes, it calls, it announces even again, or really for the first time, it convokes, it declares, and it proclaims something—more precisely, someone. In this, whatever it might want and whatever it might claim to do, it cannot fail to console others, and itself. It fortifies the desolation, and this confortation, which crushes it and leaves it without a voice, is nonetheless that—and is all the more so the failing that opens in desolation the passage for a voice—of its salute to what will not let itself be saluted. Sixteen times modulated for sixteen deceased ones, Derrida's salutation (elsewhere, other salutations, each time that someone is there to say "adieu"—and we know what a frightful sadness reigns when there is no one, and we know with revulsed knowledge what horror stretches out there where the tomb itself is refused, and with it any salvation, the tomb that is the monument to salvation)—Derrida's salutation still saves no matter what. It saves nothing from the abyss, but it salutes the abyss saved. Now the abyss thus preserved, desolate and declared in its desolation, the abyss impossible to reseal just as it is impossible to sound, gives to salutation the dignity—strange, unbearable, in tears—of the world that collapses. At the same time, the salutation gives the ruined world [*monde abîmé*] its dignity as world. To the proper name deprived of sense it gives the totality of sense. The unverifiable and manifest truth that "the world," each time, means to say.

2

What *anastasis* would designate—in the essay I wrote to deconstruct it or to turn around its value, understood as "resurrection"[5]—is nothing other than redress (*anastasis*), this raising up [*cette levée*] (and not a sursumption or a relay [*relève*])[6] of ruined sense like a truth cast forth, appealed to, announced, and saluted. Truth cannot but be saluted, each time, and never saved, for there is nothing to save, nothing to carry back up from the depths of the death [*rien à remonter du tréfonds du trépas*]: yet even that *is saluted*, hailed, each time, in the funeral oration, which is not an ornament but a necessary element of the structure or event called "dying." Through this oration, through this salutation, "death"—this supposed entity, thing, or subject, that to which Hegel concedes the name on the sole condition that "if we would thus name this nothingness"—finds itself saluted qua the dying proper to this one or that one, to him or her who was here or there (who was the world here or there), and who is no more nor shall be anywhere, at any time. In his dying, each one is saluted for himself to the entire degree to which this "himself" is desolated, intact, and no more comes back to himself than he comes back to us or will come back to us. Not coming back, lying dead, he stands aright, stands anew in a saluted truth.

This salutation effects no surreptitious return. If desolation consoles in this way, as little reassuring as it is perfectly uncontestable, then this is not by way of some dialectical machination that would convert the loss into a gain. It is not through the fantastic operation that religion appears to contrive in order to seize hold of a credulity ready and quick to gobble up salvation. In religion itself, it is not sure that the representation of salvation plays, in the final instance, the consoling role that we believe, perhaps a bit quickly, we are able to lend it, like the effect of an illusion. It would certainly not be aberrant to think that a true believer has never died nor watched another die, childishly imagining an unbroken passage toward another world just like this one, only exempt from suffering. Assuredly, religions, like metaphysics, never cease promoting a salvific beguiling and reassuring consolation. Nevertheless, "God" or the "other world" manifestly never names a continuity, and still less the continuation of this world across some furtive passage. The tomb is not a passage; it is a nonsite that shelters an absence. Faith never consists—and this, no doubt, in any religious form—in making oneself believe something in the way that one might convince oneself that tomorrow one will be happy. Faith can only consist, by definition, in addressing what comes to pass, and it annihilates every belief, every reckoning, every economy, and any salvation. As the mystics knew, without attaching any exaltation to this, faith consists in addressing or in being addressed to the other *of the* world, which is not "an other world" except in the sense of being other than *the* world, the one that each time comes to an end without remission.

"God" designates but that alterity in which the alteration of the world, of *the whole world*, makes itself absolute, without appeal, without recall. And it is the without-appeal that calls and recalls, each time, through the address to the deceased. This address is salutation. It is too contemptuous to represent humanity to oneself as though the immense majority of our peers (and we should no doubt extrapolate, varying our terms somewhat, to include animals) passed their lives—or their deaths, whichever you pre-fer—misunderstanding more or less consciously, more or less uncon-sciously, the intractable real that is dying. In a more subtle way, an infinitely more dignified way, everyone knows something of the nescience [*du non-savoir*] that befalls him and forbids him, with an extreme rigor, to claim to appropriate any part whatsoever of an object called "death," since such an object remains without consistency (in truth, it is death that is fantastic), whereas the subject who dies and he who, in saluting him, addresses him where no address can reach, these two salute each other without saving each other. They share the *anastasis*, whose elevation and rectitude cuts perpendicularly across the unsublatable recumbency of the body in the dust. There is no return, no rebirth, no reviviscence. But there is "resurrection" in the sense of the raising of a salute, of an "adieu": the departure is its own announcement; it reveals nothing; it leads to no se-cret; it effects neither thaumaturgy nor transfiguration. In a sense, there is nothing to say about this last saying, about this oration in which glimmers only the salutation, the time of a few words in a sob, in a flash of black-ness. The *oratio* is discourse or prayer; it is discourse qua prayer. Prayer is neither demand nor a trafficking of influence, it is supplication as well as praise. It is supplicating praise: at once, and each time, prayer celebrates and deplores, it demands a remission and declares what is irremissible. This is what discourse becomes when the world, liquidated, no longer allows us to link together the slightest signification. At that moment, and each time, prayer without expectation and without effects makes up the *anastasis* of the discourse; the salute stands and addresses [*se dresse et s'-adresse*] at the precise point where there remains nothing to be said.

It is unbearable: How not to bow before the fact that the living never cease bearing this and saluting it, making it even, in the final analysis, their reason for living, the only absolutely unimpeachable *factum rationis*, and the unthinkable without which none would die, that is, without which none would live?

Who then would live, ultimately, without practicing, albeit without knowing it, what I am here designating with a citation extracted by force and placed out of context: "a hymn, an encomium, a prayer" turned toward the other of the present life within life itself, "an imploration for surrection, for resurrection,"[7] such that it is this itself, this imploration, that is the resurrection?

Who then, after all, evoked a music (if not music itself) thanks to which "the my-self, dead but raised up by this music, by the unique coming of this music, here and now, in a single movement, the my-self would die in saying yes to death and would thereby resuscitate, saying to itself, I am reborn, but not without dying, I come back to life posthumously, the same ecstasy uniting in itself a death without return and resurrection, death and birth, the desperate salute of the adieu without return and without salvation, without redemption but a salute to the life of the other living in the secret sign and the exuberant silence of a superabundant life"[8]—who then, if not Derrida, the same or an other? And what is a superabundant life if not life *tout court*—yes, in all its brevity—inasmuch as it exceeds all that we could recognize and salute, inasmuch as it exceeds itself and it dies, thereby confiding and giving us over [*ainsi se confiant et nous confiant*] to superabundance and exuberance?

Exuberance is none other than the exactitude of life when existence surrenders to it. Exactitude is a word that he generously credited me with having "resuscitated."[9] This would accord too much thaumaturgy to a simple lexical trope. But let us say, simply, that without supposing God or salvation, we never lack, dead or alive, a language by which eternally, immortally, to salute ourselves, the one the other, the ones and the others. Such a salute, without saving us, at least touches us and, in touching us, *gives rise to* [suscite] that strange turmoil of crossing through life for nothing—but not exactly in a pure loss.

Translated by Bettina Bergo

On a Divine *Wink*

1

In number 44 of a text he titled, with a philosophical wink, "Faith and Knowledge," a title that is subtitled, with another wink, "The Two Sources of 'Religion' at the Limits of Reason Alone," a wink that could be considered double or triple if we reflect that "at the limits" constitutes a malicious, in the strong sense, and thus perverting allusion to "within the limits"—in that number 44, Derrida alludes to a wink, or makes a gesture in its direction that is as vague as it is precise (as the oxymoron of all winks must be). It is a theological wink, or rather, a theophanic one, since it is precisely a question, in that wink, of not speaking, which doubtless carries us immediately, in the twinkling of an eye, "to the limits of" -*logy* alone, whatever its prefix or pretext. Indeed, he quotes Heidegger apropos of the "last god": "The last god: his occurring is found in the sign (*im Wink*), in the onset and absence of an arrival (*dem Anfall and Ausbleib der Ankunft*), as well as in the flight of the gods that are past and their hidden metamorphosis."[1]

At least provisionally, I designate the German word *Wink* as "*clin d'œil*" ["wink of an eye"].[2] This word is kept, in parentheses, in German in this translation [Derrida cites one by J.-F. Courtine]. It is not the only instance of German here, since it is followed by an entire German phrase. Nevertheless, this word captures our interest; we must retain and observe it, for two reasons. First, a more extended analysis of the entire sentence and its context in Heidegger would demonstrate that the terms in apposition to *Wink*—namely, "the onset and the absence of an arrival" (i.e., of the last god), and "the flight of the gods that are past and their . . . metamorphosis"—are, in truth, less appositions than explications of the *Wink*. That analysis will be carried out later, but I anticipate its result. Second, mention of the word *Wink* imposes itself on the translator, whoever he or she may be, in a far more imperious (dare I say "sovereign"?) way than does mention of the other terms. *Wink*, properly speaking, is untranslatable. In a conceptual context, and where the use of the French word *signe* ["sign"] is clearly unavoidable, it is the translator's duty to point out the presence of this irreducible word. *Clin d'œil*, an expression to which we shall return, would introduce other connotations just as suspect, and of an order more fraught or more carefree than that of *signe* understood in the sense of *Zeichen*, of signifying sign, of sense-to-say—precisely because that is not what is involved here.

In a general sense, the mention of a word in the original language (as, e.g., to stick to German, the words *Witz* or *Wesen*) indicates that the word chosen as an equivalent translates the original one poorly or inappropriately. Thus the translator informs us of the impropriety, warns us of it, without going into all the intentions, implications, and idiomatic innuendos. When the translator must, or wants to, avoid an explanatory and hermeneutic note on the untranslatable that thus remains untranslated (a note that quite often would run the risk of becoming a philological, philosophical or, in my case, theological compendium), the translator must be satisfied with a gesture that does not produce sense but indicates, on the contrary, the proximity of a sense that is other, a sense that does not mean in the language into which the text is being translated, a sense that does not succeed in sense from one language to another. A sense whose arrival is suspended between its onset and its absence, to return to our original motif.

Now it is quite true that the general situation of translation is to be subject to the double postulate in the form of the *double bind*[3] of an integral signifiability and a residual in-signifiability, which turns out also to be originary, an exception that makes the rule, since it exposes and imposes the irreducibility of the language, its idiosyncrasy, without which there would be no need for translation—nor any languages, for that matter.

To this consideration of the mention of *Wink*, that is, a consideration intended to open up a passage toward the thing or the role that is "essentially deployed" in this word and to which Derrida alludes here, two scholia should be added.

1. The translator's gesture, indicating that the word is improperly translated, is itself a *Wink*, that is, a "sign" (the term used in place of a translation), in the sense of a "signal," a "warning," a "portent" [*intersigne*], as one used to say not so long ago. It is an indication given at once from afar and in passing, without explanation, without any true sense, evasive as to sense but specific as to direction: pay attention to this area. This should be translated differently, but later or elsewhere: for the moment, we'll put this word on hold—awaiting its own true sense.

We will return to this question. The *Wink* is a sign of awaiting, or of putting expectation in the position of a sign. It is suspended between hope and disappointment. We must await its interpretation, but that waiting is, in itself, already a mobilization, and its mobility or motility is more important than its final interpretation. The most current model of the *Wink* (model in the sense of example or of modalization), is given in the *clin d'œil*. A wink is always to be translated, but at the same time it has already gone beyond its translation by its gesture. It has jumped in one bound, in the twinkling of an eye, beyond the sense it has prompted us to await. It is still, it will always be, to be translated. It will not have its own fully accomplished, determined, saturated sense. The *Wink*—and the word *Wink*, for the French translator, but also, in the final analysis, for the German reader . . . appropriates the impropriety constitutive of a sense that is defective or excessive, labile, evasive, allusive, or deferred. (As I write "deferred," I add here, in parentheses, a word that is all the less translatable for not being a word: *différance*.)

2. The exception of the untranslatable constitutes the law of translation. The latter's logic is a transportation of sense made possible by a general law of language [*langage*], according to which a sense can be said in multiple languages [*langues*], but entailing the fact that *some* sense, if not *the* sense, refuses or eludes that possibility. That retention or subtraction appears in exceptions, in the form of such and such a word, *Wink*, or *Witz*, or *Wesen*, but these exceptions reveal the truth of the language [*langue*], that is, the retreat of the idiomatic this side of or beyond the law of sense. Where there is exception, there is sovereignty. What is sovereign is the idiom that declares itself to be untranslatable. (And as we know, in the end it declares itself such in all of its words and all of its turns of phrase.) Each signifier in a language signifies and *winkt* at the same time. There is always excess, lack, or curvature of sense: *winken* is, in fact, first and foremost to curve or bow, to angle, vacillate, wobble, list. I speak here of the *clinamen* of sense without which there would be no languages, but only characteristics. I speak of the *clinamen*, which creates a world of sense, while hinting at its truth in non-sense.

Sovereign is the translator who decides to suspend the translation, leaving instead the word in the original. Equally sovereign, moreover, is the translator who, taking it to the next level, decides in favor of a solution by "equivalence," as we say, or by periphrasis, analogy, or some other procedure. But the latter's decision, too, consists in leaving the order of signification proper (if there is such an order) for a different one: that of sense in the sense in which each language is a world of sense, and in which translation jumps from world to world by winks, with neither instruments nor passageways. From the genius of one language to that of another there can be nothing but winks, blinks, and scintillations in the universe of sense, in which truth is the black hole into which all these glimmers are absorbed. Sovereign here is thus, as in the State, he who appropriates the absence of ownership, of a suitable foundation, an available code, of guaranteed attribution and secure presence.

Thus it is that we can establish, on the one hand, that the *Wink* is sovereign, and on the other, correlatively, that the sovereign *winkt* (as it can be expressed in German, a language in which it is impossible, however, to adequately render "sovereign"). (*Herrschaftsbereich des Winkes* is an expression used by Heidegger three lines further on the same text.) The fact is, a *Wink* departs from the established order of communication and signification by opening up a zone of allusion and suggestion, a free space for invitation, address, seduction, or waywardness. But that departure beckons toward the ultimate sense of sense, or the truth of sense. Here, sovereignly, sense excludes itself from sense: such is the wink's monition.

But the fact is also, correlatively, that the sovereign *winkt*. Nothing is more specifically characteristic of sovereign majesty than the frown, the wink, the expression said to be "imperceptible," the reply to which is called a "sign of complicity" [*signe d'intelligence*], in the sense that, in that complicity, connivance precedes and exceeds understanding, in the sense that complicity has already understood whatever it is that has not been openly offered up to the understanding, but is expected. The *Wink* opens an expectation at the same time as an impatience to which the decision to understand without waiting, in the twinkling of an eye, responds.[4]

2

To return to this topic for a moment, just as the mention of the word *Wink* is a sovereign gesture on the translator's part, so this gesture confers upon the German word a sovereignty whose ambivalence is immediately obvious. It is a composite of a subtraction of sense and an access of (or to) literalness, according to one of those privileges regularly invoked by the Cratylism and the idiomaticity that are irresistible to philosophers (and of which Hegel's *Aufheben* is the most outstanding example). It is by being untranslatable that the *Wink* takes on its (un- or hyper-) signifying charge. And it is by being noted, not translated, by the philosopher-translator that it acquires the force of a concept or thought. We may even note in passing the following remark: All the interrogations of the difference (with or without *a*) between philosophy and literature can be reactivated and deployed on the basis of the simple fact that a literary translator does not normally mention the terms used in the text being translated. Literature loses the sense essentially, while philosophy thematizes the sense to the point of excess, to the point of an incalculable exceeding that approaches literary expenditure.

Here, in this text by Heidegger to which we are led back by its translation, it is a philosophical sovereignty that is invested in the *Wink*:[5] that is, a position in excess of sense (and, consequently, of "truth"). I could show, by appealing to the entire context of the *Beiträge*, that this word receives no sense more determinate than that of its current value in German. No conceptual work is performed on the regime of sense and signification designated by this "sign." All one can say is that the *Wink* is regularly associated with several variants of the expression mentioned by Courtine and Derrida: *Anfall und Ausbleib der Ankunft*, an expression that is itself cumbersome to translate and that designates the double nature of sudden surge and sustained absence of, or in, the arrival of the last god (as well as in the "flight of the gods" prior to him, as the rest of the sentence goes on to say, which repeats nearly word for word a sentence from the preceding paragraph). Without exploring in greater depth what is at stake in this context, but in order to give a general sense of the approach, I will just say that the *Wink* has its concept, or quasi-concept, its insight, by and in its association with what Heidegger also calls, in these pages, *Vorbeigang* ("passage," with the force of "in passing") or, earlier in the same book, *Blickbahn*,[6] a rare term with the sense literally of "pathway of the look" and bringing together the values of "perspective" and "glance." The *Wink*, here, in its function of sign or divine signal—of god-signal, one would have to murmur—is identified as fugitiveness, as the beating of the instant according to which what arrives leaves and, *in leaving* (a word French can use here in a double sense)[7] remains absent, remains outside its own arrival, while in the midst of or through this throbbing there is launched the glance that gives (and/or?) receives the signal. The privilege of *Wink* consists, in short, in the fact that its sense is spent in the passage immediately stolen away, in the hint suddenly hidden of a sense that vanishes, and whose truth consists in vanishing. This, then, is why the "essence of the *Wink*" (an expression used in §255) is analyzed or determined no further than as the batting or twinkling that harbors, hidden within itself, what the same text expresses as "the secret of the unity of the most intimate approach in extreme distance." (Writing these words, can Heidegger not sense some evanescent allusion to Augustine's *Deus interior intimo meo, superior summo meo*?[8] I leave this question open for debate.)

Ambivalence, ambiguity, oxymoron, *Witz* as the affinity of opposites, *Aufhebung*, or even—why not?—the meeting of *Witz* with *Aufhebung*, and of the wink with the speculative: such is the character of the *Wink* as outside signification, which confers on it, in the original text, as in its mention maintained by its translators, this sovereign privilege that prompts Heidegger to write, in the same place, that it is a question of "the onset and absence of the coming and flight of the gods and of their sovereignty [*Herrschaftstätte*]."

Ambivalence is constitutive of sovereignty: it combines absolute power and excess over legality, which necessarily belong together. According to the formula of Carl Schmitt, law suspends itself in the sovereign act. In order to be *all*-powerful, *omnipotence* must extend to a point no power precedes, founds, or dominates. In order to be *absolute*, power must absolutize itself, that is, *absolve itself* from any tie or responsibility other than that of being answerable for itself and self-authorizing. Hence this omnipotence is absolutely not of the order of "power" in the sense of potentiality. It is not *dunamis* but *energeia*, an efficacious act that precedes all possibility, a reality of power that cannot simply be equated with a brutality ignorant of laws, since it is the laws, the juridical construction as such, that must not know the arcane secret of their unfounded foundation.[9]

If ownership is always de jure and never just de facto, if property (whether as sense or estate, wealth, consciousness, or body) is only such by the mediation of a right that signifies and guarantees a grounded and exclusive ownership, then the sovereign exerts—he actualizes and enacts, in the juridical sense of the term—an unmediated ownership that falls short of or exceeds any appropriation. That is why he *winkt*: he sets something in motion by means of a signal, instead of and before establishing it within a signification. The sovereign opens up possible sense, just as much as he closes off or suspends already available senses. That is why there is, in the *Wink*, or in *winken* ["to wink"], an energy that its sign per se does not possess. And that is why, definitively, a *winken* accompanies all *bedeuten* ["to mean"], all intending of sense [*vouloir-dire*] and sending of signals [*faire-signe*], which, unaccompanied by it, would not have the power to send a signal or, consequently, the power of its own "willing" [*"vouloir"*] or its own "doing" ["*faire*"]. There is in sense an active power that arises at the moment of the signifying act and that, in terms of sense, goes beyond it and gives way to it at the same time.

The *Wink* triggers; it acts and it activates a play of forces on the sly or in counterpoint to the sense. A wink, as we are well aware, can trigger the greatest of surprises, release an incongruous desire, disrupt the norm, just as it can confer favor or disfavor at the whim of the prince, whose "gracious majesty" is majestic precisely in proportion to his sovereign power to dispense favor or disfavor—a power whose specificity can be seen in that its omnipotence is exerted not only *by*, but *in* "the blink of an eye." The rapidity of the wink engages the efficacy of presence in the very blinking of its passing instant.

3

At this moment I happen upon another passage by Derrida, the passage in a much earlier text in which he wrote, picking up on a passage from Husserl:

> As soon as we admit this continuity of the now and the not-now, perception and non-perception, in the zone of non-primordiality common to primordial impression and primordial retention, we admit the other into the self-identity of the Augenblick: non-presence and non-evidence are admitted into the *blink of the instant*. There is a duration to the blink, and it closes the eye. This alterity is in fact the condition for presence.[10]

As we see, this is not just any passage. At issue here are structure and movement; movement—the wink—as the structure of différ*a*nce, whose motif or motivation is in the process of moving Derrida toward what always motivated him: the absenting of presence at the heart of its present and its presentation, and, correlatively, the spreading open of the sign at the heart of its relation to itself, and then the hollowing out of a non-signifying passage at the heart or *joint* of the sign. The wink gives us the structure of différ*a*nce, and more than the structure, it gives us its excess or lack of signification (it is "neither a word nor a concept," as Derrida will later say), and it makes its eclipse shine forth. It suspends the present instant for an instant, for the time of a furtive duration during which onto-chronology is suspended.

We could follow in Derrida the destinies of the wink intertwined with those of différ*a*nce, in which the *a* twinkles, scintillates, or *winkt*. In 1986, for example, in *Parages* the wink is introduced to qualify another decisive element, the "supplementary characteristic" that qualifies the genre of a work of art or of a text—the characteristic that itself belongs to no genre and that "belongs without belonging," in such a way that the "without," here, "appears as but the time without time of a wink."[11] We could, no doubt, let ourselves be guided by the hypothesis that the wink always gives the modality of donation of a supplementary or excessive truth.

Similarly, we could follow, in Heidegger, the pathways of the *Wink*. But my purpose lies elsewhere. As the reader will have understood, what concerns me, and what in my opinion should concern us in a necessary, or even imperious (sovereign) manner, is the relationship that must be discerned between this *a* and the *Wink* of the last god. Need I say it? Not only am I not attempting to theologize différance (which would be difficult, since it is clearly from the god of onto-theology that presence is being unsealed or removed); I am not trying theologize the "last god," whose nature or essence, whose *Wesung* or *Götterung*, as Heidegger writes, I do *not* believe to be theological. It is not theist, in any event, and the same §256 makes a point of rejecting "all the theisms" as being allied with "metaphysics" and "Judeo-Christian apologetics."

(The fact that Heidegger bypasses, intentionally or otherwise, another dimension of Judeo-Christian faith—and not "apologetics"—and that he either ignores or is unaware of what, within that faith, involves a *Destruktion* of theology is another question, which will have to be taken up elsewhere.)

The idea is not, therefore, to theologize but to discern what is divine in the *Wink* as different, radically different from *theos*, and at the same time as irremediably deferring its theological being. In other words, and consequently, it is a matter of discerning—even if by winking—a divine trait in différance—and yet in so doing to behave quite the opposite of what has accusingly been called a "theological turn in phenomenology."[12]

This is, above all, because it is not a question of phenomenology. As I will show, with the *Wink* and the *a*, the *a* that *winkt*, phenomenology goes to the end of its own reversal. Not only does appearing become that of the non-apparent—which was already accomplished—but the whole problematics of (non)appearing opens the way for a dynamics of passing by, of the *Vorbeigang* of the *Augenblick*.[13] The question is no longer one of being or of appearing, and it is no longer a question. There emerges an affirmation of passing by, that is, of the passerby. Not being and the individual being,[14] but the individual being and the passerby.

But let us resume.

The *écart* of the wink, the lapse of its instant, the interval at once opened and closed, and, as it were, the self-sameness of the present, like the self-sameness of time itself, which does not pass in its incessant pass-ing, and thus the identity *to* itself grasped in that other "to" [*à*] that relates it to itself—that is what the *a* of différ*a*nce makes scintillate, and what is made to scintillate by it—by the supplement of a grave accent (the affair is in fact grave; there is nothing more serious). (*Scintiller, clignoter*: these are the values of the English forms *to twinkle* and *to blink*, while in Ger-man *ein Winker* is a blinker [*clignotant*].) With and without the accent, positing and eclipsing in turn all the directional value of the *ad*—just as the value of the *zu* must be in *Sein zum Tode*, in the being-toward-death; that is, in the being qua being-in-passing—the *a* forms simultaneously the present's adherence and expectation toward itself. It presents them and retains them.

This is what the *Wink* does, that *winkt zu* and *winkt ab*, that *winkt uns zu dem von woher er sich uns zuträgt*, if I may allow myself to rearrange another passage from Heidegger[15] (it motions to attract, to brush aside, it motions us toward the place from which it came toward us). This is about access to the presence whose threshold, lapse, or wink [*clin*][16] opens the gap of the present's own self-presentation. That access is formed, then, in excess of itself, or else in lack. Appropriation appropriates presence *to* itself by this wink, by this inclination that, in inclining the same toward (*zu*) the same, even in order to incline itself in this way, to give it that narcissis-tic inclination, separates itself from itself, renders itself absent and differ-entiates itself into the other.

The *Wink* stretches and curves the punctuality of the identical and the patent evidence of truth. The complicity of the wink, of différ*a*nce and the *Wink*, is played out in this *clinamen*, in this batting and dynamic diag-onal in the midst of the vertical fall of sense, falling infinitely back upon itself.[17] It thus signals sense, it signals the proper signification of sense, its terminal truth, by way of a relation analogous to that which connects the moral law to Kantian freedom: a *ratio cognoscendi* intersecting a *ratio es-sendi*, which responds to it, but without the former being in a position to unveil the latter. It is *ratio* itself—*ipsa ratio ultima et sufficiens*, sovereign reason—that is curved, disfigured, not coinciding with itself. (The fact is—and I insist on clarifying this point—that this Kantian arrangement does not offer us a simple analogy; or if it does so, it is an *analogia entis*: it is a question of the same thing, just as it would be if we were to consider the relation between the singular and the absolute in Hegel. It is always the slant [*clin*] of the other in the same, which metaphysics never stops declining according to a ruse of reason that thus passes behind reason's own back and from there, winks at us.

4

There is, then—but "there is" in the most matter-of-fact, chronological way, in the sense of *es gibt* and of *that happens, that comes to pass,* and *that passes*—there is a sovereign gesture[18] that signals a literal sense's own non-return to self. Différance is not a concept *because* it does not signify but only motions, because it is, or rather makes, a gesture. And because it makes rather than is, its gesture is that of one who passes by.[19] So it is that, willy-nilly, whether inclined by an evil genius or not, Derrida will have (according to this future perfect he favors as the tense of différance), by a parenthesis of untranslatability, winked toward the *Wink* from différance. From différance, since the passage in which the *Wink* is cited concerns the future or the absence of a future, Levinas and Heidegger placed side by side as the double figure of the god who comes and the god who passes, and almost, if I may extrapolate, as two gaits of passing, toward presence and toward absence, *zu* and *ab*, or *à* with an accent, and *a* without one. As if Derrida were winking in putting them before us side by side, *zu* and *ab* the one for the other, the one *with* the other, *apud, ad,* in a proximity that dominates the infinitesimal calculus of the touch, the derivative of the difference with and without *a.*

In denouncing the sense of the sign that they are not, but that they make, in withdrawing truth from a present in favor of a *prae(s)ens* that exceeds being, in favor of a pre-sence always shaken by a beating that separates it from itself, the *Wink* and différance engage one another in a sort of co-designation or co-appropriation of what, exceeding sense, must signal that very exceeding. What the passing designates is not something situated beyond being, or, in consequence, beyond the individual being, the being of which is merely being. It is not the sense of the other or of an other, but the other of sense and an other sense, an always other sense that begins freely—if freedom consists in the beginning, and not in the completion, of a new series of events, a new sending back and forth of sense. This inaugural and never terminal freedom accedes to that excess of sense—which is its sense, which is to say also *the sense of being*—as if to a climax, a supreme or a sublime that we cannot (and this is precisely the point) call "supreme being," and that corresponds rather to the suspension of the supreme or of the foundation by which sovereignty declares itself.

Now, if the sovereign is not the Omnipotent or the Supreme Being, that is, if there is no extremity of being—but only the ex-istence in which it founders—then the access in question cannot consist in accession to the end of a process, no more in the "ontological proof" than in the authorized attestation of some "witness of god," martyr, prophet, or mystic. But access comes and withdraws. It comes in passing, in withdrawing. Such is the passage, the *Vorbeigang.* But this passage cannot be the passage of the god, either. If the god *winkt* and *is not,* if he is not even the non-being of being, or its withdrawal, since there is no such thing to "be," it is because he only motions toward, about, and from a distance—*that there is no such thing.* (No such thing as the Supreme Being or the Supreme Entity, and nothing *of the sort,* absolutely, nothing that can properly exhaust (mean) the *suchness* [talité] or the *quality:* nothing that is properly in and unto itself.)

The god is therefore not the designated but only the designating, the making-a-sign. There is no passage of the god, but this is the passing of the passage, the passage of whoever makes a sign. The passage of the one passing by—whose coming becomes more distant in the instant—makes the gesture that hails from afar and that at the same time puts the distant itself at a distance: the ever-renewed distancing of the other in being, and of the absent in the present.

5

Why must this passerby be named *god*? Why must the *Wink* and différ*a*nce be declared divine? This is indeed the crucial question. It is obvious that one cannot answer by showing how *winken* and *différer* would be the attributes of god or of the god, since what is proper to the divine itself would have to have been presupposed. We must, on the contrary, establish the divine nature of both gestures by a transcendental deduction.

"The last god," Heidegger specifies, is not to be understood in the sense of the last in a series—or not only so (for it does correspond to a turning point in history, after which there are no more gods). It is last in the sense of extreme, and that extremity, being the extremity of the divine, delivers the divine from itself in both senses of the expression: it frees it from the theological and disengages it from its own gesture. What one should probably understand from this is that the god is gesture: neither being nor a being, but gesture in the direction of the in-appropriable being of beings (an appropriation that Heidegger names *Ereignis,* whose analysis will have to begin by noting that it is toward the *Ereignis* that the *Wink winkt* and within it that différance differs, and that it consists, perhaps, in nothing but a wink).

Whether or not it is necessary to speak of a god is uncertain. Be he last, first, or whatever, nothing confers apodictic evidence upon the use of this noun—if it is a noun, and if so of what sort? (Common? If so, common to what class or what type of being? Proper? But to whom or about whom?) Here one can only lie in wait and hope to take by surprise the eventuality that this word, *god*, will turn out to be appropriate to designate the in-appropriation of the wink. Could we not say, in a preliminary way, that the word or name *god* cannot be said without some form of a wink or blink of the eyes? When we say "god," whether we "believe in him" or not, as they say, we also declare, in one way or another, that we cannot signify properly or without remainder what we are saying or whom we so name. Only when reduced to the principle of supreme being does "god" have a sense: but then he no longer needs his name, and this is what is announced by saying, proclaiming, and shouting that "God is dead." But the name *God* does not die with that supreme being. And that should perhaps make us decide to consider it a proper name. A proper name does not die; what's more, the only thing proper to it is immortality. This proper name, *God*, insists, as if it should be the name that remains in the vacancy left by that individual being, in the vacant heart of sovereignty—and in this sense, as "the last god." But that expression would then mean that "god" is always the last, the name of the last extremity of all names and all senses. The name, therefore, for an excess and an absence of sense that would not allow this noun to be properly meaningful, would on the contrary demand that it name the unnameable nonmeaningful. I have said that this disposition is valid for all, believers or nonbelievers, "theists" or "atheists" (by which it will be seen, moreover, that if it is simple and necessary to be an atheist, it is not so necessary to be "without God").

Whatever the unnameable nonmeaningful may be, the retreat of being into its *différance*, the bearer of the name, signals it. (And perhaps all bearers of a name signal it—perhaps *God* is present/absent at the heart of every name; we shall have to return to this point.) It signals the unnameable nonmeaningful without signifying it. It signals it in passing, since it cannot be stabilized in a presence. He who signals in passing is the passer himself. The passer passes, and in order to pass, is someone. Some *one* who passes, is but the tread of the passing, not a being who would have passing as an attribute. One should not speak—Heidegger himself should not—of the passing *of the* god: but God is in the passing. God is the passerby and the step of the passerby. This step is his gesture, which, in passing, *winkt* and differentiates itself from itself ("the step negates itself and carries itself away," writes Derrida, interpreting [I mean playing] Blanchot).[20]

Someone who passes: his unity and the truth of that unity are in the passing. The unity is that of the step, and consequently that of the wink, which forms a different step, a different beat, a different syncope. It is someone who is not a subject, or is only one with the proviso that he only exists (and it is, in fact, a question of ek-sisting) step by step, singularly step by step. But it is someone; it is *who* and not *what*. That is the first reason to name it. The name *God* does not answer the question "What?" But neither does it answer the question "Who?" It signals this: that there is no question "Who?" (unless it is a question that comes down to "What?" as when in asking "Who are you?" one wants to obtain a true, substantive identity, not differ*a*nt from itself in itself). The name *God*, or some name of god, whatever it may be, or that way of saying the god of someone (the God of Akhenaton, the God of Abraham, of Isaac, and of Jacob, the God of Jesus Christ, the God of Muhammad, and also "my God," the God of myself, a God in each case mine, *etwa eine Jemeingötter-ung*). The "last god" would also designate the extremity at which the name *god* expires in that "my God," in my utterance of a différ*a*nce that is incommensurable and in-appropriable in me—to me, and to whomever.

It is, moreover, for this reason that différ*a*nce is "neither a word, nor a concept": it is a calling from one toward the other, from one *to* the other, the calling of a thought to itself as to the unthinkable that is its ownmost.

6

It is not, therefore, a question of the "ineffable being no name could come close to: God for example," which Derrida contrasts precisely with the other "unnameable," that of différ*a*nce.[21] If the last god is also the last, ultimate articulation of the name *god*, it is because this quality of ultimate-ness belongs to this word not as a signification but only as an utterance,[22] and as "my" utterance *to the precise degree that it comes to me from the other who, in passing, gives me a sign*, and whose *Wink* I respond to with "my God!"—without my having actually to say this word, whose "sense" is to name or rather to mark, to remark, and to exclaim the passing itself and the passing not as a thing or a state but as a passerby whom I call to or address, having perceived his step and the signal of that step.

"To address" here does not mean to designate someone and require his or her attention, let alone submission. It only designates the exchange of signals, without which there would be neither signals nor winks. There is no assignment of persons or things. There is no intentionality. The wink in fact closes the phenomenological gaze and opens another one, or rather opens a *regard* [égard] in place of a gaze [*regard*]. The blink [*clignement*] is also the gesture of one who tries to adjust his eyesight in very bright light. Trying to adjust entails a focusing on objects, but blinking indicates that he is dazzled and discerns poorly or not at all. At most, he catches a glimpse. His blinking attunes itself with the luminous scintillation and loses the distance of vision. In the wink that has the value of a *Wink*, it is not a question of looking or of distinguishing forms; it is, on the contrary, a question of sending toward the other the light of the eye, the eye as *lux*. In fact, the wink brings about that modification or that modalization of the eye: it makes the eye into a signaling, not a seeing, organ. The wink belongs to all non-phenomenological looking, that is, to all looking that looks at the look of the other and takes the other into account in his or her look. Every reciprocal look is a wink that can go on and on, go to the limit of blurred vision as well as to the height of emotion, which is why it usually does not last, or lasts the length of an eternity in the midst of time. Thus I find myself both close to and far from Levinas . . .

This instant, withdrawn from the instant and from the triple determination of time within it, pulsates only with the difference between those dimensions, with the difference that time properly *is* and according to which it never catches up with itself and defers itself in its being as well as differentiating itself from itself. Now, that difference, as the tread of the passerby, forms the difference of gait, and of the passing as a putting in play of a difference of forces. One cannot take a step without activating the walking machine. But the difference between the forces makes force itself, its essence, if you like, since a force is never present but always raised, upright, activated against another (the foot lifted against gravity). Such is definitely the lesson of Deleuze that Derrida received explicitly in his analysis of différance.[23] If, with the passing of the last god, it is only a question of glimpsing and interpellating, that is because everything comes to pass *between*; indeed, everything takes place in the between (which also can be written with the *a* that is not heard).[24] The silent force of the passerby activates the difference of gait. And the singularity of the passerby, the singularity of his or her personal unity, if you like—"one passerby"— articulates the singular unity that operates *between* the forces (between his foot and the earth, between his body leaning forward, off balance, and the machine that holds it back, that holds itself back in the advance itself; a machine ahead of itself, on the brink of itself).

If this passerby lets himself be addressed by this name-word (non-word?)[25] *god*, by this thought that calls "god" in or to it, it is because this word, which appears to express ultimate power, omnipotence (differing only from the powerlessness of all his creatures),[26] in fact says nothing more than a difference. More precisely, it says the difference between omnipotence and the feeble strength of the created. Still more precisely, and to say everything *exactly*, that is, to the last extremity of the act in question (i.e., of divine designation), it says that difference in the sense that the power of everything is nothing, nothing but the instantaneous act in which the world of beings "comes to be," as we say, that is, comes from nowhere and goes nowhere, but thus passes or happens, takes place; it says, therefore, the difference between that power-outside-power of the totality and the feeble strength according to which an individual being ek-sists, that is, is outside of itself in order . . . not to be, but to find itself arrived, taken away, and dedicated to its own self-sameness. (I thus translate very rapidly *ereignet, enteignet*, and *zueignet*, while specifying that "dedicated," which I have chosen to translate *zueignet*, was also meant to express "declare" and "reveal.")

"God" says difference as the opening between the excedance of the outside-all and the eksistence of the someone (and/or the something). "God," in fact, says the difference of day—*dies*—and night, the division light/darkness by which everything takes place, taking place *between* those two modalities, those two accents or those two sides of the same peak or the same height of being, of the same ontological sovereignty that thus reveals itself not to be, and not to be ontological any more than theological. Nor phenomenological, as I have said, and consequently, strictly, passing. The name *god* names the divergence and the step across the gap between nothing and nothing—let us call it the *res ipsa*, the thing itself.

The resource of the Latin *divus/deus*[27] should not produce any etymological or Cratylian illusion, not even any properly significant one, not even and especially not, since the name *God* would be the pro-noun of the Unnameable as the superessence of arch-significance. On the contrary, *god* is the common name of the separation between light and darkness, seeing and not seeing, day and night, something and nothing, without that—namely, that separation, that step—being properly named. *God* names, rather—and in all languages, according to their various resources—the opening of the name to its own non-sense, yet also that very opening as a calling out. As we have already seen, "God!" only takes on "sense" in calling, in being called, and even, if I may say so, in calling himself.

We are thus once again approaching a super-appropriate super-nomination, where identity would be bound by the name of the unnameable, of the non-nomination of the Name—even the indefinite, poetic or musical, jaculatory, or arch-silent self-transcendence of nomination and of the sign in general. It suffices to point out that, rather than any of these ecstasies of beyond-sense, "god" proposes simply a common name in the guise of a proper name, and in a manner that does not subsume the common under the proper, no more than it assimilates the proper into the common. Let us say, rather, that "god"—with an exclamatory or invocatory intonation that gives it its wink, its accent, its verbal *clinamen*—sends its *Wink* sideways, alongside all names, from the most prestigious to the most modest. In a sense, it is the sovereign word, the name beyond all names, and in another sense it is the non-naming name that twinkles in the open space between all names—a space that is the same as the one that appears between the eksistant *and* the being that "-izes" it (transitive verb) and not that it "is" (supposedly a verb expressing a state).

The signal of the passerby is, then, nothing but his or her footfall. It is not a signalization or overarching signage. The twinkling does not come from a neon sign but simply from the ordinary alternation of days and nights, comings and goings, births and deaths. "The step of the truth becomes non-reversible into the truth of the step," writes Derrida.[28] Such is the divine truth of the *Wink*: it stems from the fact that there is no wink *of* god, but that the god *is* the wink. He does not do it, he winks himself there, just as he states his name in it, properly common and commonly proper—the name, in sum, of every person.

In the midst of the wink, the eye closes, and it is in the batting of the open/closed, the synthesis in syncopation of common sense and the call proper ("You!" goes the *Wink*, "Your turn!" "Come!" or "Go away!") that the passerby passes by. The passing and the existent enter into a fleeting complicity, the différ*a*nce of their senses, passing through the difference between them. When both eyes close at once, whether the eyes of both parties or just those of an existent in response, this is acquiescence. In Latin it is called *conniveo*, formed from *nictor*, the verb "to wink." To wink with both eyes at once—and to wink in the being-together or in the being-with of *the caller* and the called, who can no longer be discerned (or barely can, since one has to blink)—is to enter into *connivance*. Man is in connivance with God. Connivance is mute; it is content with the *Wink*, and, in it, it exceeds sense, the look, and, finally, the god himself. That is the divine trait or gesture: God is exceeded in his own passage. In fact, he comes there and leaves from there; he is the passing of it. God exceeded is not the supreme individual being, put to death. It is god who succeeds God, as Jabès wrote in another passage quoted by Derrida.[29] But it is the succession that is divine. It is the passing—the passing of the witness and the passing of the step [*passage du pas*]. The step is the divine place, the only one, the place in which the power of the passing manifests and transcends itself. There remains, nonetheless, the possibility that the look, in the violence of its fixity, may catch and capture the connivance. Then the god no longer passes: he becomes God. Then différ*a*nce turns—not into transcendence (for in truth, is transcendence not an echo of the movement of transcending [itself]?), but into transcendence installed as domination.

The god who passes is a passerby who is not us, but who is not "an other" either, in the sense of another subject or another being, or the "Other" of all beings and/or all sameness. Rather, an other than the other-of-the-same or than what could be called "the other same," or, yet again, the Same-other (who is usually called "God"). An other who is only his step, and in this step, the *Wink* of/toward that alteration of sense: for, after all, what he shows is more an alteration than an alterity. His step changes even the coming or the advent of the event: it does not arrive, it passes. The *Wink* of the *a* and the *a* as some*one* who passes—and this passer as this god who passes. *The passing of the god is identical with his retreat.*

In this step, "the time of a wink [*für einen Augenblick*], the e-vent properly arrives, leaves, and is dedicated [*das Er-eignis ist Ereignis*]. This wink, this instant, is *the time of being* [*die Zeit des Seins*]."[30] This could be translated: its eternal and instantaneous différ*a*nce. Or again: the transitivity transfixed by which it is communicated to the existent as nothing. It is this sudden communication in the absolute gap that the passerby signals—and passes by.

Rimbaud, that "considerable passerby," as Mallarmé called him, wrote:

It has been found again.
What?—Eternity.
It is the sea, gone
With the sun.[31]

Translated by Michael B. Smith

An Exempting from Sense

There is no sense that is not shared [*partagé*]. But what is sharing, and what sense is revealed in it? Perhaps the two questions overlap: that is, one shares only that which is divided in this sharing, that which separates from itself, and a shareable sense is a sense separated from itself, freed of its completion in a final or central signification. A value of the end or of the center, in a general way, is a value of sense—in the sense that sense is understood as the concentration and crystallization of an absolute *value*. It is only in a value that has value in and for itself, that is not relative to anything else, that there can be an assuaging, a fulfillment, and a conclusion of the movement by which sense or value (whether these words, or this double name for the same concept, are taken on the level of language, of ethics, or of metaphysics) is referred to a horizon or a subject in which it is absorbed and in whose substance, in sum, it is "realized," as we say of a financial value or capital. Of course, it is no accident that we thus touch upon the order of monetary value, and consequently that of general equivalency, which is the condition of a monetary economy—which in turn seems to regulate today the horizon of sense and its sharing.

Value or sense can be absolute in only two ways: either in the order of a supreme, ultimate value that measures everything else without itself being measured by anything, or in the system of a general equivalency, in which everything has worth by the same thing as everything else, while at the same time value consists in producing value and in reproducing that productivity. The first sense is deposited in the German word *Würde*, close to the word *Wert*, which means "value," and with which Kant designates the absolute *dignity* that he places in the "human person." The second sense is the word *capital*, which also designates, by metonymy, the process of an indefinite valorization of the production of exchangeable value.

It should also be said, to be more precise: the absolute value of the person, which also constitutes, when transposed into Marxist terminology, the human value of the productive act of production, and consequently the incalculable value added by man to the work [*œuvre*] (or as the work) is equally what capital converts into general equivalency.

And we are thus at the heart, today, of the tension that tears apart, before us and within us, history, politics, culture, even science, and the world—hence sense, or its truth. That is, the tension that distends within itself the equivalency of these absolute values that human beings are supposed to be.

Roland Barthes placed the entirety of his work beneath the sign of a preoccupation he called "morality of the sign,"[1] characterizing it as a care of sense regulated by a double refusal: that of "solid sense" (acquired and fixed sense) and that of "zero sense" (that of the mystics of liberation, he says). To keep, to protect sense from being filled, as well as from being emptied—that is *ethos*.

It is worth pointing out that this "morality of the sign" bears some resemblance to the concern for "simple saying" in which Heidegger wishes to invest the requirement of what he designates as being the sense or originary value of an ethics. The connection I thus suggest (one that also involves Levinas) will disturb only those for whom the names *Heidegger* and *Barthes* are saturated in advance with some sense or value, whatever it may be. I do not say this in order to enter into a comparison, which obviously would soon encounter the issue of a very considerable difference in *tone*, and consequently of *ethos* as much as *pathos*, between them. I only bring it up to indicate that the concern with sense (and there are a good many other names I could mention among contemporary thinkers on this score) is not one concern among others, but defines for us ("we others," as Nietzsche said, we latecomers, we the good Europeans . . .) the concern with thought itself, the concern with its *morality* (to retain this word); that is, the concern with a type of conduct and behavior that measures up to the requirements of a time for which sense, or the sense of sense, causes a problem, a concern, or an aporia.

This preoccupation proceeds from a self-understanding of our time as one of nihilism. "Nihilism" designates what might be called the lapse of sense. There is no need to belabor the point: history or destiny, subject or process, market or ethical value, this very word *ethical* as well as the word *aesthetic*—and to end this list that is in principle endless—*sense* as signifying, sense as in the five senses, and sense as direction, our condition of thought and therefore of *morality*, encounters, no matter what, assuming we reject vain restorative attempts and feigned incantations, a lapse of sense. And assuming we reject the tragic and cynical versions of nihilism (sublime heroism or ridiculous catastrophe) as well as negative theologies that reveal sense outside sense. In all respects, sense or senses are out of date. They are no longer valid, no longer have any true market value, unless it is only, miserably, an artificially controlled market intended to conceal actual poverty.

The self-understanding of a period no more expresses the whole truth than does that of an individual. But at least it indicates where the truth resides: that is, for us today, in the necessity of understanding sense, or the sense of sense, otherwise.

That is why I have found, on this occasion, on which I am to speak at the Roland Barthes Center, a *kairos* that leads me to reemploy an expression he used in order to try to blaze a trail toward a different understanding or a different way of hearing sense—namely "an exempting from sense."

I will be asked (I have already been asked) whether it is not preferable simply to give up on "sense," not in favor of the nonsensical (as if to exacerbate nihilism), but in favor of a stoic bearing in the ascesis of a truth devoid of any sense, or in favor of an infinite dissemination of sense itself. Such a question proposes drying out sense or scattering it in all directions, or in any case giving up on its weighty concept, the most weighty of all. To this there must be added the Freudian warning that to wonder about the sense of existence is already to be neurotic. It would seem that it is not possible, these days, to ignore sense, or to keep it at a distance, or to be cured of it—not to mention those who would rehabilitate it. In a certain way, I have the definite intention of taking into account all these retreats or refusals and of making them into so many a priori conditions—but conditions for opening up, and obstinately so, the sense of sense. So, rather than somehow confirming the lapsing of sense, I would like to consider an exemption from sense. That is the expression Barthes gives us, and it must hold our attention all the more due to the circumstance that he himself did not furnish us with a real analysis of it but left its sense in limbo, attached only to a few occurrences, elusive at best.

"The Exemption from Sense" is the title of a chapter in *The Empire of Signs*.[2] Without any inspection of the selected term, the chapter is devoted to characterizing the relationship to sense in Zen and haiku as one of detachment: neither excavation nor the "mise en abyme" of a sense whose negativity or sublimation keeps on reiterating, always a little further on, the promise of a final signified, albeit a silent, yawning, pallid one, like death and God conjoined (which would represent the deep movement of all Western thought), but the detachment and abandonment of sense itself. The "exemption" in that chapter is clearly the opposite of the "effraction of sense" that, in the preceding chapter, designates the imperious, indiscreet, and eager seizure of sense that would interpret the simple words of a haiku. What "exemption from sense" must involve is withdrawal from that signifying will, a retreat from a wanting-to-say that can step aside to give pride of place to saying. Barthes writes: "The haiku does not want to say anything."

Wanting-to-say, which Derrida introduced at the same time—'68 is both the number and the sense—in the guise of a translation of Husserl's *Bedeutung*, indicates, within sense, the prevalence of willing over saying. Willing is subjectivity making itself into its own work [*œuvre*]: it is the projection of an assumed interiority into the reality of an exteriority. (Kant defines the will [*le vouloir*] as the faculty of "being by its representations the cause of the reality of these same representations."[3]) Sense qua will (i.e., *sense* in the absolute sense, as we understand it at the very beginning, "we others") always comes down to that self-instituting projection of the will. To take the example of the most famous and publicly scrutinized of senses, recently fallen into desuetude, a *sense of history* comes down to the accomplishment, by history, of a will already given: this sense thus proceeds to the strict annulment (in all senses of the word) of historicity itself. Similarly, a *sense of life* bridles life with the will for its completion. In this sense, all sense is death-bearing, or morbid, as Freud suggested.

ॐ

We could, then, stop here and bid sense farewell. That is not what Barthes does. The expression "exemption from sense" is not taken up again in its proper sense. It is fleetingly, in the chapter, made analogous to "a lapsing of sense," in order to designate the result of the Zen operation of suspension, arrest, or destitution of sense.[4] Generally, the word gives way to "suspension," and when it is taken up again further on (in the chapter "Tel"), the same substitution of "suspension" takes place without any further examination. Five years later, in the text titled *The Rustle of Language*, the word *exemption* reappears when Barthes speaks of a use of the language that would allow us to "hear an exempting from sense." From one occurrence to the other, there has been a displacement of form and content. A displacement of form, because from the wording "the exemption from the sense" [*l'exemption du sens*] we have moved to "an exempting from sense" [*une exemption de sens*]. A displacement of content, for, in 1975, Barthes specifies that it is not a question of "foreclosing" sense, and that the latter remains on the "horizon," that is, on the horizon of what he calls "the utopia" of the "rustling of language," of a kind of purely sonorous effusion of the pleasure of language, from which sense would nevertheless not be excluded, but on the contrary be "the vanishing point of intense pleasure."

This time, then, it would seem to be a question of exempting without lapsing, and within a context that no longer plays on a contrast between East and West but rather attempts a maneuver that disorients the Occidental way of signifying, so to speak. In keeping with this, it is no longer a question of "*the* exemption from sense," a general, categorical formulation, but of "*an* exempting from sense," a formulation indicating a circumscribed, circumstantial operation, the formulation suggesting an opportunity to be seized in language, in the interstice between the wanting and the saying phases of sense [*vouloir-dire*], and something like a murmur of saying at the level of the grain of the voice.[5]

How is this to be understood? How are we to understand a disorientation that would be tantamount neither to a pure aberration (of the nihilistic sort) nor to a reorientation (such as "salvation through *zen*," another nihilistic motto)? And how are we to understand an exemption that would remain somehow regulated by what it exempts? As I have indicated, I do not want to do a commentary on Barthes himself. I am taking up at my own risk a clue that he, willingly or otherwise, left in suspense and that he exempted himself from explicating.

What is the sense of "exemption"? We know perfectly well. To exempt is to relieve of an obligation, to free, to exonerate from a duty or debt. In order to conceive of an exempting from sense, first sense must have been posited at the level of an obligation, an injunction of some sort. To make sense, to produce or recognize its instance and form—would be for us first and foremost an imperative. (It can be shown to be the essence of the Kantian imperative.) Indeed, referral to a reason or purpose, an origin or destination, a reference point or value, seems indispensable to us for the constitution of a being, or of being itself. That being is for some purpose, even if it is for the very purpose of being, is one of the strongest motivating forces behind our thinking—"we others, thirsting after reason."[6] There, in a certain way, is the pure and simple schema of our late thought. Thus it is that being is always reduced to what should be, what can be, and what we desire there to be—to what always also includes the dimension of a production and an effectuation, a *realization* of *value*. We have to make sense and produce sense, or else produce ourselves as sense. In that way, sense is always constituted inevitably as end-oriented sense, and end-oriented sense itself tends, at least asymptotically, to conduct itself and to develop as unique sense.[7]

An exempting from sense would be, then, a lifting of that imperative. It would not be a denial on principle but only a single and exceptional dispensation. Whether we imagine it as temporary, spasmodic, or rhythmic, or represent it as invested solely in certain individuals among others (these are other questions), it is undeniably a question of a privilege. But this is no slight privilege. Once the general law authorizes exceptions, it exposes and is exposed to a beyond-the-law that will no longer be reassimilated. Now, the law of sense seems to authorize exception in two ways. On the one hand, it always ends up postponing ultimate sense, placing it outside language, in the ineffable. The unsayable unnameable realizes the apogee of sense. On the other hand, conversely, this apogee of sense must be given up in order for us to go on speaking. Between the unsayable of the ineffable and the too-much-said of a last word (I allude, of course, to Blanchot), saying itself thus requires an exempting from sense.

Hence the formally sublime dignity of the "person" and anonymous monetary circulation present the double face of the economy of unsayable sense. The unsayable or the supra-sayable produces the rage—indeed, the sickness—for the imposition of sense. In order to keep language, in both senses of the word *keep*, one must except oneself from its *goal-oriented* regimen. That which withdraws from the injunction of sense reopens the possibility of speaking.

Along the same lines, the privilege that confers exemption lifts the teleological obligation, and paradoxically in that same gesture does not excuse us from speaking but on the contrary calls us to a renewed, refined, and ever more finely honed word [*parole*], in its concept as well as its image: the word of the writer, the lover, or the philosopher; poetry, prayer, or conversation—but thus a word always closer to its birth than its closure, always more governed by its saying than by its said, by its reserve more than by its last word, by its truth more than by its sense.

The wanting-to-say commanded by sense always consists, in sum, in a wanting-to-have-said ("I have said" is the word of the master). An exempting from sense, by contrast, designates a wanting-to-say in which the wanting melts into the saying and gives up wanting, so that sense is absent and makes sense beyond sense. The beyond is no longer ineffable; it is in a surplus of speech, and consequently it is no longer beyond. Instead of pronouncing the end of History—in both senses of the word *end*—we, the speaking subject, "we others . . ." open another history, a new narrative—a recitation even. Rather than completing signification, it recites its own signifying, and it is in that signifying that it finds its extreme pleasure [*jouissance*], the sense of which becomes its "vanishing point."

The vanishing point is the inverted figure of the last word. Intense pleasure derives from the circumstance that it does not have a last word, and that its words or its silences are not those of conclusion but of opening and calling out. Not "I have said" but "tell me," or "allow me to say." One does not say (as in Sade) "I'm coming" [*je jouis*] or "you're coming" in order to express a sense, but one says it to feel the saying resonate with the coming.

Just as orgasm is a pleasure that is neither terminal nor preliminary, but pleasure that is exempted from having to begin and end, similarly orgasmic sense is sense that ends neither in signification nor in the unsignifiable. "Jouis-sens,"[8] as Lacan says, but it must be understood that orgasm is always about sense in all senses. To have an orgasm is always to feel, and since to feel is always also to feel oneself feeling, thus presupposing an alteration and an alterity, to have an orgasm is to feel oneself through the other and in the other.

As for sense, you have to feel it go by, and doubtless we must even assert: sense is precisely that: the fact of feeling it go by, and of its feeling itself going from one to the other (from one person to the other as well as from one sense to another).

This might well be called "consenting": neither a consensus, nor submission, but consent to feeling the other and being felt by him or her, consent to the other person's feeling him or herself, and thus infinitely fleeing the very flight of orgasm, whose breaking away is at the same time identically the consent to orgasm. Sex, from this point of view, is the sense of the senses. Not that it constitutes the only paradigm for this, but that it offers the syntax for it. That is relationship—by which sense regains sense. It is nothing other than relationship, the back and forth from one to the other. Sense depends on nothing but a receptivity, an affectability, a passibility: what there is of sense is what comes to me, strikes me, disturbs me, moves me. Its truth is the instantaneous touch; its sense is the movement to and fro.

There is no sense for just one, Bataille said. What makes sense is what does not cease circulating and being exchanged, like coins in fact, but coins whose currency is incommensurable with any possible equivalent.

Sense is shared, or it does not exist. The contrasting couple of the exclusive ineffable and the general equivalent, or, if you prefer, of negative theology and monetary ontology, is the result of the disintegration of sharing itself, in which each of two senses falls to a single side. Unique sense, in sum, is always unilateral, and no longer has any sense for that very reason. Nor is it a question of juxtaposing multiple senses. Here's the point: What *makes sense* is *one person speaking to another*, just as what *makes love* is someone making love to someone else. And one being the other by turns or simultaneously, without there being an end to these comings and goings. The goal—if we must speak of a goal—is not to be done with sense. It is not even mutual understanding: it is to speak anew.

We know this already, and yet when we find ourselves standing on the edge of a vacuum of sense—whether in the domain of history, art, matters of state, sexuality, technology, or biology—we stand nonplussed. Yet it is precisely there, in the place of our relinquishment, that the truth becomes available, not within easy reach or within shouting range, but within the range of language.

The lesson is very simple, as always, but the task is awesome. We, we others, have no lesser task than that of understanding and practicing the sharing of sense—of the sense of the world, no less. That doesn't mean dialogue and communication, which drag themselves listlessly along like saturated significations and the latest conventional chit-chat, but it wants to say—or no longer even *wants* but simply says—something other, for which the proud and solitary word [*parole*] is worth as much as mutual conversation: that the truth of sense is properly nothing but its being shared, that is, at once its passage between us (we who are always other than ourselves) and its internal and sovereign dehiscence, by means of which its law justifies its exception, by means of which sense is exempted from itself in order to be what it is, and by which its *jouissance* is not its sensed result but the exercise of its very sense, its sensitivity, its sensuality, and its feeling. Again it is Barthes who spoke of a "love of the language": that love is every bit as *worthy*—the expression is particularly apt—as the love of one's neighbor, and might even be said to make up all the latter's value and sense. And there we have, if I still dare use this word, an ethics for our time—and more than an ethics.

Translated by Bettina Bergo

"Prayer Demythified"

For Michel Deguy

1

Who can require of the present time a prayer, and of us, the godless who live this time as our own? It's not surprising it should be a poet who dares to do so, or dares at least to ask what such a prayer, if there is such a thing, could be.

That poet's name is Michel Deguy, and he writes:

> Let us quote Adorno, who writes that music, "*Prayer demytholo-gized*, freed from the magical result, represents the human attempt, *however vain*, to utter the Name itself instead of communicating meanings."
>
> *Prayer demythologized*? That is a powerful oxymoron, a tidal bore in which the movement of belief (the *credo* of the prayer) and the movement of mis- or dis- or un-belief collide: if demythologization recedes from credence, from the momentum of confidence or credu-lity in.[1]

Michel Deguy is a poet; he is also a philosopher, by training and by practice. Adorno is a philosopher; he is also a poet, at least to the point at which poetry is inevitably attained by a philosopher who cannot be satis-fied with philosophizing, whatever his speculative power and perhaps pre-cisely in proportion to that power.

Let us maintain that philosophy and poetry together indicate something they name with this word *prayer*. Let us also maintain that what they mean to designate with this word is a modality of language, whose property is to exceed the resources, possibilities, and horizons of both poetry and philosophy. Adorno motions in the direction of music—the art always considered the closest to language, though remaining obstinately separate from it. But Deguy, in his commentary, neglects that suggestion of music. He wants to proceed immediately to the element "prayer" denotes, without bothering to give it a place in advance, an artistic localization that would ipso facto temper the spiritualist or mystical ardor the word *prayer* unfailingly awakens, whether through disdain for that ardor or by attraction to it.

Deguy passes over Adorno's metaphor and demands that "prayer" be considered in itself, according to its own value. Without such a passing over, the "powerful oxymoron" would not be generated, but "prayer demythologized" would only remain a paradox so long as "prayer" has not been stripped of its character of—well, prayer. The new twist Deguy gives the text comes down to simply taking Adorno at his word rather than in his imagery, and driving him to take cover behind his formula. It is time for us to ask straight out: How can a demythologized prayer be a prayer? Even more uncompromisingly: How can a demythologized prayer pray?

What is the effect of this sentence that thus literalizes the metaphor of Adorno, forcing his figurative logic into a literal one and flushing out in him a disposition and an intellectual posture he might not have been able to admit? (A posture that, Deguy admits, takes on, claims even, all the more easily since he does not take shelter behind any metaphoricity.) It produces a discomfort, no doubt, among the atheists we are (along with Deguy), and at the same time a worry, because we immediately know we will not extricate ourselves from this dilemma by turning to some metaphor, since that is what has just been objected to, or calmly pushed aside and ignored.

The term *oxymoron* also has a literal value: it contains conjunction, collusion, or collision of opposites, and even contradiction. Not only do prayer and demythologization repel one another (since you have to posit the existence of a recipient of the prayer in order to pray): they mutually exclude one another. One who is outside the myth cannot pray. One who prays cannot have divested him or herself of all mythology.

Now, Deguy proposes that we maintain this contradiction, requests that we confront this "clash." Moreover, even if the *prerequisite* remains implicit, it is clearly not a question of treating the contradiction by imposing on it a conciliatory dialectic. We won't waste time here refuting that sort of hypothesis. If the "oxymoron" is "powerful," it is so to the degree that its power comes from a tension to be maintained rather than reabsorbed.

Perhaps the history of the idea of contradiction—of its resolution and/or non-resolution, that is, the history of the "dialectic" in all its forms, which modulate in every case the same *dialogical* tension—recapitulates the history of thought in general. The *dialogical* is a matter of the tension that the *logos* itself is, in that it involves nothing other than the effort of *saying*—provided we understand this verb in the way that the entire history of thought suggests. For what it says, what it *wants to say* always comes down to this: to say *the thing itself*, to say the thing in itself, for itself and by itself, and, in addition or perhaps consubstantially, to say the itselfness of the thing, by which it *is* the thing it is. That is sometimes called "truth," sometimes "the name," sometimes "the manifestation," among other possible designations. All the dialectics are, in this sense, dialogical: tensions of saying that are strained and stretched to the breaking point, in order to bring about the advent of that (the thing) of which it is said at the outset that it will remain unsaid, since what there is to be said is precisely that *there is* (this or that, being or the existent, the world, the thing).

The power of the oxymoron—and with it, that of the paradox, as in Kierkegaard, as well as the power of the *Witz* of the Romantics, the Gnostic, alchemical, or Cusanian *coincidentia oppositorum*, the *sic et non* of all types, the *antinomies* of pure reason, the Hegelian *Aufhebung*, the Derridean *aporia*, and, at the beginning, the Platonic *dialogue*, along with the no less Platonic erotics—that power is none other than that of language, namely, the power of holding the thing out to us while holding us out toward it: the power of *presenting*.

As we can see, that is what Adorno's statement is about. It is about presenting, in this case qua the "Name itself," which is at least to say, as the immediate context suffices to indicate, qua removed from the regime of "signification." Signification subdues the thing to its genitive: it gives the sense *of* the thing. Nomination presents the thing. The genitive of the "name of the thing" is not of the same order as the preceding: for the "sense of" refers the thing to a different sphere than that of its thing-being, whereas the "name of" inscribes its difference (the name/the thing) within the sphere of being.

Therefore, we have to take it for granted that a "demythologized prayer" forms neither a category nor a particular linguistic operation intended for a specific goal of signification or transmission, but indicates, on the contrary, a gesture, a posture, and a postulation according to which language is tensed to its limit, at its limit, which it exceeds while maintaining itself there, extended in an unstable equilibrium.

At this point we should turn to the interrogation of music, since that is what Adorno speaks of; it will suffice to recall that he is thinking, not at all by chance, of vocal music, specifically that of *Moses and Aron*, by Schönberg. If Deguy neglects to speak of it, and if we can follow suit, it is because the question of music, and along with it that of art in general (hence of poetry itself), must not come too quickly to occupy the place of analysis. "Art" must not risk becoming the horizon, and therefore the closure, of an interrogation or hopeful anticipation that must, on the contrary, be immediately *dis-enclosed*, freed from any assignment as means or material aid, as possibility of response or provision, whatever it may be: for example, in the form of "art," whether music, poetry, or whatever. For such an assignment, in the absence of any precaution or prerequisite, could not fail to produce yet again the closure of a religion. Now, that is exactly what must be rejected, or, more precisely, it is what *is* rejected, what is dying out, or so it is in our case. (Whether Adorno himself merits being questioned, if not suspected, concerning his own relation to art and the eventuality of finding a religiosity of art in him is quite another matter, which I neither can nor care to take up here.)

2

Deguy continues his commentary on Adorno's sentence along the following lines. First, he posits that "a *truth* is trying to express itself here," that this truth is one of an "emptying out" or a "de-nomination," both these terms apparently applying to the myth content that is to be set aside: that is, the religious content. He also posits that this "emptying out" or this "deposition" (an intentional reference to the *pietà*) must also be understood as "dismissal of the hymn," an expression that he borrows from Lacoue-Labarthe (with whom, in this case, Bailly[2] is to be associated). To dismiss the hymn in trying to say a truth that would be the truth of what remains when the myth is deposed—and what is left is thus not nothing, not entirely nothing, since it is "the formula, the phrase, the vernacular not-nothing, language."

This emptied-out language, destitute—this *logos* without *muthos*—which would also be a "dialogue" without an interlocutor, dialogue suspended at its opening—should also be called "*muthos* without *muthos*," if we are not forgetful of the first sense of the word (the spoken word), and it should also give us an indication of how the oxymoron closes in upon itself: into nothing less than a contraction that could, that should, border on strangulation, or even be condemned to it.

But Deguy goes on, attaching this language that is thus almost suffocated—hoarse in any case, and broken, withdrawn from the full sonority of sense and from the possibility of a naming (since we must recall the "vanity" of attempting to announce "the Name itself"; not at all withdrawn from a silence or some form of aphonic ecstasy, but clearly withdrawn from something of poetry. He suggests it only obliquely—surely on his guard against being drawn back into some manner of re-aestheticization and artist's religiosity, and also on his guard against a certain Heideggerian tone that is enchanted with Hölderlin. He only suggests it, but suggests it nonetheless, by a thread that connects *Dichten* to the "sublimity" of a "transcendence" that, à la Mallarmé, places "the future of the repercussion *in* the élan." Here we must do Deguy's text justice, the most precise justice. It is not a matter of dialecticizing (at least not in the ordinary sense of making headway against negativity), nor is it a matter of retrieving or reinvesting ourselves in the "station of some transcendent." But it is about "retracing the steps"—of what? Nothing less than the "Gospel," the "*pietà*," and even "the Spirit." This is said only in passing, in a light and clear-headed way, firmly maintained in order to conclude by rejecting any "credulity with respect to a beyond," and yet drawn by the magnetic question: "What is the sense of 'humanity in spirit'?"

In other words, Michel Deguy sets out to seek the resource of the oxymoron—"demythologized prayer"—at the most manifest source of religious prayer in the history of our culture. And yet he must not have written the word *prayer*—he must have abandoned it after having unfolded the oxymoron, specifying: "A *prayer . . . demythologized* is a conception (not to say a concept) *emptied* entirely of what it 'contained' . . . by . . . the visit within it of its opposite, of what thwarts it, of what discountenances it and thus makes it hold on, empty, one 'last time.'"

This word thus, silently, subtends all that follows, the whole movement of emptying out, of dismissal, and of the resumption—discreet and tenacious, untenable and indefatigable, as he writes—of the movement or gesture of a "transcendence." A transcendence by which it is still, once the "*credo* of prayer" has been jettisoned, a question of no more or less than . . . praying. Praying without prayer, or the finding and forming of the wording of a prayer one would not pray: this is what it is about.

Thus it should concern a prayer not to be recited in the temple, but still to be re-cited, and in several senses of that word, on which I will not stop to elaborate right now and which would once more involve the issue of poetry, even that of the "hymn," which cannot be dismissed without receiving in its place a different phrase, a different chant. "Poetry" resists, and "prayer" can be at least one of the forms of its resistance, as well as of its deposition.

In deferring these questions for another occasion, let the following suffice. One can see, beyond a doubt, in this oxymoronic or paradoxical dialectic of "prayer demythologized" one of the most acute formulations of what is brought into play, in my view at least, by a "deconstruction of Christianity": the approach to a remnant or a "relic," as Deguy likes to put it, freed, dis-enclosed from the religious edifice, impossible to put back, but the bearer or the worker of a requirement that will not be dismissed—not as easily as the "hymn" or as poetry or art altogether, as I have intimated at least tentatively in the form of a pedagogical and prudential suggestion.

3

What we are left with, unambiguously, is this almost-nothing: How to pray without prayer? If prayer stripped of its believing, thus empty of all content, must be considered an empty container, a form devoid of matter to inform, what can it be? And, more precisely: What will it be able to say?

One answer would be that it will say whatever, as long as it says, but says at the very least according to the requirement or the desire of the saying: the desire to say the thing. On this point the worst confusion is possible: the essence of saying can turn into a "saying for the sake of saying," just as well as turning toward the thing itself. The confusion can never be simply or luminously dissipated, and that is indeed why the aesthetic mirage is a menace, above all in the form Bataille called "the gooey temptation of poetry."

It is necessary, however, to avoid confusion. But that necessity is none other than what should turn saying toward the thing—that is to say, also toward itself, toward what belongs to it by its own right and founds it, or what opens it and makes it speak (what makes us into speakers).

Now, what is prayer, if we want to consider it for a moment in its own right, since, after all, it has a consistency in itself that is not necessarily tributary to its religious use—which can also be formulated conversely: ordinary prayer, profane prayer if you will, the prayer that has its place in language when we say "I pray of you," or "Please answer" ["*prière de répondre*"]. This might well be *what is left*, the remnant that has fallen, abandoned, the not-quite-nothing of a "relic," fallen from religious faith and testifying nonetheless to the fact that there is in fact something left . . .

But what, then, might this be that thus remains behind—or rather, what is it that would be, on the contrary, qua inverted figure of the remnant, the germ, or rather the innate occasioning, of language, the tenuous vibration to which a first and instituting articulation of a spoken word attaches, henceforth neither cry nor signal, but a *saying*?

If we say that "saying" has the role of saying the thing, its being or rather even its "*that it is*" (the transitive *being* that *is* its being-ness [*étance*], as Heidegger asks—prays?—that we should try to hear it), then we should understand as well that that role consists in simultaneously positing a *said* (for example, "it is," "there is," "here is") and in obliterating that very positing, in depositing it in the *saying*'s own movement. (Few themes, no doubt, have been more worked over, reflected on, meditated, rehearsed, and variously named by our modernity than this muffled dehiscence, this intimate rending between said and saying, between the sense of the utterance and the subject who utters it, between communication and language, or yet again between signification and writing, between truth and sense, between sense and itself . . .)

If what is at stake is a deletion carried out at the same time as what it deletes is formed, two gestures modeled on one another, curved into one another and recrossing one another indefinitely, which also means that this twofold movement allows the thing to present itself. (To hone in on this point, one would have to specify how the "presenting itself" of the thing is indissociable from its "being presented": by the first, the saying is obliterated; by the second, the saying is affirmed.) Essentially, the saying exerts itself in letting the real—*res*, the thing—realize itself, that is, be what it is, and above all be *that it is*. This "letting be" is its task.

Another poet and thinker, Valéry, writes: "Prayer is perhaps the uniquely *real* thing in religion."[3] That reality is due to the efficacy of that which, in the prayer, qua prayer, is addressed to, or even, if I may say so, is erect, advanced, made to stand out and insist—in contrast to all the mythical and imaginary content of religion. The prayer, first of all, is turned toward an outside and lets it come toward it. And that is what speech does first and foremost. That outside, that real—the prayer does not signify it, does not categorize it or conceive of it; it does not even *name* it, or the very idea of the name defines the farthest reaches in which "letting be" operates in truth. What does speech do, then? It addresses this "letting be," invoking or evoking it, as we might say, coaxing our sense out of these terms. But one might say more directly, perhaps more brutally as well: it *adores* this letting be.

Ad-oration is literally the addressing of speech. But, essentially, that addressing is addressed to speech's other: the *res*. And if the adoration of idols (through which, not surprisingly in a sense, we circle back to the theme of *Moses and Aron* . . .) constitutes, throughout our entire tradition, even beyond religion, the touchstone or the *shibboleth* whose charge it is to distinguish the "true" religion (each one claiming that epithet for itself) from the others, it is clearly because "idol" represents the stupid thing, the thing without "real" presence, which truly does not hear the spoken word addressed to it by the idolater. In a symmetrical manner, the "true" addressee of adoration is the real, whose presence is not to be confused with the given present; it is the real whose presence gives or presents itself when it is "addressed."

This is why adoration, prayer in its essence, is not primarily a request made in order to receive a response, retribution, or reparation. Prayer is not primordially involved in the religious trafficking in lies about the real (about life/death, the world/nothingness, earth/heaven, etc.), nor in the related one of indulgences capitalized in the form of salvation credits. Prayer is primarily adoration: address, homage, recognition of the fact that its saying is deleted in going toward what it says (will never say). Homage, veneration, that is, simply the movement of "transcendence" as Deguy characterizes it, incessant trans-port without any "landing having been reached" or transcendence without a transcendent (which can also be expressed as transcendence immanent to our immanence, homologous with and inherent to its plane itself)—constitutes the task of saying.

Again it is a poet—Verlaine this time—who writes: "Read rather Chateaubriand on the subject of humanity's need, vis-à-vis the Celestial Powers, for a mysterious language in which (in its homage, and in the supplication that is a mere accessory to that homage) needs that are unknown to itself—poor humanity—would be implied!"[4] Abstracting from the climate of religious self-evidence in which the text is embedded (but which would require an entirely different analysis of its context as a whole), the decisive point is: "supplication," to which prayer is all too often reduced and which in fact religious piety usually *does* come down to, is but an "accessory" to "homage," because only the recognition of the excess in which we transcend ourselves, or are transcended *in* our immanence, opens onto these "unknown needs" in whose name we supplicate, implore, but not to obtain their satisfaction, because what thus reveals itself is precisely that it is not about satisfaction—or, in a more complex way, that these unknown needs are in themselves, and in their very unknowability, their own satisfaction.

Prayer does not supplicate to obtain—and thus it is that "prayer demythologized" is, in Adorno's terms, "freed from the magic of the result." Prayer does not ask in order that its request be granted, nor does it produce that result. To have one's prayers answered—that is the expectation, as self-interested as it is illusory, of religion, which consequently is doomed to content itself with imaginary satisfactions (if I am not healed, it is because an even higher good has been granted me . . .). But to be *lifted up* (for that is the word, and that is its sense),[5] that is the true efficacy of the word that rises, that is to say, that simply turns from the being-posited, given, toward the real in that it gives itself and is given, presented.

Doubtless one should not confuse (everything here, absolutely everything lends itself to confusion: the aesthetic, the political, the religious, even the linguistic . . .), one should especially not confuse the elevation of prayer itself—the freeing of the word in its very obliteration, an evaporation of sorts—and a lifting up that would like to be that of the worshipper in person, who would be hoisted above his or her condition and would come to participate in the dignity of the object of adoration. Such an elevation implies the rapture or the enthusiasm of communion in the celebration—the accents of the hymn, in fact, at least after what it has become as a result of the pomp and circumstance of the clergy, the military, the state or the partisan, and most radically the Fascists. For Fascism, in all its forms, contains, in a determining way, a co-opting of prayer and homage in an exaltation and a triumph in which the totality of a collective body, literally *carried away* and *transported* into the distance and into the substance of the thing adored, is thought to rise and be glorified. Fanaticism is nothing but the abolition of the intractable distance of the real, and consequently also the extinction of prayer and all speech, in favor of effusive outpourings, eructation, and vociferation.

(Hence we have not finished examining and carefully weighing the connections of Fascisms and fanaticisms with, on the one hand, religions properly so called—though one cannot deny, in spite of everything, the sense of the distance in question—and, on the other hand, democracy, which, stripped of both church and civic religion, labors to manage the true space of speech, which it clouds beneath "communication.")

In the elevation of prayer, a supplication also, albeit "accessory," cannot fail to intervene, for in it is revealed the "poverty" Verlaine speaks of, using a topos as poor and worn as what it conveys. The fact is, "poor humanity" may have nothing else to say but its own wretchedness, nothing else to pray. Prayer thus conceived does not enrich, does not remunerate the "poor humanity" that we today have just as many reasons to bemoan as Verlaine did in 1895. It carries poverty over to saying—and it isn't poverty but saying that is obliterated in this prayer. Does not the same apply (isn't it the same thing) to the saying of love, the saying of mourning, and the saying of speech itself?

Elevation is transcendence. Prayer does not rise toward a height, an altitude, or toward a summit (sovereign, *ens summum*), but is transcendence, or (and this is less noted) the very act of *transcending*. It is passing-to-the-outside, and passing-to-the-other: I beg of you, please [*je vous prie, je te prie*]. All address, no doubt, contains at least silently these words: "I pray that you will listen to me." And just as one who prays directs his word—himself—outward, so it is with the listener as well. Maybe when we *listen*, when we are *attentive*, it is always to a prayer—and therefore I will not avoid playing, here, once more, fleetingly, some musical instrument—the voice, for example.

Now if this is the way things are, it is because prayer (and in this it differs from the poem as well as from discourse, even though the poem also tends in this direction) is chiefly characterized as speech accompanying an act. One prays with acts of worship, a prayer ritual (hands joined, kneeling), and one always prays with a prayerful gesture, however lightly sketched out: the movement of a hand, a slight leaning forward, an eye movement, even if it is simply an intonation, which already mobilizes the entire body. In the margins of prayer there is dance—and how many rites have been danced at the same time as prayed! Prayer is the corroboration of an action, and that action is an availability to the outside, a being at the disposal of, the action of passivity or of the passion that opens itself to the outside—to the incommensurable, in relation to which we are only poor.

There is no going farther. Not a single step. We must make do with this vestige of prayer that is prayer itself, speaking beings *qua* praying beings—praying (for) that ownmost possibility of never believing our prayers to have been granted, the possibility of never believing, therefore, that we have prayed enough, of never believing absolutely, and of abiding in that unique and exclusive faith. One thing, ultimately, is indubitable: we must concern ourselves with this emptied remnant of prayer, remain faithful to this obligation. For us it has the force of a categorical imperative, for nothing today is more important than this: to empty and let be emptied out all prayers that negotiate a sense, an issue, or a repatriation of the real within the narrow confines of our faded humanisms and clenched religiosities, in order that we may merely open speech once again to its most proper possibility of address, which also makes up all its sense and all its truth.

Translated by Michael B. Smith

The Deconstruction of Christianity

As a guiding epigraph to this whole endeavor, these words from Nietzsche's *The Antichrist*: "The theologians and everything that has theologian blood in its veins: our whole philosophy." Add to it these words of Hölderlin, in their ambivalence: "Christ, I hold too fast to you!"

My question will be very simple, naïve even, as is perhaps fitting at the beginning of a phenomenological procedure: How and to what degree do *we hold* to Christianity? How, exactly, are we, in our whole tradition, held by it? I am well aware that this is a question that may appear superfluous, because it has an obvious answer. We know that our tradition is Christian, that our source is Christian. Yet it is a question that seems to me to remain obscure, because at bottom it is never confronted head on. That said, I have just learned that Michel Henry is now also taking up this question.[1] Thus it may represent a certain trait, or a certain necessity, of the times.

For my part, I will observe that the question "How and in what sense, precisely, are we Christian?" (a question Nietzsche, in his own way, answered) is no longer among those one asks. True, there have been debates on the theme "Is there or is there not a Christian philosophy?" debates that have sunk in the quagmire to which they were destined by their very formulation, but we must recognize that something of that enormous, massive Christian reference has been systematically obfuscated qua explicit reference in and by philosophy—something that not only is part of our tradition, but of which it may be said that it has constituted the very axis of our tradition since Christianity came into being. Now, this is the question: How, given the existence of Christianity, has our entire tradition, including the one antedating Christianity, found itself gathered up and launched anew?

That is the question. But in the phenomenological tradition (in that tradition par excellence, but not in it alone), what has been fertile and obvious since Husserl and Heidegger is the Greek source, not the Christian one. Beneath the Greek source it has been possible to reveal in Heidegger the presence of a latent, hidden, repressed Jewish source.[2] It seems to me that between these two references, or as a *nexus* connecting the two of them, there may be the Christian source, if we may call it that. In other words, one could wonder whether the "jewgreek" Derrida speaks of at the end of "Violence and Metaphysics" (that "jewgreek" he says is our history) is not the Christian. One could also wonder why we systematically avert our gaze from the Christian, why our eye always veers toward the "jewgreek," as if we didn't want to look directly at the Christian. Let us say, then (with a grain of salt, which is probably my way of being a phenomenologist), that the Christian or Christianity is the *thing itself* that is to be thought. Let us attempt to proceed toward it directly, by laying down two principles.

The first is: "The only Christianity that can be actual is one that contemplates the present possibility of its negation." This is a phrase of Luigi Pareysson, an Italian philosopher who was Umberto Eco's teacher. It is quoted by Émile Poulat in his book *L'Ère postchrétienne: Un monde sorti de Dieu* (*The Post-Christian Era: A World That Has Left God*),[3] the work of a Catholic Christian, which is not really a philosophical work but which I find extremely valuable as a testimony, whose essence is conveyed in that quotation.

The second principle is a correlative to the first. Parodying the first formula, I will express it as follows: "The only thing that can be actual is an atheism that contemplates the reality of its Christian origins." Underlying both of these principles, I formulate tentatively this question: "What is there, then, in the depths of our tradition, that is, in our own depths?" or, "What has been handed down to us by our own tradition from the depths of this storehouse of Christian self-evidence, which is so self-evident to us that we do not examine it more closely?"

What I propose here is not a completely finished systematic exposition. I deliberately run the risk of presenting a reflection that is still under construction, trying to find its way and unable to reach any conclusion except a pragmatic and tentative one. In a first attempt, I will distinguish the ways the problem is to be approached, then I will briefly consider three—

and only three—aspects or components of Christianity: faith, sin, and the living God. These will be, after a sort of long methodological approach, only three elements taken up from a long, programmatic list that would have to be gone through to hope to arrive at a result.

Let us go back to our title: "The Deconstruction of Christianity." It is a title that might seem provocative or seductive (i.e., seductive because provocative). But I seek no provocation—nor, consequently, any seduction derived from a provocation. Moreover, if this title were to appear to be a provocation, that provocation would be scarcely more than the dream of a somewhat dated imagination, since in fact today, when it comes to Christianity, everything is taken for granted. No one can imagine being confronted today by a Voltaire-like philosopher, having at Christianity in an acerbic tone—and doubtless not in the best Nietzschean style . . . Perhaps the reader would be more likely to have thought, reading "The Deconstruction of Christianity," that the title was not a provocation and that the vaguely sulfurous smell of such a title was destined to end up, if not with an odor of sanctity, at least in befitting considerations. The fact is, after all, that one can do virtually anything with Christianity: we have come into a climate, not only of *aggiornamento*, but of post-*aggiornamento*; a climate in which Christianity seems able to lend itself to everything and anything, provided only that we free it [*en défalque*] from a purely reactionary portion of fundamentalism,[4] in which Christianity is no longer recognizable.

I will therefore keep my distance from both critical provocation and any further step in the direction of accommodation and *aggiornamento*. I will do so for the very simple reason that there can be no question today, it seems to me, either of attacking or of defending Christianity, that is, either of damning or of saving it. Such projects are simply out of season, and it is precisely the profound, historial reasons that make them unseasonable that we have to be able to analyze. As a rough approximation, let us say that they are unseasonable because Christianity itself, Christianity *as such*, is surpassed, because it is itself, and by itself, in a state of being surpassed. That state of self-surpassing may be very profoundly proper to it; it is perhaps its deepest tradition—which is obviously not without its ambiguities. It is this transcendence, this going-beyond-itself that must therefore be examined.

Being surpassed, self-surpassing, do not mean that Christianity is no longer alive. Doubtless it is still alive and will be for a long time, but at bottom, if it is alive, it has ceased giving life—at least as the organizing structure of an experience that would be something other than a fragmented individual experience. (Moreover, is it still, in that case, an experience?) It has ceased giving life in the order of *sense*, if it is true that there is never sense for just one person. If sense is of the order of the "common," then there is no doubt that Christianity has ceased giving life—no doubt that it has passed from itself into a different status, a different realm of sense and common allotment of sense. This we all know, whether we are Christians or non-Christians. In a more general sense, Christianity's fate is perhaps the fate of sense in general, that is, what has been called in the last few years, outwardly, the "end of ideologies." The "end of ideologies" is at least the end of promised sense or the end of the promise of sense as an intention, goal, and fulfillment. That is doubtless what it is: the end of the self-surpassing of Christianity. Hence what is required of us with the greatest necessity is what we will have to call "the deconstruction of Christianity." Before revisiting this concept, I would like to reformulate these initial givens in a different way, by positing a triple axiom.

1. Christianity is inseparable from the West. It is not some accident that befell it (for better or worse), nor is it transcendent to it. It is coextensive with the West qua West, that is, with a certain process of Westernization consisting in a form of self-resorption or self-surpassing. This first axiom presupposes—as does a good portion of what I propose here—my overwhelming agreement with the work by Marcel Gauchet, *Le Désenchantement du monde* (*The Disenchantment of the World*),[5] particularly with the part related to Christianity, titled "The Religion of the Departure from Religion."

2. The de-Christianization of the West is not a hollow phrase, but the more that process advances the more it becomes manifest, through the fate of immobilized churches and anemic theologies, that what still attaches us in many ways to the West is the nervation of Christianity itself. Nietzsche put it very well in saying that the Buddha's shadow remains for a thousand years before the cave in which he died. *We are in that shadow*, and it is precisely that shadow that we must bring to light. We are *in* the nervation of Christianity; it holds us, but *how*? This second axiom posits, therefore, that *all* our thought is Christian through and through. Through and through and entirely, which is to say, all of us, all of us completely. We must try to bring to light how we are still Christian without, perhaps, remaining pious; this cannot be said in Nietzsche's terms ("how we, too, are still pious"): to ask ourselves "how we are still Christian" takes us to the very end, to the ultimate extremity of Christianity.

3. The West itself, Occidentality, is what is carried out by laying bare a particular nervation of sense: a nervation in some way empty or exposed, that of sense as a settled affair, carried to the limits of sense or of the possibility of sense. Thus to deconstruct Christianity is to accompany the West to that limit, to that *pass at which* the West cannot do otherwise than let go of itself in order to continue being the West, or still be something of itself beyond itself. In this pass, it must let go of itself; thus it is the same move—letting go of the West and letting go of Christianity. In this pass, however—and this is what I think properly and necessarily gives rise to a deconstructive move—in this pass it is a question not of rejecting a tradition, of shedding an old skin, but of meeting squarely what comes to the West and Christianity from beyond themselves, what comes toward us from the depths of our tradition as more archaic (in the sense of *archē* and not of historical beginning, of course) than Christianity. In other words, the question is to find out whether we can, by revisiting our Christian provenance, designate in the heart of Christianity a provenance of Christianity deeper than Christianity itself, a provenance that might bring out another resource—with an ambiguity that for now I take entirely upon myself—between a gesture of Hegelian dialectical *Aufhebung* and a different one that is not dialectical sublation. However that ambiguity may play itself out, if one accepts the identification of the West with Christianity one also accepts the consequence, which is that there is no way out other than by means of a resource that replaces the Christian one entirely, without being a watered-down version or a dialectical rehearsal of the same. Let us add that we do not yet even know, perhaps, what Hegelian dialectical sublation really is, that perhaps we don't know what negativity is. To find out we must plunge into its heart—a heart that risks being, if I dare say so, Christian.

Given these axioms, we can now resume, taking as our new point of departure the following. It is often said that the more or less pronounced degradation of Christianity—its smaller number of congregants, its marked disappearance as a common reference point and explicit regulative index, as well as its profound internal disaffection—is assumed to be the effect of the modern transition toward a rationalized, secularized, and materialized society. So it is said, but without having any idea why that society has become what it is . . . , unless that is because it has turned away from Christianity, which merely repeats the problem, since the defined has thereby been placed within the definition.

Let us therefore, very simply but very firmly, posit that any analysis that pretends to find a *deviation* of the modern world from Christian reference forgets or denies that the modern world is itself the unfolding of

Christianity. That denial is serious, since it amounts to forbidding the modern world to begin to understand itself, inasmuch as (and this is precisely the point) the world we call "modern" is undoubtedly constructed—and this is no accident—on the internal denial of its Christian reference. We need only reflect very briefly on the Kantian phenomenon, for example, to realize that it is open to two kinds of reading: as a manner of denial, or repression if you will, of the Christian reference and *at the same time*, as a full and total reenactment of Christian reference. Indeed, we must not forget that this sentence from the Preface to *The Critique of Pure Reason*—"I have had to suppress knowledge in order to make room for belief"—provides an opening for belief within the limits of reason. It is too often forgotten that this is Kant's purpose and that what is at stake concerning modernity is in truth something other than a deviation or an abandonment. The truth is of another order—though not the opposite one, if the opposite consists in saying that the internal decomposition of Christianity has delivered Western society to its modern loss of direction. The reader will have recognized in this opposite thesis the old model of the Catholic accusation addressed to the Reformation and Anglicanism, that of the internal self-accusation of Christianity losing itself and all the others along with it. That is, generally speaking, the "fundamentalist thesis" within each of the Christian families and between these Christian families. In an even more general way, it may be said that the conflict between "fundamentalism" and what not so long ago the Catholic Church called "modernism" is the specific conflict to which the West subjects religions (its own, at any rate), and along the lines of which it has constituted or structured its religion. The conflict between a religious fundamentalism and its dissolution by adaptation to a world that at once comes from it and detaches itself from it, rejecting and denying it—this internal conflict in the form of schizophrenia or division within itself is unrelated to the conflicts between the dogmas or between opposing beliefs. This conflict internal to Christianity (which is at present becoming internal to Judaism and Islam, though in a different way) has nothing to do with the conflict between Christianity and Judaism, if that is indeed a conflict, or with the conflicts that exist between all the great religions. Indeed, within Christianity a specific type of conflict occurs, which is probably the conflict between an *integrality* and its disintegration. It is in this specific conflict that the first indication of a nuclear property of Christianity, the first clue to the possibility of its evolution, is to be sought. Is not Christianity, in and of itself, a divided integrality? Is it not the very movement of its distension, of its opening out and of its dissolution?

Only if the response to these questions is affirmative can the gesture of deconstruction make sense, because deconstruction can then try to reach, at the heart of the movement of integrality's self-distension, the heart of this movement of opening. My inquiry is guided by this motif of the essence of Christianity as opening: an opening of self, and of self as opening.

In all the forms of opening, throughout all its reverberations: opening as distension, as interval [*écart*], but also Heidegger's "Open" (which, since the opening of Heidegger, commands a contemporary climate of thought). What of the opening of Christianity or of Christianity as opening? What of—and this is at bottom the real question—an *absolute transcendental of opening* such that it does not cease pushing back or dissolving all horizons?

That is our situation: no more horizons. From all directions horizons are asserted in the modern world, but how can we grasp what I would call "horizontality"? How can we grasp the character of horizon while we are on a ground that is not a ground of horizon(s), a ground without ground of indefinite opening? That is the question to which Christianity, at bottom, seems to me to lead.

From that indefinite opening—not from that accidental property of opening, but from opening as an essential property, from opening as Christian ipseity, hence from distension of self, from relation to self as indefinite exiting from self—I will take up for the moment, simply a first indication, evoking the complex, differentiated, and conflicted genesis of Christianity. The historical reality of that genesis is always too easily and too quickly covered over by what I would like to call "the Christmas[6] projection," that is, by a pure and simple birth of Christianity, which one fine day comes along and changes everything. Now, quite curiously, our whole tradition, as unchristian as it would like to be, still retains something of "the Christmas projection": at a given moment "that" takes place, and we find ourselves thereafter in a Christian condition. But how was that possible? We do not wonder enough how and why Classical antiquity *produced* Christianity: not how it *befell* it on Christmas Day, but how that world *made it possible*. Without undertaking extremely complex historical and theoretical analyses, I will simply highlight the difficulty by pointing out that Christianity is this very curious event in our history that imposes for its proper reading, and in its own tradition, the double schema of an *absolute happening* (which I have called "Christmas") and, at the same time, a dialectical *Aufhebung* or, if one cannot call it that, an *integration* of the entire preceding heritage, since Christianity conceives of itself as a recapitulation and *Aufhebung* of Judaism, Hellenism, and Romanity. When we consider the history of Christianity, we find three stages: a Jewish Christianity (Christianity is at first a Jewish religion, if not a sect), a Greek Christianity, and a Roman Christianity; three stages whose conjunction corresponds to the constitution of a dogmatic/ecclesiastic integrality *and* to the internal tension of an identity that can be conceived only in relation to what it negates in transcending it. Christian identity is therefore from the start a constitution by self-transcendence: the Old Law in the New Law, the *logos* in the Word, the *civitas* in the *civitas Dei*, and so on. Christianity shares, no doubt, with all other religions the schema of the constitution of an orthodoxy by defining heresies, the production of schisms, and so on, but the schema proper to Christianity is different in that it is the schema of an orthodoxy that understands itself to be the virtually infinite movement through which a faith discovers itself in relation to what precedes it, which it renews and enlightens. This faith is what it is only in revealing itself to itself progressively as the integration of what preceded it, which it carries further forward. There is something unique here: *the Christian faith is itself the experience of its history*, the experience of a plan followed by God for the execution of salvation. Thus there is, on the one hand, upstream, in the direction of the Jewish root, a history, a plan followed and oriented, whereas on the other hand, on the side of the Christian movement, this execution of salvation becomes indissociable from human history, becomes human history as such, History. From the point of view of Catholic orthodoxy, what I am advancing here is not a commentary. It is a Catholic theological thesis: that the plan for salvation is indissociable from human history is a thesis from Vatican I. It follows that the dimension of history in general, as a Western dimension, is fundamentally Christian and that the way and the life of salvation are not only, for Christianity, the modality of and the procedure for access to a specific mystery, as in all types of initiation and conversion, but the very progression of *homo viator*, of "journeying man," man en route, whose journey is not only a passage but constitutes in itself the gait and the progression of revelation. Hence, history understood as distortion, opening (with retention and protention), history as the opening of the subject as such—who is only a subject by being a historical subject, in distension with itself—is the matricial element that Christianity brings progressively to light as its truth, because it does not in fact come to pass all at once, *ex abrupto*. That matricial element, that essential historicity, posited and "thought" in Christian faith as such, that historicity—let us say—*of* the faith (not only the historicity of faith as an act of belonging, but the historicity of the very content of faith) is what ends up separating rigorously, implacably, Christianity from the element of religion in general and making of it, in Marcel Gauchet's phrase, "the religion of the egress from religion."[7]

Hence Christianity, stretched between the virtually infinite antecedence in which it never ceases deciphering the signs of its own anteriority and an infinite future into which it projects the final advent of its event in progress, is constitutively stretched between passage and presence. From the passage of God into man to the presence/parousia of God un*to* man, the consequence is valid, but that consequence from passage to presence is precisely what is called *sense*. Thus Christianity is *in* the element of sense, in both senses, significative and directional, of the word. Christianity is par excellence the conjunction of both senses: it is sense as tension or direction toward the advent of sense as content. Consequently, the question is less that of the sense of Christianity than that of Christianity as a dimension of sense, a dimension of sense that—and this is the point to be analyzed—is at once the opening of sense and sense as opening. From passage to presence, it does not cease being averred that presence always repeats passage, or that passage always leads to more opening at the heart of sense. The extreme point of that tension is attained when the absolute of parousia, the absolute of presence, ends by merging with the infinity of passage. Sense is then completed, or, to say the same thing differently, used up. It is *complete sense in which there is no longer any sense*. That is what ends up being called "the death of God," in a phrase that is not accidentally of Christian provenance (it comes from Luther), for it states the very destiny of Christianity. In other words, closer to Nietzsche, Christianity is accomplished in nihilism and as nihilism, which means that nihilism is none other than the final incandescence of sense, that it is sense taken to its point of excess.

Christianity is, therefore, not at all the obvious, aggressive, critical negation or despair of sense. It is protention toward sense, the sense of sense, acute in the extreme, beaming with its last light and burning out in that final incandescence. It is sense that no longer orders or activates anything, or nothing but itself; it is sense absolutely in its own right, pure sense, that is, the end revealed for itself, indefinitely and definitively. Such is the complete idea of Christian revelation.

This idea has never been that of the revelation of something or someone. In that sense it is certainly the surpassing, the *Aufhebung*, the Jewish departure outside Judaism, for the idea of Christian revelation is that, in the end, *nothing is revealed*, nothing but the end of revelation itself, or else that revelation is to say that sense is unveiled purely as sense, in person, but in a person such that all the sense of that person consists in revealing himself. Sense reveals itself and reveals nothing, or else reveals its own infinity. Yet to reveal nothing is not a negative proposition. It is, rather, the Hegelian proposition that the revealed is properly that God is the revealable: what is revealed is the revealable, the Open as such. It is on that sharp point that Christianity breaks and reveals itself to be what Nietzsche has termed nihilism.

So long as we do not grasp the full extent of this situation, which makes up our Christian provenance, as a Western one, to be the provenance that destines us to the revelation of the revealable, or yet again to sense as pure, absolute, and infinite, we will remain prisoners to something that has not been elaborated in such a way as to be adequate to that history and that destiny. Everything, then, is contingent on this point: to think the infinity of sense, to think truth as an infinite of sense. Or yet again, to think sense as the absolute opening of sense and to sense, but in a sense that is in a way empty, empty of all content, all figure, all determination. Let us say, punning without punning, this is "Christianity's cross," since it is exactly on that point that Christianity is simultaneously constituted and undone. Consequently, by focusing on that point it is appropriate to try to deconstruct Christianity.

Let me specify what the operation of "deconstruction" means. Deconstructing belongs to a tradition, to *our* modern tradition, and I am entirely ready to admit that the operation of deconstruction is part of the tradition just as legitimately as the rest; consequently, it is itself shot through and through with Christianity. Furthermore, "deconstruction" has this peculiarity: if we look back at its origin in the text of *Being and Time*, it is the last state of the tradition—its last state as retransmission, to us and by us, of the whole tradition in order to bring it back into play in its totality. To put the tradition into play according to deconstruction, according to *Destruktion* (a term Heidegger was determined to protect against *Zerstörung*, i.e., against "destruction," and that he characterized as *Abbau*, "taking apart") means neither to destroy in order to found anew nor to perpetuate—two hypotheses that would imply a system given as such and untouchable as such. To deconstruct means to take apart, to disassemble, to loosen the assembled structure in order to give some play to the possibility from which it emerged but which, qua assembled structure, it hides.

My hypothesis is that the gesture of deconstruction, as a gesture neither critical nor perpetuating, and testifying to a relation to history and tradition that is found in neither Husserl nor Hegel nor Kant, is only possible within Christianity, even though it is not formulated intentionally from within it.[8] Indeed, it is only from within that which is in itself constituted by and setting out from the distension of an opening that there can be a sense to seek and to disassemble.

It is important, therefore, that we not take the assemblage of Christianity en bloc, to refute or confirm it, for that would be tantamount to placing ourselves outside or alongside it. That is the move that we philosophers make too often and too soon. It has long been taken for granted that we are no longer Christian, and that is why we keep between ourselves and Christianity a distance sufficient to allow us to *take it en masse*. When we do so, it appears as an autonomous mass in relation to which we can, it is true, take all sorts of attitudes, but concerning whose point of assemblage we will remain always ignorant. But at its point of assemblage, or, as Heidegger said, at the systasis of the system, there is perhaps something to be brought to light and let play as such, something Christianity may not as yet have freed. What might be the possibility, power, or exigency, as you will, brought into play by such a disassembling? That possibility would not—would no longer be—Christianity itself. It would no longer be the Western world itself, but rather that from which or on the basis of which the West and Christianity are possible. Something the West has up till now apprehended only in the ambivalence of the upsurge of Christianity.

The deconstruction of Christianity comes down to this: an operation of disassembling, focusing on the origin or the sense of deconstruction—a sense that does not belong to deconstruction, that makes it possible but does not belong to it, like an empty slot that makes the structure work (the question being to know how to fill the empty slot without overturning in the process the integrality of the integrity of the Christianity we are trying to disassemble).

In a sense, as I have been saying, Christianity is in itself essentially the movement of its own distension, because it represents the constituting of a subject in the process of opening and distending itself. Obviously, then, we must say that deconstruction, which is only possible by means of that distension, is itself Christian. It is Christian because Christianity is, originally, deconstructive, because it relates immediately to its own origin as to a slack [*jeu*], an interval, some play, an opening in the origin.

But, as we well know, in another sense Christianity is the exact opposite—denial, foreclosure of a deconstruction and of its own deconstruction—precisely because it puts in the place of the structure of origin, of any and all origin, something else: the proclamation of its end. *The structure of origin of Christianity is the proclamation of its end.* Such is the determinate form taken by the distension I have been discussing: Christianity resides essentially in the proclamation of its end. More precisely, Christianity resides in the end as proclamation, as something proclaimed, as

Evangel, as *euaggelion*, "good news." That message is the heart of Christianity.

The Christian message of proclamation is therefore something entirely different from prophecy in the vulgar (and not Jewish) sense of divination or prevision. The Christian annunciation of the end is not at all prevision, nor is it even, in a certain sense, the promise. Of course the promise is a Christian category, but for the moment, to be clear and lay things bare, I retain only the word *proclamation*. Christianity, then, is not proclamation as a predisposition in one way or another of the end; in it, the end itself is operative in the proclamation and as proclamation, because the end that is proclaimed is always an *infinite end*. This is what truly makes up Christianity, what constitutes, as the theologians say, the "kerygma" of Christianity, that is, the essence, the schema of what is proclaimed, the schema of the proclamation. What is Christianity? It is the Evangel. What is the Evangel? It is what is proclaimed, and it is not texts. What is proclaimed? Nothing. Marcel Gauchet was attentive, as Nietzsche had been, to the thinness of the four Gospels: almost nothing. We do not think enough about the fact that this almost nothing, this bit of writing, is the *Aufhebung* of all prior *biblia*—the fact that properly Christian writing (next to nothing) consists in tracing very quickly the word *proclamation*, in saying "that proclaims," and that someone lived his life in such a way that he proclaimed.

If Christianity is essentially kerygmatic or evangelical, the question is to try to concentrate our gaze on the heart of proclamation as such, on the living, evangelical heart of Christianity, in order to go beyond the point where Nietzsche left off. Nietzsche is still one of those who separate the wheat from the tares, those who separate an original, pure kernel from its subsequent development. In my opinion the question is rather one of grasping anew—as a pure nucleus, as an Evangelical nucleus—what truly constitutes the possibility of all the rest. That must lead us not to isolate, according to a move that is well known and that might be dubbed "a Rousseauism of Christianity," a good primitive Christianity, and then to proceed to lament its betrayal.

This said, let us take a further step. To enter the heart, the essential movement of kerygmatic or Evangelical Christianity, to enter its proclamatory structure—this also must be done without having recourse exclusively to the Gospels by taking a stand against their subsequent dogmatic development. On the contrary, it is in dogmatic development that we must recover the inspiration proper imparted to this dogma by the fundamental structure of the proclamation and opening of sense. In the Christian dogmatic edifice, we are dealing with a theological construction, that is, also and primarily with a *philosophical* construction and elaboration. I say "philosophical" not in the sense in which there would be a Christian philosophy situated alongside other philosophies, but in the sense in which the original structure of the Christian kerygma developed in a specific historical relation to a philosophical history. It is, therefore, in the disassembling of the philosophical constituents of Christian dogma or Christian theology that we must perceive the philosophemes of the proclamation. It is therein that the proclamation itself must be perceived, the kerygma itself as a manifold of philosophemes, or as becoming increasingly, in the course of our history and tradition, the manifold of philosophemes that from now on will configure the articulation of our thought.

Without insisting at length on this point, I will recall the philosophical constituents of Christian theology. It is well known that the heart of Christian theology is obviously Christology, that the heart of Christology is the doctrine of incarnation, and that the heart of the doctrine of incarnation is that of *homoousia*, consubstantiality, the identity or community of being and substance between the Father and the Son. This is what is completely unprecedented about Christianity. To set itself apart from the spectrum of philosophical ontology (*Ousia, homoiōsis*, etc.), the theologian will say that *homoousia* is just a word that is appropriately used in the service of an intention of faith that must not allow the sense of the notion to be reduced to a thought of essence or of substance, and that the community of the Father and the Son is of a different nature than the singular *homoousia* that means, philosophically, a community of essence or nature. It will suffice in turn to address the following question to the theologian: Of what other nature or essence is the community of the Father and the Son if it is not of essential essence or natural essence?

Even if we assume that the sense understood by faith, that is, the sense proclaimed, awaited, and expectantly tendered by faith, is infinite, the fact remains that it is in setting out from *ousia*, taken in a determined historical/philosophical context, that that infinite remove can be thought: Christianity can only posit and conceive of the infinite remove of *ousia* on the basis of that *ousia*. In other words, the *parousia* of the *homoousia*, far from representing a difference in nature between theology and philosophy, in fact represents the infinite opening of the sense of *ousia* thought of as presence, a *parousia* of itself. Taking this as our point of departure, we can link together the entire order of reasons of theological ontology, including the Heideggerian question of the ontic/ontological difference and of the sense of being, so long, that is, as the deconstructive move does not weaken the sense of this sense. This is to say that, setting out from *ousia*, one can proceed all the way to the end of the philosophical concatenation of the concepts of ontology and find everywhere at work—as a projection into the future of the possibility of these concepts—the opening itself, beyond the conceptual philosophical systematicity to which the theologian thought to set himself in opposition.

⌘

Now let us examine the Christian categories that I announced, while trying to grasp them on the basis of the methodological principles we have set up.

Let us consider, first of all, the category of faith, since, to what has just been said about *ousia*, the theologian (or, more precisely, the spiritual man, the true Christian) will answer that all this ignores the irreducible, singular dimension of faith and of the act of faith as a dimension that it is impossible to reduce to a discourse.

In a certain way I feel bound to begin the analysis by asking: Is there another category of faith than the Christian category? Not the *act* of faith each of the faithful can pronounce in his or her heart, which it is not my aim to examine here, but the *category* of faith (for that is what can become the object of the gesture of deconstruction). With utmost respect for the act of faith considered as an act acting within the intimacy of a subject, I cannot fail to consider that the Christian category of faith is above all *the category of an act*; that of an act of and within the sphere of intimacy. That is what must be examined, knowing that it is one thing to examine this category as that of an intimate act on the part of the subject, and that it would be quite another to go after that act as such, if it takes place and where it takes place, a place into which, obviously, my discourse cannot extend.

Is not the act of faith, qua act, that which announces itself par excellence, that is, that of which the act itself, that of which entelechy, is a proclamation and not a showing? What is faith? Faith consists in relating to God and to the name of God, to the extent that God and his love are not present, shown—to the extent that they are not present in the modality of monstration. But it is not in the domain of belief, because faith is not an adherence without proof. The greatest spiritual and theological analyses of the Christian faith show that faith is rather, if we insist on expressing it in terms of adherence, *the adhesion to itself of an aim without other*. I will say, in phenomenological terms, the adhesion to itself of an aim without a correlative object, or with no fulfillment of sense but that of the aim itself. One could perhaps say that faith is pure intentionality, or that it is the phenomenon of intentionality as a self-sufficient phenomenon, as a "saturated phenomenon," in Jean-Luc Marion's sense. I understand perfectly well that Marion, in speaking of "saturated phenomena," is not talking about a phenomenon like faith, but rather of phenomena that would offer themselves as faith, or that would entail faith; nevertheless, I leave open the question of whether faith might not be such a "saturated phenomenon," or even, perhaps, saturation itself.

Faith, in any case, is not adherence without proof or a leap beyond proof. It is an act by a person of faith, an act that, as such, is the attestation by an intimate consciousness to the fact that it exposes itself and allows itself to be exposed to the absence of attestation, of *parousia*. In *homoousia*, faith understands itself as exposed to the absence of *parousia* of the *homoousia*, without which it would not be faith. If Christian faith, then, is the category of an act of intimacy that misses itself, that escapes itself, then Christian faith is distinguished precisely and absolutely from all belief. It is a category sui generis, which is not, like belief, a lack of . . . , a dearth of . . . , not a state of waiting for . . . , but faithfulness in its own right, confidence, and openness to the possibility of what it is confidence in.

What I am saying here would be perfectly suitable to our modern definition of faithfulness in love. It is precisely that, for us—faithfulness in love, if we conceive of faithfulness as distinct from the simple observance of conjugal law or of a moral or ethical law outside the conjugal institution. This is even, perhaps, what we mean more profoundly by love, if love is primarily related to faithfulness, and if it is not that which overcomes its own failings but rather that which *entrusts itself to* what appears to it as insufficiency—entrusts itself to the beyond-itself in order to be what it needs to be, that is, to be faithfulness. That is why the true correlate of Christian faith is not an object but a word. Faith consists in entrusting oneself to the word of God. Here again, our amorous faith is entirely Christian, since, as faithfulness, it entrusts itself to the word of the other, to the word that says "I love you," or doesn't even say it. At the same time, the faith in act that the theologians call *fides qua creditur*, the "faith by which one believes," actualizes, as a profession of faith by the faithful one, faith as content, *fides quae creditur*, the faith that is believed, the sense of the word of God. In other words, the veritable act, the entelechy of the *fides quae creditur*, is the *fides qua creditur*: the act actualizes the sense.

At this point, two possibilities present themselves.

1. The moment of the act as such is dominant, and the sense merges into it. In that case, we may say that the sense of faith is so intimate, so

private, that it is inaccessible to the subject. The subject of faith is, in this case, the person who puts his or her faith entirely in the hands of God's grace, as attested by these words attributed to Joan of Arc, in response to the question "Do you think you are in grace?" "If I am not, may it be God's will to put me there, and if I am, may it be God's will to keep me there." Here, faith consists in the reception of the grace of faith.

2. On the contrary, the moment of the word and of spoken, communitarian sense is dominant. In this case, all division, all dissolution of the community is at the same time the division and dissolution of faith qua communitarian attestation, qua act shared by the community and dissolving along with it. Now, this dissolution of the faith with the community represents, perhaps, the "cross" of the history of Christianity, if the kerygma and grace are, in principle, for all humanity, or if the Gospel and grace are for everyone.

Considered in this twofold schema, faith always comes down to adherence to the infinity of sense, whether it be the infinity of sense dissolved in the attestation without attestation of intimacy, or the infinity of sense spreading outside all discernible community to the outer limits of humanity. From the point of view of the Christian community, to interpret the act of faith as a subjective and existential adherence is, consequently, completely erroneous. Yet it is true that faith is the being-in-act of a nonappropriable infinite sense and that it becomes progressively, as faithfulness, faithfulness to nothing, faithfulness to no one, *faithfulness to faithfulness* itself. We are becoming a culture of pure faithfulness: the faithful assured not only to be obliged, but to want to be faithful. Faithful to what? To sense, and thus faithful to no other thing than to the very gesture of faithfulness.[9]

Second category: sin. Sin, because we cannot conceive of Christianity without sin, because it is by sin that Christianity, in the most visible and external way, has dominated—some would say that it has subjugated, enslaved—whole areas of our history and culture. But let us remark, nevertheless, that if there is nothing incongruous about speaking of Christian faith, to speak of sin today seems rather old-fashioned, inasmuch as our Christianity is no longer a Christianity of sin so much as of love and hope. But that in itself is already a sign. What is a Christianity virtually without sin? It is probably no longer Christianity. But then how is it that Christianity can, from within, free itself, rid itself, of sin? I know full well that there have long been plenty of good Christians who have bemoaned the disappearance of sin, and that Bloy and Bernanos railed in unison against the elimination of sin, and of the devil along with it.[10] But just so, *that elimination is an accomplishment.*

For how is Christian sin characterized? Christian sin presents a difference from the misdeed analogous to the one between faith and belief. A misdeed is a transgression, a dereliction that leads to punishment and eventual atonement. Sin is not primarily a specific act. (The image of confession and of recitation of articles has completely deformed our perception of sin.) Sin is not primarily an act, it is a *condition*, and an original condition. It is only through original sin that we get the full schema of the divine plan: creation, sin, redemption. Outside this divine plan, neither God's love, nor the incarnation, nor *homoousia*, nor the history of mankind has sense. Sin is, therefore, above all an original condition, and an original condition of historicity, of development, because sin is a generative condition, setting in motion the history of salvation and salvation as history, it is not a specific act, much less a misdeed.

Sin being a condition, what counts above all in Christianity is man the sinner. The original condition is that man is a sinner, thus the sinner is more important than the sin itself; moreover, this is why that which is truly pardoned is the sinner. The sinner, once pardoned, is not, of course, wiped clean—one does not simply remove from her or him the stains of sin. The pardoned sinner is *regenerated* and reenters the history of salvation. The sinner is then less one who breaks the Law than one who deflects toward him or herself the sense that was oriented toward the other or toward God. That is how the word of the Serpent was interpreted in a Christian way: "You shall be as gods." This reversal of sense self-ward is precisely what causes *the emergence of self*, the oneself, the self qua related to itself, not distended and not open to the other. Such is not only the indication of the sinful condition, but the sinful condition itself. We would never be able to go through all the texts in which the Western tradition unceasingly shows that evil is egoity or egotism. It is the self relating to itself. Consequently, sin is, in a sense, closing, and saintliness, opening. Saintliness is not (and it is this that Christianity thinks of as an *Aufhebung* of the Old Law in the New Law) the observance of the Law, but the opening to what is addressed to faith, the opening to the proclamation, to the word of the other.

The truth of our sinful condition does not, finally, lead to the expiation of a misdeed but to a redemption; to the redemption of the person who has submitted to the slavery (a slave is redeemed) of temptation. We should examine the category of temptation at great length, and ask ourselves what it is, fundamentally. Temptation is essentially the *temptation of self*, it is the self as temptation, as tempter, as self-tempter. It is not in the least a question of the expiation of a misdeed, but of redemption or salvation, and salvation cannot come from the self itself, but from its opening. Salvation comes to the self as its opening, and as such it comes to it as the grace of its Creator. Now, what does God do through salvation? Through salvation, God remits to man the debt he incurred in sinning, a debt that is none other than the debt of the self itself. What man appropriated, for which he is in debt to God, is this self that he has turned in upon itself. It must be returned to God and not to itself. *Sin is an indebtedness of existence as such.*

In other words, while Heidegger tends to detach existential *Schuldigkeit* from the category of "transgression" or of "debt" (in the ontic sense of the term), I wonder, rather, whether that *Schuldigkeit* does not realize the essence of sin as the indebtedness of existence—"indebtedness of existence" meaning, at one and the same time, that existence itself is in debt, and that what it is in debt for is precisely for itself, for the self, for the ipseity of existence.

In conclusion, the living God is what maintains the assemblage of all other elements. God, who is neither represented nor representable, but living; the Son, "the invisible image of the invisible God," says Origen, is his very presence. The Son is the visibility, itself nonvisible, of the Invisible, not in the sense of a god who would appear, but in the sense of a proclamation of presence. It is *in that proclamation*, in that address to man, in that call, that vision is made. Now, what is thus addressed is the *person* itself: the life of the living God is properly auto-affection; it presents the person to itself in the infinite dimension of itself to itself. That pure proclamation is interlocution as infinite sense of the pure person or of pure life. The living God is therefore the one who exposes itself as life of the appropriation/dis-appropriation extending beyond itself. Thus everything brings us back again to opening as the structure of sense itself. It is *the Open as such*, the Open of the proclamation, of the project, of history and faith, that, by the living God, is revealed at the heart of Christianity.

If it is in fact opening, the Open as horizon of sense *and* as a rending of the horizon, that assembles/disassembles the Christian construction (which undoes the horizontality of sense and makes it pivot into a verticality: the present instant like an infinite breakthrough), let us say, to conclude very provisionally this ongoing project, that in that (de)construction the horizon as question, *the horizon* as a proper noun for the finitude that turns toward its own infinity, is lost, but *also* springs forth.

The Open (or "the free," as Hölderlin also called it) is essentially ambiguous. (It is the entire self-destructive or self-deconstructive ambiguity of Christianity.) In its absoluteness, it opens onto itself and opens *only* onto itself, infinitely. It is thus that Christianity *would be* nihilism and has not ceased engaging nihilism, the death of God. But the question is thus posed: What is an opening that would not sink into its own openness? What is an infinite sense that nonetheless makes sense, an empty truth that yet has the weight of truth? How can one take on afresh the task of delineating a *delimited* opening, a figure, therefore, that still would not be a figurative capturing of sense (that would not be God)?

It would be a matter of thinking the limit (that is the Greek sense of *horizō*: to limit, to restrict), the singular line that "fastens" an existence, but that fastens it according to the complex graph of an opening, not returning to itself ("self" being this very non-return), yet, again, according to the inscription of a sense that no religion, no belief, nor any knowledge—and of course, no servility, no asceticism—can saturate or assure, that no Church can claim to gather and bless. For that, there remains for us neither cult nor prayer, but the exercise—strict and severe, sober and yet joyous—of what is called thought.

Translated by Michael B. Smith

Dis-Enclosure

It is difficult to make the connection between a square of wild grass growing in between two railroad tracks and . . . God, or his absence, or his
substitutes. And yet that's where it starts, with a sort of revolt that is like a
childish, twisted drive. The refusal—how to put it—of "that" appearing
before the tribunal of efficacy and meaning. . . . The multiple, the multiple
would be, yes, the disconnected part, the possibility, always on the way, of
detachment, without which there would be no surprises, or even anything
to come. Along the lines of "dormancy," such a beautiful word that has to
do with seeds, we might try something like "comancy," which would
definitely designate not an expectation, a movement of expectation, but on
the contrary a kind of immobility of coming . . . a kind of permanent dis-
enclosure, an example of which would be precisely the square of wild grass
between the railroad tracks.

—Jean-Christophe Bailly

Space is not the name of a thing, but of that outside of things thanks to
which their distinctness is granted them. Things could not be distinct in
nature if they did not also occupy distinct places. If I am taking the tree's
place (and not just "replacing it"), there is neither tree nor human being,
but something else: a sylvan divinity, for example. When the distinction
of place is hindered or rejected, a crushing, a constriction, and a suffoca-
tion is produced. That is what we can see in those geological folds and
contractions out of which come igneous fusions, conglomerates, and pud-
ding-stones, which in turn produce new types of rock—new, distinct elements in a new distribution of places and a different spatial configuration.

We can also see it when an excess of plant growth strangles some and conjoins others, weaving them into a braid, like twin trunks that sometimes intertwine with one another to the point of strangulation, growing, neither one nor two, within that embrace.

Space is a placing, and in order to accomplish this, a distribution, therefore a spacing of places, before being a distance. The spacing can be minuscule as well as immense: that does not affect its nature. It consists in the thrust of separation thanks to which "that" is distinguished, and "that" distinguishes this from that. It is the time of that thrust. This time is not the flow of the successive above the already configured spaces of the permanent. On the contrary, it forms the pace of configuration itself according to its configuring urge.

Hence this paradox of time, which is to be simultaneously pure succession and pure permanence, according to the pulsation of one in the other. Thus, even when nothing new happens, it still happens that the distinction is maintained and things do not collapse into one another. The separation and distinction of all things is not a banal, de facto given. It forms, on the contrary, the gift, the giving of things itself. It is the permanent eclosure of the world. There cannot be one sole thing that does not have a separation between itself and something else. Therefore there cannot be fewer than two things. The one-sole is its immediate negation, and space-time constitutes the structure of that negation.

That is why the "conquest of space" cannot be considered in the same way as the discovery of preexistent places. One does not discover what was previously covered up, or at least one does not just discover but one opens up as well, separating and distinguishing. Space is not conquered without space conquering its conquerors as well.

Undoubtedly, the cosmic expanses both within and without our solar system existed before our rockets, probes, and satellites were launched. But at the same time—in the very time of those launchings—the "conquest" is a moment, a scansion of the general expansion. Man not only goes far from earth, penetrating what was once another world: he also separates, in this movement, the earth from itself, and he separates himself from himself in reduplicating from the inside (if it is an "inside") the dilation of the universe. Space spreads itself out through man, whom it in turn spreads out.

When the European discovered the "New World," he engaged in an expansion in which a new world was shaped and new distinctions settled into place. A new Indies separated off from the known Indies. In the space of a century (as they say) the face of the world was changed—continents, islands, and oceans. Today, in the space of less than half a century, the configuration of that world, whose space-time is becoming that of the transmission of satellite signals, has been transformed. In a sense it is the dissolution or a dissipation of the space of clear topographical distinctions, of the space of territories and boundaries, of domains and enclosures. The space of separations is yielding to the thrust of a spatiality that separates the separations from themselves, that seizes the general configuration, in order simultaneously to spread it out in a continuum and to contort it into an interlacing of networks. The *partes extra partes* is becoming, while retaining its exteriority, a *pars pro toto* at the same time as a *totum in partibus*.

Thus what happens is the following. For the first time, the expansion or the eclosure of the world becomes identical to what was considered to be its mere instrument. The caravels of Christopher Columbus seemed to be such instruments. The *vessels* had not yet revealed the profound nature according to which they are always at once tools but also agents and locations of expansion. In truth, America had already begun on the bridge, in the stays and the astrolabe of the *Santa Maria*. A spatial vessel manifests that nature more clearly. We can see that it is itself a distinct element opening up the space around it. It is itself a world in the process of eclosing in the world, and even more in the process, if I may say so, of eclosing the world within it and around it.

Another life, another respiration, another weight, and another humanity is in the process of emerging. And consequently, what distinguishes itself today, what is in the process of spatializing itself, presents itself as spatialization itself. Faced with the "Indian" of the discovered Caribbean, we wondered: Is it another man? Is it other than man? But today we ask these questions about the discoverer of space. The one we catch a glimpse of on board our space ships—we understand that he is a variant of the same, of ourselves. In a sense, it is a return of the question: Is he another exemplar of the same, or an other than the same? But at the same time it is another question: Up to what point can the same, distinguishing itself from the same, take its sameness with it?

The eclosure of the world must be thought in its radicalness: no longer an eclosure against the background of a given world, or even against that of a given creator, but the eclosure of eclosure itself and the spacing of space itself. (In a sense, then, the word *radicalness* is inappropriate: it is not a question of roots, but of wide-openness.) A new departure for creation: *nothing*, which moves over to make a place or give occasion to *something*. Locations [*les lieux*] are delocalized and put to flight by a spacing that precedes them and only later will give rise [*donnera lieu*] to new places [*lieux nouveaux*]. Neither places, nor heavens, nor gods: for the moment it is a general dis-enclosing, more so than a burgeoning. Dis-enclosure: dismantling and disassembling of enclosed bowers, enclosures, fences. Deconstruction of property—that of man and that of the world.

Dis-enclosure confers upon eclosure a character that is close to explosion, and spacing confines it to conflagration. Thus, for the ancient Stoics, the world was thought to follow the successive cycles of a "great year" that led from sudden upsurge to implosion, from burning to extinction, and from dilation to retraction and reabsorption before the new eclosure.

Today, the conquest of space is replaying the scenario of that mythology at an accelerated pace. Probes and telescopes accompany the expansion of the universe as far as to the nonlocalizable, where stars have been dead for immemorial light-years. The end of worlds comes back to us in the launching of our own—the end, or the absolute mystery of spacing itself, according to which there is a "world," from that dis-enclosure that is preceded by no enclosure of being, but by which non-being is disclosed. Thus there is in the world something other than a unique point without dimensions, plunged deep into its own nullity.

The separation between bodies, the stellar remoteness, and the galactic distances send out toward the ever-receding cosmic extremities this point itself, this dust, this seed and this hole we have discovered ourselves to be, as well as this silence, which we call the *big bang*, whose echo haunts our voice.

Though the name *Ariadne* seems to have been given to the European space launcher out of a simple personal inclination, we cannot refrain from looking into the mythic resources. Ariadne creates the link between the inner, folded back, implosive space of the labyrinth and the open space of the sky, whose Corona Borealis she wears. In certain versions of the story, the light from this diadem of stars replaces the thread that was given to Theseus. It is she who makes possible the escape from the sinister enclosure and the return voyage on the vessel bucking the bitter waves full sail toward the open sea.

But in reopening space, Theseus also rekindles the ambivalence inherent in separation and distinction. He abandons Ariadne on an island, brief punctual expanse—less place than midpoint of a churning liquid labyrinth. In the infinitely repeated indecision of the myth, Ariadne pines away, exposed to both solitary languor and the unanticipated arrival of Dionysus.

Translated by Michael B. Smith

Appendix

Far from Substance
Whither and to What Point?
(Essay on the Ontological Kenosis of Thought since Kant)

GÉRARD GRANEL

[535] Originally, "kenosis" is the movement by which God empties himself of his divinity in the mystery of the Incarnation. Assigned to an ontological index that is no longer theological, the term indicates first the direction—we should, no doubt, better say the destiny—of modern thought in Kant and in Husserl, and second the orientation of Heidegger's questioning. Finally, perhaps we shall ourselves be fortunate enough to venture alone into a "void of being," where even Heidegger could not allow himself to be carried. But one should not promise too much . . .

This entire movement is measured, as our title indicates, as a greater or lesser distancing from Substance. What I mean by "Substance" (with a capital *S*) can in no way be reduced to the first category of Relation in Kant's table of the multiple *ptōses* of being.[1] It is a matter of the meaning of Being itself, as it obtrudes on [*s'impose*] modern metaphysics, even before metaphysics had entered into its critical period (the examples of Descartes and Spinoza suffice to illustrate this), and thereafter as it continued to reign surreptitiously [*régner en sous-main*], despite its transcendental emptying out (we will point this out, taking up various examples of what I once called the ontological equivocation of Kantian thought), and finally, as it foils all attempts at methodological radicality in Husserlian phenomenology through the face-to-face of an omni-positing subject (which is nevertheless purely and simply posited) and an ultra-constructed[2] phenomenality, which is nevertheless tributary to an impressive matter.

Nevertheless, when it is a question of determining the meaning of Being in itself and not simply of designating it by invoking historical examples, we find ourselves before the worst of difficulties: that contained in the hermeneutics of triviality. "That which stands beneath"—literally the meaning of the term *sub-stance*—is, in effect, nothing other than the thetic profanation of the most banal of evidences, that of the presence of the real. That upon which I open my shutters each morning, that in which I attend to the affairs of life, that in which I fall asleep without concerning myself with what holds Hypnos and Thanatos together as twin siblings, and, despite all that, that *of which* I am never aware.

Save perhaps in the mode of a sort of halting [*mise en arrêt*], a tiny and silent recoil before the nothing of that primitive All—let us say, a sentiment of the [536] World, or of existing (this is not an alternative, or even a difference). It is always a detail, and nothing but a detail in the immense population of things, that provokes this infinitesimal suspension: the cry of a harrier streaking the gray sky; a sudden chill that sends me back inside my skin; on another day a warm wind caressing my hair. And again. A red sun that sinks vertically down the far side of things; the tracery of branches, not to be untangled, in that great tree, whose shadow repeats it on a white wall, in an exact projection whose workings nothing gives away, and, then, on an evening in an earth of vanishing fields, an exalted color, as though it had just been laid down.

One will probably say that all this concerns the poetry of the World, and that philosophy is not poetry. For my part, I would say that there reigns here, in what writing is pointing toward, nothing less than a logic of phenomenality, a fabric of unsuspected a prioris that readily put to shame the formula we used earlier ("the presence of the real"), just as much as the one metaphysics utilizes ("Substance"). In effect, the evidence of presence carries that of representation, from which the metaphysics of Substance arises, *but also* the philosophies of the phenomenon, the Kantian and the Husserlian, despite their efforts at questioning, describing, and systematizing "far away from substance."

The word says it itself: *prae-ens*, *pre(s)ent* is that which "is there before"—and before what if not me? And this "me" is, consequently, already there, as absolute reference of the real that is present. But the inverse is likewise inevitable: a "real" is already necessary in order that a me [*un moi*] take place, present to itself among the things present. There is, here, a sort of bad schism or cleft [*sorte de mauvaise schize*], an original denial of the original affirmation. In this way, the beginning begins only by beginning anew, or again: presence presents itself only representatively.

If we consider the heaviness of all this language, we could almost cry that "it's well done." The poet—him again—is even capable of naming *that which* thus avenges itself on philosophical impatience: the most terrible Nemesis, the reserve [*pudeur*] of the World.

For it ultimately *disappears* the moment I distribute it into a matter and a form, parts and a whole, things and qualities, substances and actions—to speak successively like the transcendental aesthetic, the analytic of the concepts of quantity, that of the concepts of quality, and that of the concepts of relation. Let us attempt to follow for a moment the course of this disappearance, beginning with space and time. These are, as we know, the two a priori forms. Their "exposition," as Kant says, reveals a thinking of form that exceeds—and this is the only time we find this in the entire *Critique of Pure Reason*—or rather breaks up, expressly refuses, the validity of the first couple we named, that of matter and form. In such a couple, in effect, the evidence of matter always precedes that of form, which, short of being the form of nothing, must be conceived as the spatial arrangement (that is to say, here, *in* space) of a [537] multiplicity of given parts. But we will never think space itself—or spatiality as such—if we draw its various evidences from the intra-spatial. The ontological presupposition of a present reality, given first to sensibility, that is, as a diversity of sensations, would oblige us to conceive all form as an arrangement of sensations in space. Effected how, brought about in what way [*opera comment*]? No sensation can come out of its absolute closure to initiate the rapport of sensations among themselves. In a word, the spatial of the perceived is formal, and no form is the affair of a content [*nulle forme n'est l'aventure d'un contenu*].

What we have just rediscovered, with the tediousness of an apprentice, is what the Kantian mastery asserts from the outset: "The representation of space cannot be derived from the experience of relations between external phenomena" / "Space is not . . . a universal concept for the relations of things in general."[3] The *Critique* will thus have the audacity to declare "a priori" the spatial character of the experience [*l'épreuve]* we have of the World, and to consider that the "manifold" of this spatiality "rests . . . on limitations."[4] That this concept of limitation is frontally opposed to that of the "part," in other words, of "matter," and that, in consequence, the notion of "form" utilized to qualify space itself ("a priori form of sensibility") would thus become totally enigmatic—this is what Kant seems almost to want to smooth over by merely "exposing" this novelty ("transcendental exposition of space and time") in opposition to Leibniz's conceptuality, as though he feared having to expose himself, the thinker, to a novelty for which "words are lacking us."[5]

How are we to say, in effect (we hardly dare employ the term "describe" here, lacking any model at all that might offer itself to a painting), what he calls the *universum qua universum*, to which we are giving, for our part, its banal name, its true name: the World? Yet we must, notwithstanding, since the "a priori forms" that are space and time are forms of the World. Yet the World has no form, being nothing that would be given; it is the *formality of the gift* itself, which is something entirely different. And to think this difference, we must, in all necessity, distance ourselves from the register of reality (in the proper sense of being the *res* of a *res* ["thing"]). It will be necessary, then, to think the Whole (the World is, in effect, the Whole), while resisting the attraction of that so metaphysical *omnitudo realitatis*. We shall also have to think sensibility before and against the evidence of "sensations," in order to substitute something like an overflowing, a spillover of limitations. We can see, at this latter turn, that a certain strangeness takes hold of language, or seeks its language. Let us attempt, then, to find a language for it. A cartography of the void.

a. The All [*Le Tout*]. And yet no: already, we should say "all" and not "the" All. "Everything is sunlit this morning"; thus will we express, for example, the way in which the gift gives itself under the aspect of the weather and the atmosphere [*le temps qu'il fait*], that unique gift of [538] appearing in its integrality. A pure "how" that preserves its own unreality by avoiding—one might say "appropriately"—naming itself on the basis of what would already be "the things." For, if "everything [*tout*] is . . ."—this or that, sunlit, or again misty and gray, etc.—indeed signifies the unity of a dispensation, if it signifies the World as the pure spending of "all things," it remains that "all things" here means—likewise appropriately—neither "each thing" (none have yet *emerged* from the gift, no more than a ray of light separates itself from the sparkling of the sea), nor consequently "all *the* things."

It comes down to finding that antecedence or priority, prudently buried by Kant in the Latin *a priori*, does not mean "before." And that delivers it also from "at the same time" and "afterward." The world-space means [*veut dire*, literally "wants to say"] (and Kant silences it, rather) that any spatial given is open (to itself and for me), not *in* but *according to* an Opening that is nowhere itself open, or better: without any "itself." Space "itself" means nothing.

And yet there is indeed, if not "the All," then at least the all-form [*forme-tout*]. If we need not think this as the omni-encompassing Circle, then we must think it withal (i.e., find it, emerging from beneath the images of words, schemas, movements of meaning that fit it). We must replace, for example, "circle" by "ring," "compass," or "border" ["*cerne*"].[6] What Kant so badly names "sensibility" signifies, in effect, that we invariably dis-cern phenomena—that is to say, we have to do with them on the basis of the "Border" or "Cerne." Of this, no one has any doubts. Do we ever worry about knowing whether, perchance, the little we do see—a few houses, a swath of sky, streets, or rather segments of streets—would not stop at the edge of some great nothing; at the edge of the grand canyon of Nothingness? One might say that, even if we are assured about our good old Earth, whose rotund existence is doubtless complete, by contrast the astronomic distances that separate the heavenly bodies from our galaxy, and then the galaxies themselves (which, moreover, are speeding away from each other), are sufficient to awaken in us the terror of infinity. In-finity. Never, never, never would there come about the moment of a World. "What is man in the Infinite?" etc. Yet Pascal's text is but the rhetoric of an apologetic desire, without the slightest phenomenological foundation. When I raise my eyes toward the night sky, I no doubt have the sentiment that the stars are "far off," but even there it is not a matter of great numbers, and nothing comes to tear apart the familiar proximity of the living room [*la proximité familière du séjour*]. I marvel confusedly about that, as Kant said without saying it: "The starry sky *over my head*"—the precise correspondent, or perhaps simply the other side, of the "moral law *in me*." As though the universality of the cosmos and that of the maxim, under the apparent naïveté of a reference to man, recall that the humanity of this man is *deferred* to the World [*déférée au Monde*]. *There* we live; *there* we are, and that is why we have a gaze both universal and open upon the unreal "how" of all that is real.

A situation that is confirmed if, from the World, we now pass to things.

[539] b. "Things"—an expression we need use no more than "the All." In effect, Heidegger is right to remind us that that with which we have to do "proximally and for the most part" is not "things" (like so many sorts of units-of-reality objectively given, as the sciences find them ready and set "in nature") but *Zeuge* ["instruments, tools"] (or if you will, *pragmata*), anchoring units of "care": in no way that "object" that one can *also* call a chair, but from the outset that element-of-furniture that the chair is; in no way the thermal radiation of a celestial body, but the maternal warmth of *the* Sun [la *Soleil*] (die *Sonne*).[7]

Nevertheless, there exists for "things" a primitive mode of being that is different from the one described by the existential analytic; that is, the perceptual mode in which they are, as we say, "given." Or let us say, "that with which" (a deliberately indeterminate expression) the painter finds himself confronted. There too it is not a matter of objects. On the other side of my street stands a university building, a long crescent shape with four floors, of which I see a section. If I were to paint it, its university function would be the first determination to vanish, as it is nothing that *could* appear; but the "building" (the totality in its architectural construction) is also nothing for the eye. One will reply, "There remains but the section, then," to show that one has understood. But one will really have understood nothing! For even if, to the knowledge of the one considering it, the "something seen" is indeed the section or the side of a building, this "something" is no such thing for any kind of *seeing*. What the seeing gives us is, sooner (literally, "sooner," "earlier") a set of differences in the whites and the grays, with kinds of darker recesses, together rhythmically broken up by bars of red brick and underscored by a long trail of vegetative green. The whole thing ends at the top with geometric lines that are longer than they are high and that form a kind of notching that thrusts forward. And when I write "the whole things ends," it is not through the knowledge of the existence of a building that, despite our will to employ an *epochē*,[8] governs the description here, it is the *visual* difference between the totality, made up of tones and forms, as we have just said, *and* that which effectively forms another *part* of the given, another height (or rather, an elevation), where an *other* white and an *other* gray freely spread out—those of the vast and the luminous (*the* vast and *the* luminous, but of no thing, or what we call "the sky").

Thus, whence comes, or, if you prefer, how do we mark out the difference of belonging or adherence of what we must above all not call "the visual contents" but rather (sooner, and very awkwardly, we realize) qualities and forms? Nothing in what we have said allows us to set this question aside. *What* are we aiming at when we designate, as a perceptual "whole," something that owes nothing to the pragmatic notion of a "building" or to a transcendent concept of an "object" but that unfailingly distinguishes itself from the other "wholes" represented by the trees around it, the cars that line the street curbs, etc.? For, ultimately, the difference between this whole and the sky, which we pointed out, was the easiest to grasp. The sky, precisely, never presents itself as a "thing," [540] in whose regard forms and qualities would stand in some relationship of belonging. The sky is the paradigmatic non-thing. And, in this way, it is emblematic of the World *as such*.

Let us remain there for a moment; we rediscover "things" afterward (that is, unless they are definitively not to be found), for we are here at the very birth of the divine, as the Latin language thinks it. *Dies* means the day, more precisely, the light of the day, the Cerne or ring, compass, border of which we spoke as the condition of perceptual dis-cernment and which, for that reason, is in itself nothing that one might discern: *non cerniture dies*, as Pliny put it aptly. According to the poet Hyginus, a friend of Ovid, Dies, daughter of Chaos, is the mother of the Sky and the Earth. Moreover, it is true that the light of day, gradually erupting out of nocturnal chaos, "engenders" the first duality of the visible, according to which it "divides itself" [*se "partage"*] into the non-thing of the Sky and an Earth-of-things. The open region and the clearing of beings, as Heidegger says in *The Origin of the Work of Art*. In truth, it is the whole or totality of this division that is rightly original, and thus divine. Nevertheless, from the beginning (the "beginning" of the Latin saying), the divine is concentrated, as it were, in the Sky: *dius* or *divus* means simultaneously the light of day, the sky, and the divine. *Sub divo*: in plain day, under the sky. It goes, effectively, without saying that this Opening, in which Light itself dwells, this evidence of evidences—albeit inaccessible and ungraspable for not being, in any way, a thing—is *manifestly* of a divine order.

But again, we should not forget that Light would not be without *that which* it manifests in its turn. This is a manifold that up to now we have called, provisionally, "things," but whose mode of being we must now acknowledge as remaining multiple and generally unquestioned throughout the Tradition. The unity of appearing, from which invariably arises the dispensation of the sensible, has but rarely the style of what is "thing-like" ["*chosique*"]: for example, a tree that gleams as the daylight breaks over it confirms under our eyes the unity of a profusion in which it is obvious that the light does not pile, one upon the other, some "thing" that would be the trunk, other "things" that would be the branches, and then the twigs, all the way to a moving, shimmering multiplicity of those little-leafy-things. The tree is a unity of appearing of a non-thinglike type. There are many others, totally different from vegetal profusion: the spreading unity of the slope of a hill, for example, or, again, the two types of passing-unity, that of a passing-that-remains (the river) or that in which the passing itself passes (the flight of a bird). Profusion, spreading, passage—these are styles, veritable formalities; succinctly, we will venture this term, idealities of the visible, which we recognize without even having to think about them, as is always the case with the a priori of experience.

The question is: Why has no philosophy managed to state these a priori? Why has no philosophy so much as suspected them? Is it not the very task of philosophical discourse first to detect, then to express these "idealities," as we have called them? Or again, would there be "fine" idealities; idealities so fine that the entire Tradition would simply have missed them? At first we can hardly believe this, it is so evident that, [541] in its unfolding, what gives the Tradition its scansion is a progressive refinement of knowledge concerning *the conditions of discovery* [décèlement] of the ideal [*idéel*]. One could show that this is already the meaning of the Aristotelian critique of the Platonic inception. It is more clearly still the meaning of Kantian critique and Husserlian radicalism—to remain with the moderns here. In his attempt to distance himself from the prominence of Substance, Kant seeks out the meaning of Being in what he calls "the originally synthetic unity of experience," from which flows a "schematic" sense of the sum of categorial idealities. Husserl attempts, in his turn, to endow thinking with an unshakeable fidelity to phenomena. He does this by reducing the "object" (which is to say, I repeat, the very meaning of Being for all the moderns) to its "how" (*das Objekt*-im-wie ["*the object* in the, or its, how"]), putatively given absolutely, once every thesis about its existence and every representative construction have been "suspended" (the *Épochè*). In both cases, the fruits of these efforts will be numerous. I would even say that they are more numerous—above all, they have a stranger novelty—in Kant than in Husserl. This is so because, in the first place, while the concept states the a priori of experience only when reduced to a schema, that schema is, itself, without images—in other words, unrepresentable. One finds at least two signs for this in the *Critique of Pure Reason*: (1) the fact that the faculty of "categorizing" the phenomenon of experience properly belongs (in each block of three "pure concepts of the understanding)" not to such and such concept taken separately but to each one of them *in* the original unity of the three. Thus, for example, there is only unity insofar as it exists already in a plurality, which is therefore not several times one; just as there is plurality only as anticipated in a totality, which is therefore not the sum of a certain number of parts. The categorial triad called "quantity" is effectively not a thinking of numbers: it is a thinking of the numerous. Failing this, it would not escape the Antinomies. And again, we must clearly understand that being-numerous, precisely in its difference from number, poses a challenge to description. Try it and you will see! (2) The "unrepresentability" of the transcendental schematism of phenomenal beings is again avowed (denied and avowed) by the expression Kant uses to name the originally synthetic unity of experience: he calls this "Something = *X*." The use of the mathematical sign for the unknown is in no way haphazard. For what could this "Object in general" (the other name of the synthetic unity) really be (according to what *mode* of being), if it must be neither an object empirically given (which would effectively be the gift itself of the empirical) nor the noumenal correlate of the concept of an object taken in a merely logical generality? We are cast here, without consideration, into a void of signification.

The same goes for the correlate of the transcendental object, the other pole of the synthesis. Kant calls this the "I think," in a purely Cartesian fashion. To be sure, he "replaces" it in a certain way with something like the unity of a belonging by accompaniment: "The 'I think' must accompany all my representations, etc." And in a sense it is true that the Cogito here loses all substantiality; [542] which is to say that it ceases being the modern name for the soul, under pain of paralogism, designating merely the logical necessity of a unity of experience. Nevertheless, because this "logicity" is not only formal but also transcendental (i.e., ontological), it also names the effectivity of a void, whose existence we may conclude (by way of the deduction) but which we are incapable of *stating* for all that. I = X.

No doubt, Husserlian phenomenology is in the same situation. It may well combat—more systematically than Kant did—the "psychologism" that burdens every "naïve" noetics. Yet this praiseworthy effort cannot keep it from falling back, with each argument, into a substantializing regime of discourse presumed to be descriptive. I have shown this clearly enough elsewhere in regard to color, for example, or in light of the phenomenological doctrine of profiles [*esquisses*], or the consciousness of time. I will therefore not return to that. My purpose, here, is—alas!—more ambitious than all the critiques. It is to seek the very root of this "stubbornness" by which Substance holds us in its bonds even when we think we have undone them, or at least loosened them. The response I will venture consists in saying that what escapes us could be called *the Ungraspability of Being.*. By this expression I mean no sublime mystery, analogous to the Unknowability of God. I mean, instead, the withdrawal of the "how" that occurs in every phenomenal field—at once its finesse, its total novelty, and its unproducibility of Being, thus understood. And, since we are on the "subject," it will serve as the example whereby I attempt to follow this withdrawal, always remaining within the field of perceptual experience.

If there is something certain here, it is that perceptual experience is *my* experience. It is, we could even say, the experience-of-me [*l'expérience-de-moi*]. To suppose that someone else could look through my eyes is absolute nonsense—not because my eyes "belong to me," but because the gaze is not made "by" the eyes. The gaze is given to me on the basis of the very thing I am looking at, as also are my eyes, and even "me." Decidedly. But it is precisely here that our difficulties begin. What does it mean that seeing [*le voir*], "my" seeing, could be "given to me on the basis of the very thing" of which it is a view? There is no more, on my part, a movement of appropriation of the real than there occurs, on the side of the real, some movement of reference to me. What then? Courage! We must state the strange, or simply remain blocked here.

A sort of hollow always gathers up the seen [*recueille toujours le vu*], like some mere part of the visible, though this frontier has nothing real about it: it undoes and redoes itself with the first movement of the head, with the slightest change of angle. It signifies precisely that "to see"—whether from the side of the one *who* sees or from that of *what* is seen—is never an adventure of (or in) the real. The Open is always a "Measure of Gathering" ["*Mesure-de-Recueil*"], whereby I come to myself as the meadow turns green, or rather with it, upon it—co-participating in the space of emergence or eclosure. A "Measure of Gathering" is the exact meaning of the Greek *logos*. There is no objective quantity in this "measure"; on the contrary, it delivers perceiving from the whole avalanche of things.

What I just named descriptively (literally? I hope not) "a sort of hollow" is what Heidegger thematized as the [543] "there" (*le "Da-"*) of Dasein. The mode of being of what I call "me" is in effect a "being-there," not in the sense of in the middle of things, but rather there where they are themselves "a site" ["*lieu*"]. This is to say, there where appearing finds a measure. Perceptual unfolding always contains not only the difference between a "given" and its "horizon" (Husserl), but a sort of centering—whose difficulty is to understand that it neither supposes nor posits any "core real" [*réel central*], but rather the necessity of a form, which itself is (not) a form but a formality of appearing. In this hollow, in this "there," this "centering," "I" am. I am there in a strictly Mallarmean mode: "The one absent from every bouquet."[9]

If you have had the patience to follow me up to this point, perhaps you will be willing to pass to the final stage. It involves working through the phenomenon of the body. An escape route from the radical critique of subjectivity could be found by appealing to the robust evidence of "my body," in order to account for this marking of experience that I call "me." We must demonstrate that "me," who has no soul, has no body, either. No body for me, in any case; nor in the eyes of others, so long as they do not lay on me [*ne posent pas sur moi*] a secondary gaze, objectifying and reflective—the clinical gaze, for example. We say, "I am ill," not "my body is ill." We say, "My God, he is big!" and not "Look how big his body is!" Above all, seeing ignores everything concerning my eyes, just as much as the meaning of your words transcends their acoustics. Obviously, I do not mean to argue that we are pure spirit. Rather, it is a matter of recognizing that we are not incarnate spirit, either. My body is for me neither a point of departure nor a point of arrival, neither a means nor an obstacle. It is, rather, totally out of the picture, even when a part of it enters into the image (as when I remove a thorn from my foot, for example).

It is because he failed to notice this irrelevance of the body for the phenomenon of perception grasped in its essence that Merleau-Ponty— with his praiseworthy goal of avoiding, there as elsewhere, every objectification—invented a sort of doublet for the body, which he called either "the body proper" or "the flesh." In a phenomenology of perception, this amounts to wasted effort. Effectively, my body then becomes a "body proper" only in the kinesthetic experience of muscular effort, for example, or in the "passive syntheses" of suffering. Yet not only am I violently distracted, at that time, from the perceived world, which falls into the abstraction of an "external world," it is also not a matter of restricting perception to that of my own body. Efforts and pains: these are *felt*, they are not *perceived*.

What, then, can we say about the stubborn question, which remains inevitable despite all our disinclination, of what we cannot avoid calling "the role of the body in perceptual experience"? This much, no doubt: facing the screen where I inscribe my perplexities, facing the wall and the opening of the window, "my body" ("me"—or better, "the site of me") is a sort of black rectangle in the midst of a painting, which functions like a dispatcher of regions: there is the region of "what-is-in-front-of-me," [544] precisely, clearly offered. On its edges, the double regions of the right and the left escape from the front toward the back, in such a way that only the beginnings of this profiling still participate in the "properly perceived" (but this, in an unfocused fashion), while the "rest" loses itself very quickly in the third region: that of what is "behind me," that is, perceptively nonperceived. It is clear that the body does nothing, undergoes nothing. In a word, in no sense does the body point to itself in this ever-recommencing, spatial regionalization of the perceptive (the perceived / the perceivable), of which the body is nonetheless the principle and blind spot. The body is the site of diversification of the a priori of the visible. It is the pure ontological site.

Does that mean that it is the materialist truth of the certainty of "consciousness"? It is not this, either, since no "corporeal *matter*" enters into the spatial regionalization that we have just described: the latter is *formal*. I believe that, ultimately, we must stop at this result (at least for the time being, but perhaps also forever); it is altogether surprising, I admit, that the very thing that constitutes the purest field of thought is, as it were, *laid* upon [posé *sur*]our body. Wanting to know more about this would be like wanting to enter into the creative act of God. What then!—might we say, on the contrary, that the invention of a divine creation is only a flight, on our part, from all that is terrible in the pure and simple finitude of Being itself?

Notes

Translators' Foreword

1. See Martin Heidegger, *Being and Time*, trans John Macquarrie and Edward Robinson (New York: Harper & Row, 1962), 105n1.

Opening

1. See Friedrich Hölderlin, *Der Gang aufs Land*, adapted from Philippe Jaccottet's translation, in Hölderlin, *Œuvres* (Paris: Gallimard, 1967), 802; trans. Michael Hamburger as "The Path by Land," in Hölderlin, *Poems and Fragments*, 4th bilingual ed. (London: Anvil Press, 2004).

2. The role Christianity played in this story must be examined elsewhere.

3. Remarkably enough, this expression "theologico-political" is almost always used erroneously. One intends to denote a collusion between the theological and the political ("the alliance of the sword and the *aspergillum*"), which could well be the sense of that double epithet. The "political theology" of Carl Schmitt designates nothing like this, however, but rather the "secularization" of the theological. As for Spinoza's famous title, it refers to what is for him the necessary disjunction of the two powers. We would do much better to say that our politics is precisely without theology, which simultaneously defines it and perhaps also points toward its core problem. We should understand that the problems of permanent poverty and exploitation, of justice and equality, cannot fail to open, in and of themselves, onto the question of "transcendence"—to give it this name rather dramatically—where politics [political activity; *la politique*] is in fact summoned to state whether it is capable of facing it, or whether politics transfers it—and how—to its outer limit, to a margin whose possibility we could, *politically*, arrange and cultivate. All the rest is . . . political literature. We might well

say the same of art. It is not an accident that today art often finds no other legitimation for itself than a "political" or an "economic" one. Now there can be only one legitimation for art, which is the sensuous attestation to and inscription of the overflowing of sense.

4. As Jean Baubérot [French historian of secularization] notes in his *Laïcité 1905–2005: Entre passion et raison* (Paris: Seuil, 2004).

5. Ludwig Wittgenstein, *Tractatus logico-philosophicus* (New York: Routledge, 2001), 6.41: "Der Sinn der Welt muss ausserhalb ihrer liegen [The sense of the world must lie outside it]."

6. A seventeenth-century English version of *discloister* (borrowed from the Latin adjective *disclusionem*) was *disclusion*, defined as "emission," as in light (*OED*, 2d ed., 1999)—Trans.

7. Generally, the closure of metaphysics was claimed by Heidegger, writing after Nietzsche. There, "closure" denoted bringing metaphysics to an end by recapitulating its historical strategies. Nancy is playing on a subjective and objective genitive. He means the closure of metaphysics, in Heidegger's sense, and the enclosure that metaphysics created around itself in modern philosophy—Trans.

8. Claude Lévi-Strauss, *Tristes Tropiques* (Paris: Plon, 1955), 448; trans. John Weightmann and Doreen Weightmann as *Tristes Tropiques* (New York: Penguin Books, 1992).

9. The French text reads "ou la déclosion de son ethnocentrisme," which has two different meanings: "or the dis-enclosure of its ethnocentrism" and "or the disclosure of its ethnocentrism"—Trans.

10. No more than it is a question of envisioning, for the time being, the whole [*ensemble*] formed by the three monotheisms in this history: Christianity here denotes both itself and the core of this triplicity, whose components will have to be untangled later on.

11. *Non-indéconstructible* is a litote: the dual negation argues that the "unconditional" posited in Christian alienation is deconstructible—Trans.

12. This thesis, which should be distinguished from that of an "Indeconstructible [*Indéconstructible*]" in Derrida, will have to be more firmly established later on. If there is such a thing, the "indeconstructible," to speak like Derrida, can have no other form that that of the active infinite [*l'infini actuel*]: thus, the act [*l'acte*], the actual and active presence of the *nothing* qua thing (*res*) of the opening itself. Here and now, death, the truth, birth, the world, the thing, and the outside.

13. Saint Anselm, *Proslogion, with the Replies of Gaunilo and Anselm*, trans. Thomas Williams (Indianapolis, Ind.: Hackett, 2001), chap. 15.

14. The "rapport vide de croyance" denotes simultaneously the contentless relation that is belief in "God" and the relation devoid of belief to what one calls "God"—Trans.

15. This essay was written shortly before Jacques Derrida's death. The discussion that I hoped to pursue with him on this theme, as on the ensemble of themes of a "deconstruction" or a *dis-enclosure* of Christianity (or, indeed, of something

else again, further back behind or before "Christianity" itself) will therefore not take place. I would simply like to say that Derrida was highly sensitive to the arguments in the texts published here under the titles "The Judeo-Christian" and "Of a Divine *Wink*," both of which were addressed to him. I have no doubt that Derrida would nonetheless have persisted in resisting me, as he resisted the themes of "fraternity" and "generosity"—to his mind they were too Christian. Nevertheless, the question cannot be limited to this opposition between us, for the stakes go well beyond those debates, and I believe he knew that, albeit despite himself. It is such a knowledge—if it is a knowledge at all—that we approach here: a knowledge of a very simple, even elementary, disposition toward the "outside the world" ["*hors du monde*"] in the very midst of the world, a disposition toward a transcendence *of* immanence.

In his recent *Traité d'athéologie* (Paris: Grasset, 2005), Michel Onfray uses the expressions "deconstruction of monotheism" and "deconstruction of Christianity," committing a strange misinterpretation of the well-established philosophical meaning of "deconstruction," which he confuses with "demolition," in much the same way that he uses "atheology," misinterpreting Bataille, who was the creator and sole user of the word. These mistranslations or misinterpretations [*contresens*] no doubt result from a certain muddleheadedness, but they give rise to unfortunate confusion. The first text I published under the title "The Deconstruction of Christianity" appeared in 1998. Since then, the title, or expression, has been cited several times, notably in some texts by Jacques Derrida and myself. All these occurrences seem to have escaped Michel Onfray.

16. *Der Wink*, in German, denotes a hint, nod, beckoning, or suggestion —Trans.

17. I offer my thanks to the editors of the journals and volumes who made possible the initial publication of these essays.

Atheism and Monotheism

NOTE: This essay was written for the Italian review *L'espressione* (Naples: Cronopio, 2005) and for Santiago Zabala, ed., *Weakening Philosophy: Festschrift in Honour of Professor Gianni Vattimo* (Montreal: McGill-Queen's University Press, 2006). In a modified version, it was given as a lecture at the opening of the colloquium entitled Heidegger, le danger et la promesse, organized in Strasbourg in November 2004 by the Parlement des Philosophes.

1. Nancy will be playing throughout this essay with the notions of "principle," "principial," and even principate, or princely reign. We render *principe* as "principle" or "the premise," according to context—Trans.

2. Didier Franck, *Heidegger et le Christianisme: L'explication silencieuse* (Paris: Presses Universitaires de France, 2004).

3. The French *un rien de principe* is literally translatable as a "nothing of principle." But the phrase can be interpreted in several ways: it can mean that there lacks a principle, that there is nothing as a principle, or nothing in the place of the principle (which would make it a repetition of the preceding phrase, *rien*

au principe). Finally, it can also mean *un rien de, un peu de,* "a bit of," meaning that the nothing became a minor principle. Without positing a sophistic principle here, Nancy is playing on these senses—Trans.

4. See Jean-Luc Nancy, *La Création du monde—ou la mondialisation* (Paris: Galilée, 2002); trans. François Raffoul and David Pettigrew as *The Creation of the World; or, Globalization* (Albany: State University of New York Press, 2007).

5. Immanuel Kant, letter to Fichte, February 2, 1792, in Kant, *Briefwechsel* (Hamburg: Meiner, 1972), 553; trans. Arnulf Zweig as Immanuel Kant, *Correspondence* (Cambridge: Cambridge University Press, 1999), 403.

6. Makarios, *Le Monogénèse* 2, trans. Richard Goulet (Paris: Vrin, 2003), 23. [Makarios or Macarius was a Christian apologist at the end of the fourth century C.E. who opposed the radicality of Origen's doctrines—Trans.]

7. *Déréliction* is the French translation for Heidegger's *Geworfenheit*, which English translations render "thrownness"—Trans.

8. Rachel Bespaloff, *Cheminements et Carrefours* (Paris: Vrin, 2004), 150 (with thanks to Ronald Klapka and Monique Jutrin). Deguy, for his part, said of this phrase of Heidegger: "I understand simply that the salutary is not subject to our domination." (See Deguy, *Un homme de peu de foi* [Paris: Bayard, 2002], 57).

9. See, in this volume, "On a Divine *Wink*."

10. We cannot too much emphasize the difference, even the radical incompatibility, between faith and belief. Here, as elsewhere, I will not fail to return, and fundamentally so, to this difference.

11. Immanuel Kant, *Critique of Pure Reason*, 2d Preface (B xxx), trans. Norman Kemp Smith (New York: St Martin's Press, 1965), 29–30.

A Deconstruction of Monotheism

NOTE: Talk delivered in Cairo, in 2001, at the Centre d'études et de documentation économiques, juridiques et sociales (CEDEJ), and thereafter sent, in a revised version, to an issue of the journal *Dédale,* ed. Abdelwahab Meddeb, forthcoming.

1. For a print version of this, see *The Nation,* October 22, 2001, online: http://www.thenation.com/doc/20011022/said—Trans.

2. See Meister Eckhart, "Of Poverty in Spirit," in *Meister Eckhart: The Essential Sermons, Commentaries, Treatises, and Defense,* trans. Edmund Colledge and Bernard McGinn (New York: Paulist Press, 1981). Hallaj, *Diwan,* trans. Louis Massignon (Paris: Cahiers du Sud, 1955), 83. Hussein ibn Mansur al-Hallaj (857–922 C.E.) was an Arabic-speaking Persian Muslim mystic and poet, popularly known among Muslims as "the martyr of mystical love." As an ecstatic mystic, he was charged with heresy on account of his description of union with God, *ana al-haqq* ("I am the Truth")—Trans.

3. Ludwig Feuerbach, *The Essence of Christianity,* trans. George Eliot (New York: Harper Torchbooks, 1955), 184.

The Judeo-Christian (on Faith)

NOTE: This essay was first delivered, in French, at the international colloquium Judéités: Questions pour Jacques Derrida, held at the Jewish Community Center in Paris on December 3–5, 2000. This translation is reprinted from *Judeities: Questions for Jacques Derrida,* ed. Bettina Bergo, Joseph Cohen, and Raphael Zagury-Orly, trans. Bettina Bergo and Michael B. Smith (New York: Fordham University Press, 2007), 214–33, with slight revisions.

1. I will generally translate Nancy's *trait d'union* as "hyphen," which is standard in the translation of Lyotard. When Nancy speaks simply of *trait,* I will use "mark" or, occasionally, "hyphen," according to context—Trans.

2. In composition, the short or dashed stroke technique is found in the Neo-Impressionism of Georges Seurat and in some of Van Gogh's Seurat-influenced work. Short strokes of contrasting colors create a vibrant light—Trans.

3. The reference is to Jacques Derrida, in whose honor the conference was being held—Trans.

4. See Émile Benveniste, *Le Vocabulaire des institutions indo-européennes,* vol. 1, *Économie, parenté, société* (Paris: Minuit, 1969), 199–202—Trans.

5. A reference to Jacques Derrida, *The Gift of Death,* trans. David Wills (Chicago: University of Chicago Press, 1996)—Trans.

6. The French *s'y sauver* means to save oneself by dying and escaping one's faith. The French *s'en sauver* means narrowly to escape death. In both cases, the French verb *sauver* contains a resonance with the signifying universe of Christology and soteriology, which the English "escape" does not convey—Trans.

7. The paradoxical French reads, "La seule consistence est celle du fini en tant qu'il finit et qu'il se finit."

A Faith That Is Nothing at All

NOTE: First published in Jean-Luc Nancy and Élisabeth Rigal, eds., *Granel—L'Éclat, le combat, l'ouvert* (Paris: Belin, 2001), this essay offers a reading of the last article published by Gérard Granel, "Loin de la substance—jusqu'ou?" ("Far from Substance: Whither and to What Point?"), which can be found in the Appendix to the present volume.

1. Gérard Granel, *Traditionis Traditio* (Paris: Gallimard, 1972), 175. The article on Derrida dates from 1967.

2. Ibid., 278.

3. Ibid., 238.

4. Cited in ibid., 239.

5. Gérard Granel, *Études* (Paris: Galilée, 1995), 71.

6. Gérard Granel, "Daniélou-Garaudy: Un combat pour rien," analysis of a television broadcast, manuscript found by Élisabeth Rigal.

7. Gérard Granel, "L'effacement du sujet dans la philosophie contemporaine," *Concilium* 86 (June 1973).

8. Gérard Granel, "Loin de la substance: Jusqu'où?" *Études Philosophiques* 4 (1999). All further page references will be given in the text.

9. What word to use? We are structured so much by monotheism that we have nothing else with which to speak of its out-sides [*ses dehors*].

10. The word *scorie* belongs to the vocabulary of mining and smelting. It is the slag produced by refineries, here used as a physiological metaphor: the material that a body discharges—Trans.

11. Wittgenstein does not explicitly appear in this text. The role that he played for Granel is not, however, to be underestimated; we could try to discern his implicit presence, woven through the monograph on Heidegger, in what the text calls the "formality of appearing." That is, however, not my intent here.

12. I refer to "De la création," in my *La Création du monde—ou la mondialisation* (Paris: Galilée, 2002), 65–102; trans. and introd. François Raffoul and David Pettigrew as *The Creation of the World; or, Globalization* (Albany: State University of New York Press, 2007), 57–74. I gave the manuscript of the first version of this text to Granel, after he had given me his "Loin de la substance," and we ultimately came to agree in the main on the idea of "creation." But his illness did not allow us to undertake the analysis that I propose here.

13. I asked Gérard: "What does this change of index mean?" and he replied, "Well, old friend, we are dismissing theology!" Then his fatigue put an end to our discussion.

14. "Nothing to do with" is *rien à voir avec*, literally, "nothing to see with." Hence Nancy's comment here about "seeing"—Trans.

15. I could add more references, but that would be useless. The following citation is found in Granel, *Études*, 104.

16. The French reads: "Divin est le partage qui fait monde." The term *partage* means simultaneously a sharing or a parsing out, which is an act tied to giving ("I give you your share"), and an act of dividing. Nancy is playing on this semantic dualism—Trans.

17. The common French expression *nulle part* means "nowhere"; here, however, this "part" is not a place but a "share." It resonates with the dual sense, described in n. 16, of *partage*. We introduce the Latin to preserve what cannot be preserved with the exclusively spatial English pronoun "where"—Trans.

An Experience at Heart
NOTE: First published in *Lignes*, no. 7 (Paris: Léo Scheer, 2002).

1. What follows has, as its background, Paragraphs 28 through 35 of *The Anti-Christ*. See Friedrich Nietzsche, *Twilight of the Idols / The Anti-Christ*, trans. R. J. Hollingdale (New York: Penguin, 1968).

2. Nancy clearly follows French translations, which emphasize "anti" as "before or "ante," rather than "counter" or "opposed to—Trans.

3. The French expression is the impersonal "il remet au monde" and then "il met au monde." The first means "it returns or gives back to the world," but it can also imply *our* returning to the world: it sets us back into the world. Nancy leaves the ambiguity open. The second expression, "il met au monde," also means "to give birth to"—Trans.

4. "For example, 'I feel ill'—a judgment such as this supposes a *great and late-coming neutrality on the part of the observer*: the naïve person always says, 'terribly ill, this or that makes me feel ill,' which means he is not fully aware of his feeling until he finds a reason to find ill. This is what I call a '*lack of philology*' [*Mangel an Philologie*]: to be able to read a text *qua* text, without inserting interpretation, is the most recent form of 'inner experience'—perhaps a form scarcely possible at all," in Friedrich Nietzsche, *Nachgelassene Fragmente 1887–1889*, vol. 13 of Nietzsche, *Kritische Studienausgabe*, ed. Giorgio Colli and Mazzino Montinari (Berlin: Walter de Gruyter, 1988), 15 [90], p. 460.

5. Nancy is playing on the prefix "ex" (*é-*) and the term *à-venir*, as that which is both futural and which "happens," whether we are aware of it or not. Here, the reflexive *évenir* is formed with the same root (*venir*) and means "to come out," but in the middle voice—Trans.

6. Friedrich Nietzsche, *Twilight of the Idols / The Anti-Christ*, §34, 159.

7. Ibid.

Verbum caro factum

NOTE: This essay has not previously been published; it was written in 2002.

1. *Phaedrus*, 250d; see also, of course, *The Symposium*, 210a–211b.

The Name *God* in Blanchot

NOTE: First published in *Le Magazine littéraire*, no. 424, special issue *Maurice Blanchot* (Paris, Oct. 2003).

1. Maurice Blanchot, *L'Entretien infini* (Paris: Gallimard, 1969); trans. Susan Hanson as *The Infinite Conversation* (Minneapolis: University of Minnesota Press, 1992).

2. See *Thomas l'Obscur* (Paris: Gallimard, 1941 [first version], 1950 [second version, later published in 1992]); trans. Robert Lamberton as *Thomas the Obscure*, in *The Station Hill Blanchot Reader* (Barrytown, N.Y.: Station Hill Press, 1999); *L'Écriture du désastre* (Paris: Gallimard, 1980); trans. Ann Smock as *The Writing of the Disaster* (Lincoln: University of Nebraska Press, 1995); *Le Dernier à parler* (Montpellier, Fata Morgana, 1984).

Blanchot's Resurrection

NOTE: First delivered in January 2004, at the beginning of a lecture series devoted to Maurice Blanchot, at the Georges Pompidou Center, under the direction of Christophe Bident.

1. Maurice Blanchot, *L'Espace littéraire* (Paris: Gallimard, 1955), 194; trans. Ann Smock as *The Space of Literature* (Lincoln: University of Nebraska Press, 1982), 149.

2. Neglecting to be more precise, I list five references for these five terms, all taken from ibid., 99, 227, 244, 367, 50 / 88, 172, 184, 266, 37.

3. See Christophe Bident, *Reconnaissances—Antelme, Blanchot, Deleuze* (Paris: Calmann-Lévy, 2003).

4. An edition (Paris: Gallimard, 1941) that is difficult to find and that Christophe Bident gave me the joy of procuring for me. The passage is found there, on p. 49; it appears on p. 42 of the second edition (Paris: Gallimard, 1950).

5. *Thomas the Obscure*, trans. Robert Lamberton, in *The Station Hill Blanchot Reader* (Barrytown, N.Y.: Station Hill Press, 1999), 74.

6. This is a reversal of the well-known expression of Sigmund Freud: "Wo es war, soll ich werden" ("Where it [the id] was, I [the ego] should be"). Nancy's phrase (in German in his text) translates: "Where I was, it will be resurrected"—Trans.

7. See second edition, 100; *Thomas the Obscure*, 109–10.

8. Ibid.

9. Ibid., 101 / 110.

10. Ibid.

11. Ibid., 99 / 109.

12. Ibid. [In French the expressions *aux sens* and *au sens* (which mean "on the senses" and "on sense/sense," respectively) are homonymous. The first, which appears in Blanchot's text, is plural, but the same word could also be singular—Trans.]

13. "Lire," in *L'Espace littéraire*, 258; "Reading," in *The Space of Literature*, 196.

14. See, e.g., Maurice Blanchot, *L'Écriture du désastre* (Paris: Gallimard, 1980), 97; trans. Ann Smock as *The Writing of the Disaster* (Lincoln: University of Nebraska Press, 1995), 57. In the same work, there are several attestations of the thought that can be qualified as "of resurrection." Thus p. 214 / 141, where we read that K. in *The Castle* "is too tired to be able to die: in order for the advent of his death not to change into an endless non-advent, that 'non-advent' is 'resurrection.'" Still, there occurred between 1950 and 1980 a partial deletion of Christian terminology and references. As Christophe Bident notes, in connection with *Thomas*, after the second edition "his Christian name will give way to other, atheist figures of generosity, such as *the last man*, or *the friend*." See Bident, *Maurice Blanchot: Partenaire invisible* (Seyssel: Champ Vallon, 1998), 290. One issue remains to be examined: that "deletion" itself—its modality, its possibility. What takes place in the passage from a proper to a common name, and, in a general way, in the tenor of such an "atheistic" substitution, which would nonetheless maintain an undeniable continuity—precisely that of thinking of dying.

15. See, in this volume, "The Name *God* in Blanchot." Concerning the question of myth in Blanchot, one could take up the discussion opened by Daniela Hurezanu, in *Maurice Blanchot et la fin du myth* (New Orleans: Presses Universitaires du Nouveau Monde, 2003).

16. *L'Écriture du désastre*, 191 / 124. The following quotation is from 71.

17. *L'Espace littéraire*, 189 / 146.

18. Ibid., 259 / 195. All the following quotations are taken from this page and the following one.

19. The fact that Blanchot quotes the Latin of the Vulgate rather than the Greek or the French bespeaks both a time and a character permeated with Catholic habits. Other passages in his work corroborate this, and the phenomenon would merit a more detailed examination.

20. *L'Espace littéraire*, 261 / 197.

21. Ibid, 260 / 197, the following quotations are also from this page.

22. Ibid., 261 / 197.

23. Ibid., 193 / 148.

24. Ibid.

25. Ibid., 193 / 149.

26. Philippe Lacoue-Labarthe, "Agonie terminée, agonie interminable," in *Maurice Blanchot—Récits critiques*, ed. Christophe Bident and Pierre Vilar (Paris: Farago / Léo Scheer, 2003), 448.

27. Cf. ibid.

28. See *L'Écriture du désastre*, 35 / 18.

29. Ibid., 37 / 20.

Consolation, Desolation

NOTE: First published in *Le Magazine littéraire*, no. 430, special issue *Jacques Derrida* (Paris, April 2004).

1. Jacques Derrida, *Chaque fois unique, la fin du monde* (Paris: Galilée, 2003). [Based upon Jacques Derrida, *The Work of Mourning*, ed. Michael Naas and Pascale-Anne Brault (Chicago: University of Chicago Press, 2001)—Trans.]

2. Jacques Derrida, *Le toucher—Jean-Luc Nancy* (Paris: Galilée, 2000); trans. Christine Irizarry as *On Touching: Jean-Luc Nancy* (Stanford, Calif.: Stanford University Press, 2005).

3. The reference is to Jean-Luc Nancy, *Noli me tangere* (Paris: Bayard, 2003); trans. Sarah Clift in *Noli me tangere: On the Raising of the Body*, trans. Sarah Clift, Pascale-Anne Brault, and Michael Naas (New York: Fordham University Press, forthcoming).

4. Jacques Derrida, *Adieu à Emmanuel Lévinas* (Paris: Galilée, 1997), 27; trans. Pascale-Anne Brault and Michael Naas as *Adieu to Emmanuel Levinas* (Stanford, Calif.: Stanford University Press, 1999).

5. Nancy, *Noli me tangere*.

6. *Relève*, understood as raising something to a higher level and as taking the function of something, was Derrida's proposed translation of Hegel's *Aufhebung*—Trans.

7. Jacques Derrida, *Mémoires d'aveugle* (Paris: Réunion de Musées nationaux, 1990), 123; trans. Pascale-Anne Brault and Michael Naas as *Memoirs of the Blind: The Self-Portrait and Other Ruins* (Chicago: University of Chicago Press, 1993), 121.

8. Jacques Derrida, "Cette nuit dans la nuit de la nuit . . . ," a lecture on Marie-Louise Mallet, *La Musique en respect* (Paris: Galilée, 2002), published in *Rue Descartes* (Paris: Presses Universitaires de France, 2003), 124–25.

9. Derrida, *Le toucher*, 17 / 7–8.

On a Divine Wink

NOTE: In French, this essay was delivered in Coimbra in the fall of 2003 at a colloquium organized by Fernanda Bernardo on the work of Jacques Derrida. That essay was published in the proceedings *Derrida in Coimbra* (Viseu, Portugal: Palimage, 2005).

1. Jacques Derrida, "Faith and Knowledge: The Two Sources of 'Religion' at the Limits of Reason Alone," trans. Samuel Weber, in Jacques Derrida and Gianni Vattimo, eds., *Religion* (Stanford, Calif.: Stanford University Press, 1998), 55; trans. modified. The first French edition, "Foi et savoir: Les Deux Sources de la 'religion' aux limites de la simple raison," in *La Religion*, ed. Jacques Derrida and Gianni Vattimo (Paris: Seuil, 1996), 73, has a mistake in the Heidegger quote (*défection* in place of *accès*), an error subsequently corrected. Courtine's article quoted by Derrida ("Les Traces et le passage du Dieu dans les *Beiträge zur Philosophie* de Martin Heidegger," *Archivio di filosofia*, nos. 1–3, 1994) constitutes, along with other texts by Courtine and a set of references he supplies, a well-informed and necessary preliminary work for the examination of "the last god" of Heidegger. If I take a very different, even an opposite direction, this is less a question of differing interpretations than of an interpretation, such as Courtine's, as opposed to the extrapolation and free use of the texts upon which I venture.

2. This decision is a bit abrupt and requires further precautionary remarks. After the Coimbra colloquium, Ursula Sarrazin presented me with some observations that were both nuanced and knowledgeable, for which I thank her. They can be condensed as follows. *Wink* has more the sense of a gesture (a movement of the hand or the head) than of a *clin d'œil*: the former is indicative or imperious, or else indicates a leave-taking (*Winke, Winke* designates the way little German children wave "bye-bye"); the latter is more complicit. But a rapprochement between the two meanings is entirely possible, and even has in its favor etymological attestations through English. A poem by Goethe titled "Wink" makes explicit connections with the *clin d'œil*. It is quite remarkable that the earliest examples given in the Grimm Brothers' dictionary are taken from the religious domain. Thus Ursula Sarrazin quoted for me (from a *Reformatorische Flugschrift*): "gott hat uns yetzt gewuncken / im folgt manch frommer Knecht [god has now made a sign to us / more than one pious servant is following him]." The fact remains that, with varying degrees of emphasis, this word has its center of gravity in nonverbal indication. Fernanda Bernardo told me that the Portuguese *aceno* presents a semantics very close to that of *Wink*: derived from *cinnus*, a sign or blink of the eyes, it refers to a movement of the hand, the head, or the eyes to suggest or communicate something without recourse to the spoken word. It is a signal or hint of availability, desire, or promise. ("It took no more than an *aceno* for her to throw herself in his arms.")

3. In English in the original—Trans.

4. Werner Hamacher analyzes the dominating power of the imperial and imperious look (power and violence of the ideal, as well) as that of a look that no

longer sees, "not that it becomes lost in its sight, but because it *shows* its sight"; this is "the violence of the showing of staring [*Starren*]" ("One 2 Many Multiculturalisms," in *Violence, Identity, and Self-Determination*, ed. Hent de Vries and Samuel Weber [Stanford, Calif.: Stanford University Press, 1997], 284–325; "Heterautonomien: One 2 Many Multiculturalisms," in *Gewalt Verstehen*, ed. Burkhard Liebsch and Dagmar Mensink [Berlin: Akademie Verlag, 2003], 157–201). The fixed and petrifying look constitutes the ultimate or central possibility of the blink, and, consequently, the latter's ever-present ambiguity. I will return to this theme in my conclusion.

5. Of course, the use of the word *Wink* throughout Heidegger's work deserves a special study—a project that has in fact been partially undertaken in a few works outside France, whose results such a study would have to address. Heidegger makes repeated use of the term, in the commentaries on Parmenides and on Hölderlin, in borrowings from Rilke, and in other circumstances.

6. *Beiträge*, §42. Heidegger seems to favor the word *Blickbahn*, which is little used. That deserves closer examination. [In vol. 65 of Martin Heidegger, *Gesamtausgabe* (Frankfurt am Main: Vittorio Klostermann, 1975–).]

7. The French is "ce qui arrive part et, *partant*." The last word can mean either "in leaving" or "therefore"—Trans.

8. Augustine, *Confessions*, bk. 3, chap. 6: "God deeper within me than I myself am, higher than my highest." My translation. For a different English translation, see *St. Augustine's Confessions*, with an English translation by William Watts, vol. 1 (Cambridge: Harvard University Press, 1977), 119, 121—Trans.

9. As Kant, that tutelary genius of law, knew and said. See *The Philosophy of Right*, pt. 2, section 1, A.

10. Jacques Derrida, *Speech and Phenomenon*, trans. David B. Allison (Evanston, Ill.: Northwestern University Press, 1973), 65; *La voix et le phénomène* (Paris, Presses Universitaires de France, 1967), 73.

11. A commentary follows on the fact that the wink allows us to see what it hides for an instant: the day itself (Jacques Derrida, *Parages* [Paris, Galilée, 1986], 264). Further along, on p. 296, the wink designates the time of an obviousness that would be that of "the folly of the law. . . . of order, of reason of meaning, of the day."

12. This was, of course, the title of the much-noted work by Dominique Janicaud, *Phenomenology and the "Theological Turn": The French Debate*, ed. Dominique Janicaud et al., trans. Bernard G. Prusak (New York: Fordham University Press, 2000); *Le Tournant théologique de la phénoménologie française* (Paris: L'Éclat, 1991).

13. The passage or passing of the moment (literally, the blink of the eye)—Trans.

14. Here and henceforth the French word *étant* is translated as "individual being," and *être* as "being"—Trans.

15. Martin Heidegger, *On the Way to Language*, trans. Peter D. Hertz (New York: Harper & Row, 1971), 26; *Unterwegs zur Sprache* (Pfullingen: Neske, 1971), 117.

16. The use of the French word *clin* here seems to constitute a bridge between the *clin d'œil* and *clin* used alone, which evokes the notion of slant or incline and will dominate the next paragraph—Trans.

17. Cf. Lucretius, *De rerum natura*, 1.216–93. Lucretius theorizes that some atoms, instead of raining straight down, fall at an incline, thus colliding with others and causing things to arise—Trans.

18. The connection between *Geste* and *Wink* is made by Heidegger in the same text.

19. The gesture of this "making," however, is not a *poiēin*: it is quite clearly a *prattein*. There is, in the *winken*, a *praxis*: that of the god who makes himself divine in this gesture.

20. Derrida, "Pas,"in *Parages*, 31.

21. Jacques Derrida, *Margins of Philosophy*, trans. Alan Bass (Chicago: University of Chicago Press, 1982), 26; *Marges de la philosophie* (Paris: Minuit, 1972), 28.

22. This should be put in relation to what Derrida proposes, in "Faith and Knowledge," on the subject of how language generates "God."

23. Derrida, *Margins of Philosophy*, 17/18. This moment is a remarkable point of encounter between the two forces of these two philosophers, a differential encounter on the differences Derrida revisited on the occasion of Deleuze's demise. See his text on that occasion in Jacques Derrida, *The Work of Mourning*, ed. Pascale-Anne Brault and Michael Naas (Chicago: University of Chicago Press, 2001), 189–96; *Chaque fois unique, la fin du monde* (Paris: Galilée, 2003), 235–40.

24. The French word for between is *entre*; Nancy is suggesting that it could be written "*antre*," a natural hole or lair, the home of ancient gods, which, like Derrida's différ*a*nce instead of the normal *différence*, would be an inaudible difference—Trans.

25. French *nom-mot* is homonymous with *non-mot* ("non-word")—Trans.

26. The fact that Heidegger gives monotheistic "creation" the most banal, pejorative, and also erroneous interpretation is a different problem, belonging to the larger issue of the entirety of his tortuous relations with Judeo-Christianity.

27. See Jean-Luc Nancy, "A Faith That Is Nothing at All," in this volume. The root of *divus* is the Greek *dios*, to which *Zeus* is connected. *Gott/god* is linked to a completely different and uncertain etymon, which may refer either to a calling or a libation, but in both to a relationship to distance, to a "hailing" or "pouring far," constituting another modality of separation.

28. Derrida, *Parages*, 67.

29. Jacques Derrida, *Writing and Difference*, trans. Alan Bass (Chicago: University of Chicago Press, 1978), 294–95; *L'Écriture et la différence* (Paris: Seuil, 1967), 429.

30. Heidegger, *Beiträge*, §279. [In vol. 65 of Heideger, *Gesamtausgabe* (Frankfurt am Main: Vittorio Klostermann, 1975–).]

31. The first (and last) stanza of Rimbaud's "Eternité," the third poem in the group "Fêtes de la Patience"—Trans.

An Exempting from Sense

NOTE: The first version of this essay was delivered in January 2003 at the Roland Barthes Center, directed by Julia Kristeva, at the University of Paris VII.

1. Roland Barthes, *Roland Barthes* (Paris: Seuil, 1975), 101; trans. Richard Howard as *Roland Barthes* (Berkeley: University of California Press, 1994), 97.

2. I am indebted to Jean-Pierre Sarrazac for valuable information on the occurrences of this expression of Barthes and their context. I cannot be sure that I have an exhaustive list of these occurrences. Since the completion of this presentation, I have discovered that they are numerous, but unless I am mistaken Barthes has never bothered to explicate or unpack his notion of this phrase.

3. See Kant's 1788 Introduction to the *Critique of Practical Reason*: *Kritik der Praktischen Vernunft* (Leipzig: Philipp Reclam, 1983), 15–16n. The underlying Kantian term, *Begehrungsvermögen*, is closer to the faculty of desire than to that of will—Trans.

4. A synonymity of *exempter* ("to exempt") and *périmer* ("to terminate") can be found, at any rate, in Barthes, *Roland Barthes*, 168 / 165.

5. This may be an allusion to a collection of interviews with Roland Barthes, titled *The Grain of the Voice: Interviews 1962–1980*—Trans.

6. Nietzsche, *The Gay Science*, trans. Walter Kaufmann (New York: Random House, 1974), §319, p. 253.

7. French *sens unique* has two meanings: "one way" (e.g., street) and "one sense," or "unique sense." The notions of unidirectional and of univocal sense are probably co-intended here—Trans.

8. *Jouis-sens* translates literally as "enjoy-sense," but its French homonym *jouissance* means "orgasm," among other things—Trans.

"Prayer Demythified"

NOTE: This essay was originally composed for a volume honoring Michel Deguy prepared by Jean-Pierre Moussaron, forthcoming [at the time of the French publication of the present book, 2005].

1. Michel Deguy, *Sans retour* (Paris: Galilée, 204), 109. This passage brings to bear not only several themes that are to be found elsewhere in Deguy's book but also others (or the same ones) from his *Un homme de peu de foi* (Paris: Bayard, 2002). I am not interested in reconstructing the more or less tightly knit systematization connecting these themes. Suffice it to say that these words on prayer concentrate the essential elements of an insistent problem: how to give meaning, or more simply credibility—refraining from meaningful construal—not to a painfully revived religion but to the "relics" (as Deguy likes to call them, thus bringing into affective play the meaning of a religious term) that an extinguished religion leaves in its wake—such as prayer, faith, the name *God* itself, and a few other attestations to an irreducibility of language.

2. Nancy is referring to the writer Jean-Christophe Bailly, with whom Lacoue-Labarthe had a series of conversations, filmed on the Île Saint-Pierre (Switzerland) in 2006 by Christine Baudillon and François Lagarde. Bailly is the

author of many works of art, most recently *Le Champ mimétique* (Paris: Seuil, 2005)—Trans.

3. Paul Valéry, *Cahiers* (Paris: Gallimard, 1974), 2:605.

4. Paul Verlaine, "Confessions," in *Œuvres en prose* (Paris: Gallimard, 1972), 467.

5. Nancy is drawing the attention of the reader to the homonyms *exaucé*, "to have one's prayers answered," and *exhaussé*, "to be lifted up"—Trans.

The Deconstruction of Christianity

NOTE: This essay was first delivered as a lecture at the University of Montpellier in 1995. It was recorded, transcribed, and then edited by Emmanuelle Soler, Vincent Chekib, and Pierre Rodrigo, to whom I express my gratitude for having been willing, in the urgency of the moment, to carry out that thankless and delicate task. It has retained the marks of a certain improvisation, the spoken language, and a very tentative stage of the work. Only the two last paragraphs were added after the fact. It was published in *Études philosophiques*, no. 4 (Paris, 1998). I have left this text in its original state (barring a few minor corrections), as a witness to the first moment in a questioning.

1. See, now, the book that he was working on at that time: Michel Henry, *C'est moi la vérité: Pour une philosophie du christianisme* (Paris: Seuil, 1996); trans. Susan Emanuel as *I Am the Truth: Toward a Philosophy of Christianity* (Stanford, Calif.: Stanford University Press, 2002). After the colloquium, which he attended, M. Henry expressed to me his total disagreement with my intent.

2. See Marlene Zarader, *La Dette impensée: Heidegger et l'héritage hébraïque* (Paris: Seuil, 1990); trans. Bettina Bergo as *The Unthought Debt: Heidegger and the Hebraic Heritage* (Stanford, Calif.: Stanford University Press, 2006).

3. Émile Poulat, *L'Ère postchrétienne: Un monde sorti de Dieu* (Paris, Flammarion, 1994).

4. I have followed the usual practice of translating *intégrisme* as "fundamentalism." In the following pages, however, it is important to relate *intégrisme* to a certain holistic sense of the fundamentalist movement, which then becomes subject to "disintegration" and to losing its "integrity," that is, its internal coherence—Trans.

5. Marcel Gauchet, *Le Désenchantement du monde* (Paris: Gallimard, 1985); trans. Oscar Burge as *The Disenchantment of the World: A Political History of Religion* (Princeton, N.J.: Princeton University Press, 1997).

6. French *Noël* has an etymological connection with Latin *natalis*, "of birth," which English, and therefore my translation, lacks—Trans.

7. One could, though I will not do so here, abandon oneself at this point to a Hegelian variation, since Christianity is in fact characterized as the unhappiness of consciousness, in the Hegelian sense in which "unhappiness" means distension of consciousness. And this "unhappiness," considered by Hegel to be properly Jewish, lends, in this view, its tension (no more "unhappy" than "happy," but . . . tensed) to all monotheism. But if consciousness implies tension, does not

culture in general imply religion? . . . (Note added after the fact.) See Gauchet, *Le Désenchantement.*

8. It is true that Luther spoke of the *destructio* of a certain ecclesiastical tradition (as Derrida recalled apropos my own expression "deconstruction of Christianity"). But before closer examination of the uses of this term in Luther (and during his era, because within it we find, e.g., a *Destructio cabbalae*, as well as a *Destructio destructionis*, which translates the title of Averroes against Al-Ghazali; in these cases the force of "destructuring" is unclear) and also before an eventual revisiting of *Destruktion/Zerstörung/Abbau* in Heidegger and of *Abbau* in Husserl, I will restrict myself to what is, after all, the essential: a gesture of an opening or reopening in the direction of what must have preceded all construction. That will undoubtedly have to be elaborated later. Moreover, the flat, deformed senses in which *deconstruction* is so widely used today, so that it has become synonymous with "critique" or "demolition"—a usage due to a great extent to the success of a Derridean *vulgate*—prompts one to use the term sparingly . . . (Note added after first publication.)

9. I find it rather remarkable, e.g., that someone like Alain Badiou, in his so unchristian book on ethics (*L'Ethique: Essai sur la conscience du Mal* [Paris: Hatier, 1993]; trans. Peter Hallward as *Ethics: An Understanding of Evil* [London: Verso, 2001]), should put at the heart of his thought a category of empty faithfulness. Badiou seems not to suspect that, under that faithfulness, it is possible to make *fides* reemerge: but I *believe* he does more, in reality, than suspect it.

10. Léon Bloy (1846–1917) and Georges Bernanos (1888–1948), Catholic novelists associated with an orthodox, strongly antimodernist traditionalism (now looked upon as the beginning of *intégrisme*), gave Satan and sin a very prominent role in their works. See Bernanos's first novel, *Sous le soleil de Satan* (*Under Satan's Sun*, 1926)—Trans.

Dis-Enclosure

NOTE: This text was originally written to go with an extended report on space in the journal *Java*, no. 25/26 (Paris, 2003). [For an explanation of the term *dis-enclosure*, see the Translators' Foreword—Trans.] The epigraph is from a conversation between Jean-Christophe Bailly and Emmanuel Laugier, published in *L'Animal*, no. 17 (Metz, Fall 2004), 85.

Appendix: Gérard Granel, Far from Substance: Whither and to What Point?

NOTE: This text was first published in *Études philosophiques*, no. 4 (Paris, 1999). Granel treasured this text: he sent it to me, asking where he could publish it. I proposed it to Jean-François Courtine, who immediately published it in this journal. The pages to which my previous text refers are indicated here in brackets. The text is reproduced without any modification.

1. *Ptosis*, or the plural *ptoses*, is generally a medical term for the prolapse or drooping of viscera or flesh. From the Greek *piptein*, it means originally the act of falling, by extension befalling, occurring; as though Being fell into modalities noted by Kant in his table of the categories—Trans.

2. The French term is *archi-construit*, in which the common prefix *archi-* denotes an absolute intensity or degree—Trans.

3. Kant, "Transcendental Aesthetic," *Critique of Pure Reason.*

4. Ibid.

5. This is the remark Husserl made at the end of his *Phenomenology of the Consciousness of Internal Time*, after reducing immanent time to a flux in which temporal positions remained more or less fixed—Trans.

6. The French *cerne*, the root with which French and English form *discern* and *concern*, comes from the same Latin root that gives us *circle*: *circinus*. The term in French also means a circular trace or round shadow: eyes have dark *cernes*; a tablecloth has the round traces (*cernes*) of coffee cups; etc. Hence our dual use of border and ring—Trans.

7. In German, the word for "sun" is feminine; in French, it is masculine. When Granel writes *la Soleil*, he is emphasizing the maternal warmth he contrasts to a "scientific" characterization of the sun, any sun—Trans.

8. *Epochē* refers to Husserl's technique of phenomenological bracketing, by which the objective existence or the subjective reality of intentional focus is provisionally set outside consideration—Trans.

9. The French uses a feminine noun here, *l'absente*, implying the flower absent from every bouquet—Trans.